Dialogue of One

William J Grimm

Dialogue of One

Homilies for Sundays and Feasts in Years A, B and C

William J Grimm

Adelaide
2019

Text copyright © 2019 remains with William J Grimm.

All rights reserved. Except for any fair dealing permitted under the Copyright Act, no part of this book may be reproduced by any means without prior permission. Inquiries should be made to the publisher.

© Cover art work by Kim En Joong
cover design by Myf Cadwallader

ISBN: 978-1-925612-80-6 soft
      978-1-925612-81-3 hard
      978-1-925612-82-0 epub
      978-1-925612-83-7 pdf

Published by:

An imprint of the ATF Ltd.
PO Box 504
Hindmarsh, SA 5007
ABN 90 116 359 963
www.atfpress.com
Making a lasting impact

Table of Contents

Introduction: Thoughts on Preaching   xi

1. **Sacred Seasons**
   Advent and Christmas   1
      First Sunday of Advent Year A   3
      First Sunday of Advent Year B   5
      First Sunday of Advent Year C   7
      Second Sunday of Advent Year A   9
      Second Sunday of Advent Year B   11
      Second Sunday of Advent Year C   13
      Third Sunday of Advent Year A   15
      Third Sunday of Advent Year B   17
      Third Sunday of Advent Year C   19
      Fourth Sunday of Advent Year A   21
      Fourth Sunday of Advent Year B   23
      Fourth Sunday of Advent Year C   25
      Christmas Midnight Mass   27
      Christmas Day   29
      Holy Family Year A   31
      Holy Family Year B   33
      Holy Family Year C   35
      Epiphany Year A   37
      Epiphany Year B   39
      Epiphany Year C   41

2. **Sacred Seasons**
    Lent, Easter, Trinity and Corpus Christi   43
        Ash Wednesday   45
        First Sunday of Lent Year A   47
        First Sunday of Lent Year B   49
        First Sunday of Lent Year C   51
        Second Sunday of Lent Year A   53
        Second Sunday of Lent Year B   55
        Second Sunday of Lent Year C   57
        Third Sunday of Lent Year A   59
        Third Sunday of Lent Year B   61
        Third Sunday of Lent Year C   63
        Fourth Sunday of Lent Year A   65
        Fourth Sunday of Lent Year B   67
        Fourth Sunday of Lent Year C   69
        Fifth Sunday of Lent Year A   71
        Fifth Sunday of Lent Year B   73
        Fifth Sunday of Lent Year C   75
        Passion or Palm Sunday Year A   77
        Passion or Palm Sunday Year B   79
        Passion or Palm Sunday Year C   81
        Holy Thursday Mass of the Lord's Supper   83
        Good Friday   85
        The Easter Vigil   87
        Easter Sunday Year A   91
        Easter Sunday Year B   93
        Easter Sunday Year C   95
        Second Sunday of Easter Year A   97
        Second Sunday of Easter Year B   99
        Second Sunday of Easter Year C   101
        Third Sunday of Easter Year A   103
        Third Sunday of Easter Year B   105
        Third Sunday of Easter Year C   107
        Fourth Sunday of Easter Year A   109
        Fourth Sunday of Easter Year B   111

Fourth Sunday of Easter Year C	113
Fifth Sunday of Easter Year A	115
Fifth Sunday of Easter Year B	117
Fifth Sunday of Easter Year C	119
Sixth Sunday of Easter Year A	121
Sixth Sunday of Easter Year B	123
Sixth Sunday of Easter Year C	125
Ascension Year A	127
Ascension Year B	129
Ascension Year C	131
Seventh Sunday of Easter Year A	133
Seventh Sunday of Easter Year B	135
Seventh Sunday of Easter, Year C	137
Pentecost, Year A	139
Pentecost, Year B	141
Pentecost, Year C	143
Trinity Sunday, Year A	145
Trinity Sunday, Year B	147
Trinity Sunday, Year C	149
The Body and Blood of Christ, Year A	151
The Body and Blood of Christ, Year B	153
The Body and Blood of Christ, Year C	155

3. **Sacred Season**

Ordinary Time	157
First Sunday of the Year, Baptism of the Lord, Year A	159
First Sunday of the Year, Baptism of the Lord, Year B	161
First Sunday of the Year, Baptism of the Lord, Year C	163
Second Sunday of the Year, Year A	165
Second Sunday of the Year, Year B	167
Second Sunday of the Year, Year C	169
Third Sunday of the Year, Year A	171
Third Sunday of the Year, Year B	173
Third Sunday of the Year, Year C	175
Fourth Sunday of the Year, Year A	177

Fourth Sunday of the Year, Year B	179
Fourth Sunday of the Year, Year C	181
Fifth Sunday of the Year, Year A	183
Fifth Sunday of the Year, Year B	185
Fifth Sunday of the Year, Year C	187
Sixth Sunday of the Year, Year A	189
Sixth Sunday of the Year, Year B	191
Sixth Sunday of the Year, Year C	193
Seventh Sunday of the Year, Year A	195
Seventh Sunday of the Year, Year B	197
Seventh Sunday of the Year, Year C	199
Eighth Sunday of the Year, Year A	201
Eighth Sunday of the Year, Year B	203
Eighth Sunday of the Year, Year C	205
Ninth Sunday of the Year, Year A	207
Ninth Sunday of the Year, Year B	209
Ninth Sunday of the Year, Year C	211
Tenth Sunday of the Year, Year A	213
Tenth Sunday of the Year, Year B	215
Tenth Sunday of the Year, Year C	217
Eleventh Sunday of the Year, Year A	219
Eleventh Sunday of the Year, Year B	221
Eleventh Sunday of the Year, Year C	223
Twelfth Sunday of the Year, Year A	225
Twelfth Sunday of the Year, Year B	227
Twelfth Sunday of the Year, Year C	229
Thirteenth Sunday of the Year, Year A	231
Thirteenth Sunday of the Year, Year B	233
Thirteenth Sunday of the Year, Year C	235
Fourteenth Sunday of the Year, Year A	237
Fourteenth Sunday of the Year, Year B	239
Fourteenth Sunday of the Year, Year C	241
Fifteenth Sunday of the Year, Year A	243
Fifteenth Sunday of the Year, Year B	245
Fifteenth Sunday of the Year, Year C	247

Sixteenth Sunday of the Year, Year A	249
Sixteenth Sunday of the Year, Year B	251
Sixteenth Sunday of the Year, Year C	253
Seventeenth Sunday of the Year, Year A	255
Seventeenth Sunday of the Year, Year B	257
Seventeenth Sunday of the Year, Year C	259
Eighteenth Sunday of the Year, Year A	261
Eighteenth Sunday of the Year, Year B	263
Eighteenth Sunday of the Year, Year C	265
Nineteenth Sunday of the Year, Year A	267
Nineteenth Sunday of the Year, Year B	269
Nineteenth Sunday of the Year, Year C	271
Twentieth Sunday of the Year, Year A	273
Twentieth Sunday of the Year, Year B	275
Twentieth Sunday of the Year, Year C	277
Twenty-First Sunday of the Year, Year A	279
Twenty-First Sunday of the Year, Year B	281
Twenty-First Sunday of the Year, Year C	283
Twenty-Second Sunday of the Year, Year A	285
Twenty-Second Sunday of the Year, Year B	287
Twenty-Second Sunday of the Year, Year C	289
Twenty-Third Sunday of the Year, Year A	291
Twenty-Third Sunday of the Year, Year B	293
Twenty-Third Sunday of the Year, Year C	295
Twenty-Fourth Sunday of the Year, Year A	297
Twenty-Fourth Sunday of the Year, Year B	299
Twenty-Fourth Sunday of the Year, Year C	301
Twenty-Fifth Sunday of the Year, Year A	303
Twenty-Fifth Sunday of the Year, Year B	305
Twenty-Fifth Sunday of the Year, Year C	307
Twenty-Sixth Sunday of the Year, Year A	309
Twenty-Sixth Sunday of the Year, Year B	311
Twenty-Sixth Sunday of the Year, Year C	313
Twenty-Seventh Sunday of the Year, Year A	315
Twenty-Seventh Sunday of the Year, Year B	317

Twenty-Seventh Sunday of the Year, Year C	319
Twenty-Eighth Sunday of the Year, Year A	321
Twenty-Eighth Sunday of the Year, Year B	323
Twenty-Eighth Sunday of the Year, Year C	325
Twenty-Ninth Sunday of the Year, Year A	327
Twenty-Ninth Sunday of the Year, Year B	329
Twenty-Ninth Sunday of the Year, Year C	331
Thirtieth Sunday of the Year, Year A	333
Thirtieth Sunday of the Year, Year B	335
Thirtieth Sunday of the Year, Year C	337
Thirty-First Sunday of the Year, Year A	339
Thirty-First Sunday of the Year, Year B	341
Thirty-First Sunday of the Year, Year C	343
Thirty-Second Sunday of the Year, Year A	345
Thirty-Second Sunday of the Year, Year B	347
Thirty-Second Sunday of the Year, Year C	349
Thirty-Third Sunday of the Year, Year A	351
Thirty-Third Sunday of the Year, Year B	353
Thirty-Third Sunday of the Year, Year C	355
Thirty-Fourth or Last Sunday of the Year, Year A	357
Thirty-Fourth or Last Sunday of the Year, Year B	359
Thirty-Fourth or Last Sunday of the Year, Year C	361

4. **Sacred Days**

Major Feasts	363
January 1: Mary Mother of God	365
February 2: Presentation	367
June 24: Birth of John the Baptist	369
June 29: Peter and Paul	371
August 6: Transfiguration	373
August 15: Assumption	375
September 14: Triumph of the Cross	377
November 1: All Saints	379
November 2: All Souls	381
November 9: Dedication of the Lateran Basilica	383

Introduction: Thoughts on Preaching

A teenaged member of a parish I served in Japan came to me one day with a complaint. The parish church only had Mass on alternate Sundays because I went to celebrate twice a month at another parish. On Sundays when no priest was present, members of the parish conducted a communion service during which parishioners would share thoughts on the readings.

The boy's complaint was simple: 'Every night at dinner, I have to listen to my father preaching. Now I have to listen to him in church, too.'

Preaching is, in the minds of most non-preachers and poor preachers, the quintessential monologue. One person stands before a crowd of others and talks at them. The audience is expected to keep quiet and merely listen. The reality, as any real preacher knows, is more complicated. Though only one person appears to be speaking, there is, in fact, a dialogue in progress.

The community responds in many ways: body language, snores, laughs, bored or rapt looks, whispered conversations, shouted *Amens*, walking out, applause.

In addition to this feedback during the homily, there are the day-to-day life and concerns of the community that must form part of the preacher's talk. The listeners tell the preacher a lot in church and out, and a good preacher responds to them. Though one speaks out loud, it is a dialogue.

Hence, the name of this book. The phrase comes from the poet John Donne (1572-1631) who was a noted preacher in his day, though he originally used this phrase in a poem.

I have called what follows 'homilies', but they are homiletic essays more than true homilies. They are merely intended to give homilists ideas that may be useful in their own preparation for preaching and to give non-preachers ideas for understanding the Scriptures they read and hear.

If what follows helps others deepen the hope that is in them, these essays will have served their purpose. If they help my fellow preachers proclaim the Word in the pulpit and in their encounters with our brothers and sisters beyond the church walls, they will have done more than I should hope for. If they help even one Christian draw closer to Christ in his word and world, I will be a happy man.

Why do we have preaching in the Church? Is it meant to be an opportunity for the preacher to show that he or she is holier, wiser or more competent than the rest of the people gathered to worship? In the case I know best, that is certainly not the situation.

So, why do we do it? It is so much a part of our worship that perhaps we never give a thought to the fact that it is actually unusual. Many religions do not make preaching a part of their worship. It was not part of worship in the Jerusalem Temple, which was more like a slaughterhouse than a meeting hall. The synagogue is the source of the Christian custom of preaching, a custom referred to in Luke's account of Jesus in Capernaum (Lk 4:16ff). The custom moved into Islam, probably under the influence of Jewish and Christian practice.

A distinguishing, though not unique, characteristic of these three religions is that they define themselves in terms of an interpersonal relationship with God rather than in terms of rites. It is a relationship that should permeate every aspect of a believer's life. In other words, Christian faith, to limit ourselves to one tradition, is not something that happens in Church.

That presents a difficulty. If religious faith were merely a matter of the proper carrying out of rituals, there would be little question of how to live. Religion would be like making a bowl of instant noodles. Just follow the directions to the letter and you get the desired results. Once you have gotten them, you move on to other concerns.

But, if faith has at least as much to do with our daily thoughts, actions and omissions as it has to do with worship, then problems arise. Can I be sure that God is actually involved with me in my day-to-day life? Is it possible to take the general truths given by Scripture and the traditional teaching and practice of the Church and make them fit into an ordinary life, my ordinary life?

Preaching is the 'Yes' answer to these questions. The job of the preacher is, above all, to give encouragement to the People of God by showing that faith does bear some relation to our lives outside the church. Preaching is the part of liturgy that affirms that the timeless realities of Word and Sacrament we celebrate on Sunday morning can, must and shall have some connection with Tuesday afternoon or Thursday evening.

The homiletic essays that follow were originally video presentations by UCA News, the news agency of and for the Church in Asia. Published in four volumes, they are here brought together in one, reedited and with new material.

One summer when I was a boy, my friend Rickey and I, two city kids, stayed at a relative's farm, the fields of which were rented to a local farmer. One hot afternoon, an old man came on a tractor to mow and rake alfalfa. After he had worked in the sun a long time, Rickey and I brought him a pitcher of cold water. We talked for a while, telling him we were on summer vacation from high school. He looked at his big, muscular black hands as he spoke of how a lack of education could condemn a man for life to doing someone else's work. Then, with sadness and hope in his eyes, he said, 'You go to school, now, and study hard, and learn. Don't be like me'.

That man did more for my education than any teacher I have had, any book I have read or any course I have taken. I have listened to those teachers, read those books and taken those courses in obedience and service to that man. May God bless him. I dedicate this book to him.

William J Grimm, MM
Tokyo, Japan

Sacred Seasons:

Advent and Christmas

First Sunday of Advent (A)

When a race starts, is the waiting over, or has it just begun? How about a theater performance? A concert? A football game?

In one sense, the wait is over. When the starting gun fires, the curtain goes up, the baton comes down or the ball is kicked, the participants can at last do what they have come to do. The tense build-up is ended, the action has begun.

In another sense, though, a new wait has begun. Now, there is an action wait, a doing wait. Who will cross the finish line first? How will the play work out? Will the concert be a success? Which side will win the match?

Waiting for the result is common to the participants as well as to the spectators or audience. When it comes to waiting, all are engaged in the same activity. Beginnings mark a new wait.

With the first Sunday of Advent, we begin the Church's season of waiting.

What kind of wait is Advent? For those to whom it is the Christmas shopping season, this is a build-up season. Excitement builds as we wait for the feast. Once it comes, the waiting is over. We put away the Advent wreathes and calendars. The celebration begins.

But, perhaps Advent is about the other kind of wait, the doing wait, the moving wait, the heading toward a goal wait. Perhaps it is more like riding on a train than like sitting in a theater before the show starts.

Actually, it is both kinds of waiting, but backwards. We are not waiting for something to happen and ready then to wait and see it through to completion. We are waiting to see how things already begun will turn out, but we are also waiting for something to begin. The activity is in progress. The onset is yet to come.

What is it that we await? I am living my life day to day, making a story the end of which is still unknown. I am the lead character of my life and I am waiting to see how the story of my life forms a plot.

Of course, since I am the chief actor of the story, my waiting is not a mere 'waiting around.' I am like the actor, the musician or the athlete who is fully involved in the process.

Like theirs, mine is not a solo performance. Others are involved, most of them people I do not even know. There are my family and friends. There are the people whose work makes my life what it is: farmers, engineers, miners, journalists, transport workers, civil servants, etc. There are even the dead, men and women of the past who made the world in which I live, the world that has shaped me, that challenges me and supports me. There are my ancestors, both human and nonhuman.

They are part of my waiting to see what my life means. They wait with me because part of the meaning of their lives is linked to mine, as the role of each character in a play is defined by the other characters.

How our lives intersect is a mystery to us all, a mystery that will be answered by the other wait, the onset wait.

The onset for which we wait is the one we pray for in the Lord's Prayer: 'Thy Kingdom come.'

The coming of the Lord to bring the completion of the Reign of God will give the meaning to the waiting I live today. Just as a race is defined by the finish line (100–meter dash, marathon), so, too, is my life. The run is good in itself, but is fulfilled in the finish.

That finish takes two forms. The most obvious is the end of my life, when my run ends. The other is one that gives the ultimate meaning to my life, the coming, the advent, of the Lord as judge and ruler of the universe at the end of time.

In that, the mystery of all the people and events of all our lives will become clear. So, we wait in joyful hope for the ongoing completion of our own story and for the coming of our Savior, Jesus Christ. Advent is a time to remember that we are waiting and to examine the way we wait, both in loving activity today, and in hope for the future.

First Sunday of Advent (B)

Though Advent has four Sundays, we celebrate with three virtues three comings of Christ in three tenses. Three threes!

With Christmas decorations all over, it is easy to forget that Advent is a time of coming rather than a preparation for Christmas. The Gospel about the coming of the Lord when we least expect him makes it clear that we are not merely preparing for December 25.

That day, we celebrate the past tense coming of the Lord, the birth of Jesus. He was born like us, grew up like us, died like us. He had a mother, a father, relatives, teachers, friends and foes. He worked as a carpenter. He called followers, and directed them to a new way of life before God long ago and far away. And we believe in him.

Faith is our love of that man. We love him in the life he led, in the Scriptures that teach us of him, in the Church that guides us to him. We gather each week to remember him by breaking bread. We commit ourselves to saying that he was real, not a legend. He was someone we can love as we love other people we have known in the past, people no longer present.

But, there is a difference, because his coming in the past is not all. We also await his future coming. He 'will come again in glory to judge the living and the dead.'

I'm not sure I want to meet the One who knows all there is to know about me. At some time in the future, I will face the absolutely just judge who will know exactly what I deserve, and will render the fairest judgment on my life: 'Guilty.'

Yet, we wait in joyful hope for his coming. Do we look forward to being forced to see how sordid our lives have been? No. We look forward to the full verdict: 'Guilty, but forgiven.'

That is the source of our hope, love in the future tense. We love the Lord who will come bringing final forgiveness and healing and joy to our lives.

I fall into problems, though, if I concentrate solely upon the past and future comings of the Lord. Especially as Christmas approaches,

I get sentimental over Christmases past. Eventually, I forget the real man Jesus altogether.

If I focus upon his future coming as Judge and Savior, I get complacent. After all, we've already waited two millennia. In addition, the future is an abstraction. At least I've lived through the past and have some idea of what it was. The future may be daydreamed about, but my guesses are empty speculation. So, I don't bother; I sit back and forget.

That is why the most important coming of Christ is neither in the past nor the future. It is his coming today, in the present tense. He comes in my time, my life.

Ironically, this most important coming is often the hardest to recognize. His past coming is available to us in the Gospels. His future coming is not available to us, though when it comes, there will be no mistaking it.

His present coming is paradoxically present, yet hidden. It is too present, too quick, for us to devote time to recognizing it. He sneaks up on us, demanding instant recognition and instant response. And he does it in disguise. It takes a ready heart to see him. It takes the fullness of the love that shows itself as faith and hope, love in itself.

Jesus comes in someone needing help, the child lost in a crowd, the lonely neighbor, the family member across the table. He is the child who asks a wise question, the adult who gives a wise answer. He may be a poet, a politician, a pauper or a prince. Sometimes I even catch a glimpse of him in the mirror. He comes in so many disguises that I usually miss him.

When Jesus comes in the present, he looks for real, practical love. Not an emotion, but action. My faith means nothing if I can't see and love him today. My hope is wasted if I refuse his invitation to love him now. If I'm not willing to see the Lord today, I have reason to fear seeing him at the end.

Faith, hope and love are virtues directed toward past, future and present. In Advent, we remind ourselves to be ever ready to meet and love the Lord who has come, who shall come, who comes.

First Sunday of Advent (C)

If someone said to me, 'nations will be in anguish' or, 'people will be terrified to death at what is going to happen,' how would I answer?

'So? What else is new?'

Nations are always anguished over something or other, usually with good reason. Peace and justice always seem to be one more negotiation, one more election, one more ceasefire away. When things are going well politically, some sort of natural disaster seems inevitable.

When it comes to people being terrified, we know that is a description of each of us at least sometimes. Children live in a world of giants who say and do inexplicable things. Young people fear rejection by their peers. Students worry about courses and their future. Adults worry about their work and their children. The elderly worry about their health, their past and their future.

Perhaps that is the reason people in every age think theirs is the one of which Jesus spoke. So, let's assume that the Lord is talking of our age and our lives. What then? There must be a better answer than fearful concentration upon an impending doom that never quite arrives, yet whose threat never quite disappears.

'When these things begin to happen, stand up straight and raise your heads.' Is that the way to face the anxieties of my life? Stiff upper lip? Forced cheerfulness?

But, there is more to Jesus' answer than platitudes like 'keep on keeping on.' He says the reason we should not give up is that our 'ransom is near at hand.' We have all been in situations where we needed some sort of 'ransom,' some rescue.

However, we will not be able to see that our ransom is at hand unless we are prepared to receive it. Jesus warns us to 'be on guard' and singles out indulgence, drunkenness and worldly cares as the dangers we must avoid. Why point to them in particular? Why doesn't he warn us about wrong ideas or inadequate faith?

The thread that unites those dangers is cowardice. When I choose them, I have decided to run away from tensions and troubles to embrace oblivion or to crowd them out of my life with frenzied activity. But, though I may try to avoid them or close my eyes to problems, they will not go away. Even if I spend a lifetime at it, I will not be able to avoid the inevitability of death.

In order to be ransomed by the Lord, I need courage to accept the pain, confusion and disaster in my life. Only then can the Lord rescue me. The reason is plain: the Cross is the ultimate pain of the world and the healing of that pain. God Incarnate tortured to death rescues us. Only when we are willing to stand by our own crosses, confident that the Lord is with us, can the healing ransom offered by Christ be ours. If I run from the pain, I run from the place where I can meet the healer.

Advent ('Coming') is our time of waiting for the Lord, the Lord who will come at the end of time, but who also comes to us whenever we are willing to stay at the cross—whether his or our own. The Lord has acted, and will act in the midst of pain and confusion.

Can I believe that when troubles come the Lord comes as well? How can I deepen my faith in that coming? The Lord's answer is 'Pray constantly.' That does not mean spending all my time on my knees. It means being constantly aware, or at least constantly reminding myself that the Lord is really with me.

In Advent we nurture our awareness that the Lord really has come and really comes. One way to do that is by remembering. Let's spend this season remembering how he has come many times when we were afraid and confused, and how the Lord brought us through. The remembering will enable us to 'stand secure before the Son of Man.'

Second Sunday of Advent (A)

The first people who took the trouble to go into the desert and look for John returned home and told others about the man in the wilderness who lived on bugs and honey and dressed in camel hair. They also told how abusive he was, attacking some of them for coming in the first place: 'You brood of vipers! Who warned you to flee from the wrath to come?'

And what happened? Did folks say, 'That guy has been out in the sun too long—he's crazy, and maybe even dangerous'?

No. John became a celebrity! 'At that time Jerusalem, all Judea, and the whole region around the Jordan were going out to him.'

Did folks like to be abused? Is that why they made the dangerous trek into the desert? Did they go out of curiosity, to see the wild man in the wilderness? There may have been another reason for their going: they knew John was right.

The psychiatrist Karl Menninger wrote a book titled, *Whatever Became of Sin?* It was a good question. A growing understanding of the psychological causes that lie behind many of our actions, combined with a reaction against a spirituality that seemed to make an awareness of sin rather than of God's sin-forgiving love the center of the Christian life seem to have decreased some of our consciousness of sin.

There is much good in this tendency. Sometimes we are not fully responsible for our actions because of psychological or social factors that influence and even control us. In addition, instead of weighing our consciences and trying to keep mental or even written lists of sins to take to the confessional, we have come to a deeper appreciation of God's forgiving love embracing us at all times.

However, I sometimes move from there to a sort of self-forgiveness. I decide that sin is not a reality in my life, that none of my problems are due to sin—mine and the world's. I sometimes forget that God's forgiving love is precisely that—*forgiving* love. In 'what I have done and in what I have failed to do,' there is something that requires forgiveness.

John's problem with people who went to the desert was not that they were sinners. His problem was that some of them seemed to think that all they had to do was go through the motions. They would admit to being sinners (the more vaguely, the better), go out to the desert for John's baptismal ritual, and then get back to living as they always had.

John warns such folks, 'Bear fruit worthy of repentance. Do not presume to say to yourselves, 'We have Abraham as our ancestor.'' He then speaks about 'the one who will follow me.'

John moves his listeners from focusing on past sins or present hypocrisy to the future, the time of hope.

'Advent' means 'coming' and coming is something that happens from the future. At this time of year I remind myself that my whole life is lived in expectation of something that is coming, and that does not merely mean December 25.

I have a past and a present. They have made me the person I am. However, the story of my past and present is not the real story of me. My real story is in the future, in God's call to draw closer and in the opportunities (including death) that will bring me closer and closer to God. God calls to me from out of the future rather than pushing me from the past.

Every moment is an advent. In every moment God invites me to move away from the past and the present into a new future.

But, there are obstacles. My obstacles are those that brought people to John in the desert, the sins of my past and my tendency to not let go of them in the present.

They prevent my meeting the advent of the future because one of the characteristics of sin is that it is directed to the present. I sin because of what I want to have or want to avoid in the present.

The people who went to the Jordan River had to repent and abandon their sins if they were to meet the one who would come, Christ. The same is true of me. That does not mean abandoning the present. It means living a present that can worthily come with me into the advent of the future. The eternal future to which God calls me must shape my present.

Second Sunday of Advent (B)

In this Church year, we will reflect upon the Gospel of Mark, the first of our four gospels to be written, and the only one to call itself a Gospel. The word is actually two Old English words put together: *gōd* ('good') and *spel* ('news'). Good news. It is a translation of the Greek word that Mark uses in today's reading, *euangelion*.

'Here begins the gospel of Jesus Christ, the Son of God,' is the way Mark opens, and this one sentence sums up his entire text. Right from the start, Mark declares that what he has to tell is good news.

Let's stop for a moment and think about that. Do I really think of my faith as good news? Sometimes, I suppose, I do. But I'm more inclined to think of it as ideas to which I give assent, moral rules which I obey (or disobey), a structured community living in history (including my history).

Does the world at large think of our faith as good news? If folks believed it to be good news, there would be more of them joining us. Perhaps they don't see it as good news for themselves because we don't show that it is good news for ourselves.

Why do you suppose that is? Is it possible that our faith in the Good News is so weak that we fear putting it up against the bad news? Are we afraid to match the gospel to the pain, confusion, doubt and evil we see around us and within us? Perhaps we fear that the gospel won't measure up, or even that it is irrelevant to what bothers the world. Do we fear that the bad news will smash our gospel faith, and so we keep it safe to be brought out like fancy dinnerware only on Sundays and holidays?

Yet, for the Good News to be good, it must face what's bad. Most of us are experts at bad news. Being experts at bad news is, paradoxically, good. At least we know where the Gospel is needed in our lives, know the shape of the hole in our lives that the Good News must fill to really be good news.

The answer to it all is a relationship with Jesus Christ. And so Mark says, 'the gospel of Jesus Christ.' The bad news in my life has an answer in the One who went to the Cross. He knows the bad news, because, like us, he lived with it. He knew the confusion of childhood, the insecurity of adolescence, the betrayal of love, the fear and agony of death. He knew his own bad news, and he knows mine.

We are very busy people. Just getting to church on Sunday seems to be about as much as I can handle. Give time for prayer or quiet reflection? Give time to read Scripture and other faith-nourishing, faith-challenging things? Spend time and energy with and for my neighbor? I'd love to, but I'm just too busy. And yet, that is where I will develop the relationship with Christ that will be the Good News for my bad news.

Why is that? Mark also proclaims that in his first sentence. Jesus Christ is 'the Son of God.' In knowing Christ, I know the Son of God whose death on the cross became the source of life. God's love is stronger than the bad news. The resurrection of Christ is the guarantee of that strength. Our baptism into the death and resurrection of Christ is the guarantee that we share it.

That's good news for you, for me, for everyone. And good news is for sharing. Just as we recommend good restaurants and good films, once we know Christ as good news, we recommend him. How? By living lives that really look as if they are touched by good news.

Once I really know Christ as good news, others will want to know the secret of my joy in pain, my confidence in confusion, my hope in the face of death. The pain, the confusion, the death will not go away. They will be, however, the place where I meet Christ more deeply because I'm not afraid to bring my faith there. The pain, confusion and death will be the bad news where the Good News happens.

And so, in Advent we make a bit more effort to welcome the Lord into our lives and into our hearts, so that we can indeed know him as Son of God, as Good News.

Second Sunday of Advent (C)

We know we will be taken to a world of adventure when a tale opens with words like 'Once upon a time.' They prepare us for marvels—for knights in armor, damsels in silks, fierce dragons, talking animals, magic potions, helpful elves, mischievous gnomes and mysterious fairies.

Compared with that, Luke's story of John is boring. How much adventure can we expect from a story that begins with names of rulers who mean little or nothing to us, detailed yet incomprehensible information about some date, and names of places that are hard to pronounce and that don't even exist anymore?

Why couldn't the evangelist have just written, 'Once upon a time in a land far, far away the word of God was spoken to John son of Zechariah in the desert'?

The Bible does have 'once upon a time' tales. The two creation accounts in Genesis, the Tower of Babel, Noah's Ark, Balaam's talking donkey, Jericho's walls falling to trumpet blasts—all are such tales. Like poetry or good fiction, they are true, but not factual. It is true that God created the world in power and love to be good. That is the truth of the creation stories, which are not factual at all.

Luke tells us that wonderful things are going to happen. 'Every valley shall be filled and every mountain and hill shall be leveled. The windings shall be made straight and the rough ways smooth, and all flesh shall see the salvation of God.'

That sounds like a 'once upon a time' tale, and if it were a fairy tale, we would listen to it in a certain way.

However, Luke is not telling a fairy tale. His story is real, the most real story, the truest story that ever was. In this story, God's truth and the world's facts are not merely close, they are together in Jesus.

Therefore, we know that the way of the Lord will be prepared for real, and all shall see the salvation of God for real.

Reality—that is Luke's message. He tells of a reality that can be located in time and place. So, we get facts of geography, chronology and history. It is Luke's way of saying, 'Hear this story as you hear no other. This story goes beyond what you think of as fact or truth.'

That is an important message for us in Advent. This is the season in which we recommit ourselves to live in anticipation of the fulfillment of God's promises. It is a time to recall that those promises are real and that God intends them to be true in the real world, the world in which we live in flesh, not fantasy.

The vocation of John the Baptizer is the vocation of us Christians, the Church. He was a herald announcing the coming of God's Kingdom. So are we. He came in a particular time, 'the fifteenth year of the rule of Tiberius Caesar,' to a particular place, 'the entire region of the Jordan.'

Each of us lives in a particular time and in a particular place. And in that time and place, the word of God is spoken to each of us, giving us the vocation to call upon the world to 'Make ready the way of the Lord.'

We live in expectation of the coming of the Lord. That coming is not a once upon a time thing nor a someday, somewhere, somehow thing. The coming of God to me, the call of God to me, and my response to that call are something that happens today. It happens in a certain time and a certain place. It calls me to respond with my real life here and now.

Advent is the season in which the Church recommits itself to living a great adventure. We are a band of companions walking through a world of marvels and dangers to a promised goal, eternal life with God. The band is real, the world is real, the marvels are real, the dangers are real. The goal is real.

Third Sunday of Advent (A)

Some people want God to be vengeful. Some even appoint themselves the instruments of that vengeance. Of course, such self-appointed condemners and avengers for God seem insensitive to their own sins and their own need to repent.

They forget or ignore what St Paul said about vengeance: 'Beloved, never avenge yourselves, but leave room for the wrath of God; for it is written, 'Vengeance is *mine, I* will repay, says the Lord." In other words, 'mind your own business.'

People who think God is about vengeance do, however, have a precedent in John the Baptizer. In last week's reading from Matthew, John launched into a tirade against the Pharisees and Sadducees for trying to 'flee from the wrath to come' and said that 'every tree that does not bear good fruit is cut down and thrown into the fire.'

When Jesus came speaking about beatitudes and hope, John naturally had doubts about him. Shouldn't the message of 'the one to come' be an intensified word about God's wrath that is drawing near? So, John sent some of his disciples to question Jesus. 'Are you the one who is to come, or are we to wait for another?' The answer they brought back may have only increased John's doubts.

'Well, John, we asked him what you told us to ask, and all he said is that good things are happening. The blind receive their sight, the lame walk, the lepers are cleansed, the deaf hear, the dead are raised, and the poor have the good news brought to them.'

And John said, 'You're sure he said nothing at all about the wrath of God? Nothing about punishment for sin and evil? How can he be the One? Didn't I say the one to come will burn the chaff with unquenchable fire? Well, then, he must not be the One.'

'By the way, John, he did say one more thing: "blessed is anyone who take no offence at me"';.

The kingdom of God is 'righteousness and peace and joy in the Holy Spirit,' says St. Paul. Like it or not, we are called to joy. The

Gospel really is good news; the coming of the Lord is healing, peace and reconciliation.

What, then, is the task of the followers of the Lord? Are we to keep quiet in the face of sin and evil? No. I should combat sin, beginning with the sin in my own heart. In addition, I must shine the light of God's will on the sin of the world, that of individuals, of groups or of the entire world—especially, perhaps, those groups and those parts of the world that support my livelihood or comfort. But, I must do all that out of love for the sinner—whether myself or others.

Christians are supposed to be signs of the Kingdom, of the coming of the Lord. That means more than putting up a Christmas creche or even a cathedral. It means more than spending an hour each week in a building with a cross on the roof.

Being signs of the Kingdom means that we imitate Christ. Someone who looks to us to find out if God's Kingdom has come in Christ should be able to see that the sufferings of the world are relieved, that the causes of suffering are banished, that new life is given to all, that the good news is proclaimed to the poor. We should be able to reply as Jesus did.

John tried to live as a prophet of God as he understood God. A wrathful God should have wrathful prophets. So, John was 'hellfire and brimstone.' We try to live as signs of God who is present to us in Jesus Christ. So, we show the forgiving love of God to the world. That is where we are greater than John. We are not better than he; we merely know something about God that John did not know, that God would rather go to the Cross than inflict wrath on the world.

Now as we practice the carols of 'peace on earth, good will to all' it is time to renew our commitment to live as Christ who came not to condemn sinners, but to embrace and save them. That's good news for the whole sinning world, including me.

Third Sunday of Advent (B)

A minister described his vocation in the words of John the Baptizer: 'a voice in the desert, crying out: 'Prepare the way of the Lord!"

That is a description not only of the Baptizer's vocation or the minister's, but of the vocation of every Christian. We are all meant to be voices in the desert, calling upon the world to prepare the Lord's way.

TV nature shows teach us that the desert is full of life, color, beauty and documentary makers. But, for people who lived in the cities and towns of the Middle East two millennia ago the desert was home to scorpions, vultures, poisonous snakes and demons, a place of loneliness, barrenness and death.

That's the sort of place where John felt called to proclaim the coming of the Lord. Why? Well, it doesn't take much thought or experience to admit that loneliness, barrenness and death can be true, if partial, descriptions of the whole world. Especially when viewed without faith, the world looks like a desert. John was in a place that symbolized the world of those who heard him.

We, too, are sent into the desert to do what John did. Our sandy wastes may be paved and our vultures may carry smart phones, but where we live can be as much a desert as the area around the Jordan River.

We are in the desert, and like John we have a vocation here. We must issue a call to prepare the way of the Lord.

But, what is this way of the Lord? The English word 'way' is an excellent starting point for reflecting upon what it is that we are called to do with our faith. Two of its many meanings will suffice.

The first meaning, the one Isaiah used, is a road from one place to another. A way has a starting point and a goal toward which one heads. To prepare the way is to make sure the road is ready for travel.

Ways are defined by where they go. Where are we headed? The object of our journey is the full, uninterrupted, unweakened and unending experience of the love of God. We have to name it, so we call it heaven. Jesus called it the Reign of God.

So, preparation of the Lord's way to which we call our fellow desert creatures is preparation to experience the love of God. Since we learn best by doing, we invite, challenge and offer opportunity to our fellows to love and be loved. That's where the way of the Lord moves into a second meaning of 'way'—a style of doing or being.

The style of those journeying toward the Lord is characterized by certain ways of dealing with fellow travelers: love (of friends and foes alike), justice (in the Biblical sense of taking special care to look out for the weak) and peace (not the mere absence of conflict, but an environment in which all can live as children of God).

Since every human being is in the desert, since every human being is on the journey to the Lord, preparing the way is a vocation for all men and women, Christian or not.

This is the reason we, the Church, have something to say about the way the world runs. Society, politics, economics, religion, the arts, the sciences are all subject to encouragement or correction as they aid or hinder preparing the way of the Lord.

That's a big responsibility. It's so frightening that perhaps our greatest sins are due to our fear of what calling the world to prepare the way of the Lord might cost. After all, John the Baptizer lost his head. Jesus was killed on a cross. What will the neighbors think? I need a lot more courage. Where can I find it?

Courage comes from the conviction that I am not alone. We are a community of saints and sinners who call the world to journey toward the Lord, to live in the way of that journey. What is more, we journey with the risen Lord who called himself The Way.

The place we really live our faith is not in a church. It is in the desert of our workplaces, our schools, our streets, our homes. There is no other place for the world to hear our call to prepare the way of the Lord, to join us on the way of and to the Lord.

Third Sunday of Advent (C)

Among the popular features of many publications and the internet are advice columns. Readers send questions, and writers then provide answers.

We like to get answers to our problems. If someone is able to suggest a quick fix to them, we are happy. It has always been that way, and probably always will.

Various people came to John the Baptizer in the desert to get advice. He gave it.

He told the crowd in general to share. He told tax collectors (a notoriously corrupt group in his time) to be honest. He told soldiers to not abuse their power by abusing people.

We are not told how they reacted to John's advice, but since group after group asked for it, we can assume that folks liked what he had to say. We can be less sure that they actually followed it. My own experience of giving and receiving advice makes me suspect that they did not.

Apparently, the people who heard John were looking for something other than advice. Otherwise, they would have followed it, and the world would be a different place. Equally apparent is the fact that I am not really looking for advice, though I may listen to talks, read books and scan articles which I then ignore. I have some other desire, a desire symbolized by my hopeful search for good advice.

What are we really looking for? Answers or an answer? Occasionally, we see signs or hear people who say, 'Jesus is the Answer.' The irreverent comeback is, of course, 'What's the question?'

Well, what is the question? What am I looking for? What is the desire?

I think it is a special kind of relationship. Perhaps that is the real meaning of those 'Jesus is the Answer' declarations. John offered advice. The One who came after, who was 'mightier' than John, seldom offered advice. Frequently, we see him ignoring requests for advice. Instead, he invites people to a new kind of relationship with God and other people.

A common question at this time of year is, 'What do you want for Christmas?' When I was a child, my father used to reply, 'All I want is some well-behaved kids.' We always found it easier to give him a necktie.

The Lord asks each of us the same question. 'What do you want for Christmas?' His asking frees me from the necessity of thinking of one more thing that will clutter my life. I can turn to him and say, 'Lord, all I want is to know you, to know how close to me you are, how much you love me.'

It's a cliché in Advent and Christmas time to mouth wishes for world peace, but the Lord does not even offer that. What he offers is himself. If we really accept that gift, we will find peace.

The acceptance is the key. When John offered advice, people could accept it or reject it and carry on with their lives. If they accepted it, they became nicer people and the world became a nicer place. Nicer, that's all. It remained the same old world. If we become nicer, the world would still be the same old world.

The Lord comes to clear it all away. 'His winnowing fan is in his hand to clear his threshing floor.' The Lord offers something totally new, totally different. He offers a world where advice is not needed, where our baptism 'in the Holy Spirit and in fire' will make of us a new creation.

What we really want has already been given us. We do not have to wait until Christmas Day to receive it. We do not have to wait until we start following all the good advice we have received.

We can spend our lives looking for John the Baptizer, looking for the right advice, the right rules, the right morality by which to live. Or, we can accept the Christmas gift offered us at every moment, the loving presence of Jesus Christ the Lord.

Fourth Sunday of Advent (A)

There was nothing extraordinary about the name Yeshua that Joseph was ordered to give the child. There were probably other kids in town with the same name. As the Aramaic version of Joshua, it was a popular name.

(This might be a good point to make a little digression into the question of how 'Yeshua' came to be called 'Jesus.' The language of the early Christians outside of Israel was Greek. That is the reason the New Testament was written in Greek. Now, when Greek speakers wanted to speak of Yeshua, they had two problems. For one thing, they had no sound in their language that corresponds to the one we write 'sh' in English. The closest they could manage was an 's' sound. Another problem was that to Greek ears, 'Yesua' would sound like a woman's name, since names ending in 'a' were feminine. Since Yeshua was a man, they changed the last sound to a masculine ending, another 's.' So, in Greek, Yeshua is called Iesus. When Christians moved into the Latin-speaking world where a different alphabet from the Greek was used and where 'I' and 'J' were interchangeable, we got Jesus. The hard 'J' pronunciation in English comes from the fact that in English, we pronounce 'J' and 'I' differently.)

So, Joseph was told to name the child Yeshua, and we name him Jesus. But, that is only one of the names by which we call him. The name Yeshua sounds similar to the Hebrew and Aramaic phrase, 'he will save,' and so the angel said, 'you are to name him Jesus, for he will save his people from their sins.' That is something else we call him. Jesus was one man who was really true to his name, a savior.

His disciples called him 'rabbi' or 'teacher.' The Church has called him 'Christ' and 'Lord' and 'God-Man' among other titles. Today's Gospel passage, applying to him a verse from Isaiah (another variation on the same name as Jesus) calls him 'Emmanuel, which means "God with us"'.

But, when all is said and done, perhaps the best title he has for us is the simplest, the one his parents and playmates used in Nazareth, the one his disciples used on the road, the one the Romans put on his cross: Jesus.

Think about your own name or the name of someone you love. Is it a mere word, a few syllables that provoke no more response from you than any other sound? No, a name is special. When I say that I am So-and-so, I mean more than when I say I am a jogger or a stamp collector or a bank robber. My name *is* me.

If I say your name, I say a word that carries with it all I know about you and all my feelings about you. I mean not merely one of many human beings, but one who looks and sounds a certain way, has certain interests, does certain things. Your individuality is captured in your name.

And that brings us back to Jesus and his name. In one sense, it is not a special name. It is not unique. Many people had the same name. In Spanish-speaking societies, many people still have it.

That is part of the wonder we are preparing to celebrate at Christmas, that God has become present among us not in some unapproachable, exalted way, but as someone with a name, an ordinary name because that extraordinary man is in a real way as ordinary as you and I. Jesus really is a normal human being with a normal name.

And when I say that name I declare my relationship with him, my beliefs about him, my hopes in him. By saying his name, I say that it is possible for me and other normal human beings to know him and to call upon him with the same familiarity as his playmates in Nazareth two thousand years ago. He is God, but he is also my friend.

The one whose birth we are about to celebrate has many titles, but one name, the name he shared with so many other people in his land. It is wondrous because it is so common. The mystery that we celebrate in his birth is that the God of the universe is met in someone like us, someone with a simple name, an ordinary Tom, Dick or Yeshua.

Fourth Sunday of Advent (B)

The angel appears to Mary and says, 'Rejoice, O highly favored daughter! The Lord is with you. Blessed are you among women.' But Mary is 'deeply troubled by his words.' Why would anyone be troubled to hear that God favors her?

Let's imagine the scene. Mary has been doing laundry, and is drying her hands on her apron while the messenger of God speaks to her. She is no one special, just one of the many women in Nazareth who expect to spend a lifetime bearing babies, baking bread, cleaning house and looking after their husbands and children. Though there have been great women in the history of Israel, they are long dead. Why should she expect anything special from God or anyone else? Yet, here is an angel telling her she is specially favored by God.

There is a problem in being specially favored by God. It usually means God has chosen one to do something special, given a call that requires a break from a comfortable everyday existence to do something that may make no sense.

Mary's society may not have offered her much of a life, but at least it was secure. It was the life her mother, her grandmother and all the women she knew had lived. There was security in it and even some personal fulfillment according to the terms she had been taught to seek. What if God's favor meant abandoning that security and being someone other than her society envisioned?

That's the trouble with God. Just when we think our lives are going smoothly—not great, but not bad—God shakes us up with a call. Frequently, it's less pleasant than we think the appearance of an angel might be. It may be something that can drive us to despair.

The difficulty is that we are willing to settle for less than what God offers. We are offered God, and want the world instead. Sometimes it takes wrenching separation to prepare us to accept God's offer.

And what of Mary? The angel offers her an unplanned pregnancy, the risk of a broken engagement, the likelihood of ostracism by family and friends. Had she answered, 'Thanks, but no thanks,' she would have been a very sensible woman. Yet, Mary was not sensible.

It takes unsensible people obeying unsensible calls to do unsensible things in order to bring Christ to the world.

But, why Mary? There would have been a rabbi in town who had dedicated his life to the Law of God and service to God's people. Just about any man would have been better educated than Mary. There would have been more powerful people, more socially prestigious people. Even among the women in town, there would have been wives of prominent men, mothers of many sons. Why did God favor an unmarried girl?

God doesn't choose the way we would. God chooses worldly weakness to proclaim divine power. That's the reason Mary was chosen and the reason we have been chosen.

All of us know deep down that we are poor weak sinners, lost in the world and hoping that no one will notice we're not really grown-ups yet. And God has chosen us to be bearers of Christ for the world.

We share Mary's vocation. She was chosen to bear the Savior. In our Baptism, we have been appointed to do the same, to bring Christ to the world, to be Christ for the world. Mary gave Jesus a body. So do I. So do you.

The story of Mary is our story, too. Or, it can be. The key is in our response. The whole story of Christmas depended upon one woman's willingness to say, 'I am the handmaid of the Lord. Let it be done to me as you say.' Am I willing to say the same?

As we celebrate our final Sunday before Christmas, Mary's willingness to say 'yes' is an example and a challenge to each of us. Am I as ready as she to say 'Yes!' to God's call to bring Christ into the world? Am I as ready as she to risk what doing the will of God might mean in my day-to-day life? If I can follow Mary's example, then my life will be Christmas for my brothers and sisters, the coming in unlikely circumstances of the Savior of the world.

Fourth Sunday of Advent (C)

Sometimes, I meet someone and know the child he or she once was because the child has grown up, but has never been outgrown. There is a spontaneous friendliness, a wonder at life and grace that could only belong to that child.

On the other end of life, I look at an infant or child and wonder what sort of grandmother or grandfather I am seeing. Will this child grow in wisdom and grace and be a blessing to all? Will she live a full lifetime? Will he be marred terribly by the injustice, pain and suffering that are inevitable in any life? Will she be forced to endure more than a fair share of that injustice, pain and suffering? Will he cause joy or pain?

Luke's Gospel presents two pregnant women. Luke tells us that each had reason to believe the child she carried was a son. We are also told that each of them was pregnant through an extraordinary act of God. Otherwise, they knew as little as any mother does about the child she bears. What their children would become was as much a mystery to Mary and Elizabeth as any child is a mystery to us.

Elizabeth's child became a desert-dwelling religious teacher who taught his disciples how to live before God. His forthright fulminations against evil eventually cost him his life.

Mary's child followed his father's trade as a carpenter. Later, he became an itinerant preacher. Eventually, he, too, paid with his life for what he became.

What would Mary and Elizabeth have done if they had known in advance the lives their sons would live? Would they have despaired? Would they have terminated their pregnancies? Would they have done all in their power to prevent their sons' choosing the paths they eventually traveled? We don't know.

We are about to celebrate the birth of Jesus. We see pictures and statuettes of the child in the manger. We watch movies and television programs about children and 'the spirit of Christmas.' In many places, Christmas has become a festival for children.

Christmas is, of course, much more than a child's feast. But, it is, indeed, a time for us to reflect upon children and the gifts we give them, the legacy we leave them. It is not always a good one.

One of the dispiriting things at this time of year is adults' supporting unbridled selfishness in children. For many, Christmas is the season of 'Give me'. But, the point of gifting is the giving, not the receiving. I knew a child who at Christmas time would go with her parents to an orphanage to share her parents with children who had none.

There is much that we do throughout the year to our children that warps the promise with which they are born. We provide them with 'entertainment' that is, in effect, a form of child abuse, because it will malform the child that God has given to the world as a unique gift. We may bring the child to church and provide for some religious education, but then show that our day-to-day lives bear no relation to the Gospel we claim should be the guiding principle of our lives.

A speaker once asked her audience, 'If you die tonight, will your children go to heaven?' That simple question contains the challenge and the glory of a parent's vocation. But, it is not limited to parents. We all play a part in raising the children of the world. Are we giving them all they need to be children of God through all eternity?

Mary and Elizabeth could not protect their children from the dangers of life. They could, however, raise their sons to be men for whom faithfulness to God was more important than life itself.

Can we do the same for our children? We will not be able to protect them from life, but we can point out to them the road to heaven. We can take them with us as we journey along that road. Can there be a better Christmas gift than that?

Christmas Midnight Mass

The children at a parish in Tokyo were preparing a Nativity play and needed a donkey. They decided I was perfect for the role. So, after several rehearsals, I found myself in front of the congregation on my hands and knees with a leash around my neck and Mary sitting on my back.

As rehearsed, Joseph led me to the door of the inn and knocked. As rehearsed, the innkeeper gruffly asked, 'What do you want?' As rehearsed, Joseph said, 'My wife is having a baby and we need a place to stay.' As rehearsed, the innkeeper said, 'No room. Go away.'

Then, *ad lib*, Joseph turned to Mary and said, 'I *told* you to make reservations!'

The accommodations for the birth of Jesus is an important matter for Luke. In fact, it may be the major point of his account. He was not trying to make his story more poignant or sentimental. He was engaging in a form of ancient Jewish Scripture commentary, *midrash*.

Midrash, too simply put, is the practice of using the details of a story to bring the rest of Scripture to bear on a point.

Luke's account of the birth of Jesus is an extended midrash, using various details to make his readers or hearers think of parts of Scripture that tell us important things about Jesus. The birth in the stable is one of those details.

If Mary had, in fact, called ahead for reservations, how would the story have continued? Joseph would have checked in, and Jesus would have been born in an inn. Is there any problem with that? There is if you ask yourself, what is an inn?

An inn is a place for travelers, for people who are passing through. They do not plan to stay long, just long enough to get some rest, conduct some business and move on. The fact that there is no place for Jesus in the inn refers to a verse in the Book of Jeremiah: 'O hope of Israel, its savior in time of trouble, why should you be like a stranger in the land, like a traveler turning aside for the night?' It is a prayer that God stay with the people of Israel, that divine care be present for them in time of need.

Jesus is not born in the inn because he is not 'a stranger in the land . . . a traveler turning aside for the night.' He really is Emmanuel, 'God With Us.' By saying that 'there was no place for them in the inn,' Luke is not talking about overworked hotel staff. There was no place for them in the inn because an inn is not an appropriate place for the birth of Jesus. He is not passing through. He has come among us to remain with us. He is not a traveling stranger, but a native of our world, and he will not move on. He's here to stay.

For Luke, the key detail of the account of Jesus' birth is the manger. He mentions it three times. It is the detail that guarantees the message of the angel to the shepherds. 'This will be a sign for you: you will find a child wrapped in bands of cloth and lying in a manger.' It is important because it tells us why this 'God With Us' is with us.

Isaiah talks of how the people of Israel have turned away from God: 'The ox knows its owner and the donkey knows its manger; but Israel does not know, my people do not understand.' Luke is telling us (three times!) that the time has come to know God. No matter that we may be as dense as an ox or as stubborn as a donkey, we can now know God because in Jesus God is as really present as hay in a barn. (That's why we put an ox and a donkey in our Christmas creches.)

What is usually in a manger? Food. Jesus is found in the manger because he is nourishment and strength, 'good news of great joy to all the people.'

And who are those people? The first announcement of the birth of Jesus is to shepherds. In our Tokyo performance, the shepherds were cute kids. Shepherds in Israel two thousand years ago were a very different group. Shepherds were outcasts. They had a reputation for being thieves, wandering the wilderness with their sheep, and attacking unwary travelers they happened upon in their wanderings. They had reason to be afraid when 'the angel of the Lord stood before them.'

The first people to hear that God is now with us and will never leave us, the first to hear that in Christ God is clearly present as one who will give us life, is a group that most needs that kind of good news. Christ has come for sinners. In other words, Christ has come for me, for you and for all the world.

Jesus will not stay at an inn, but in the manger. He will always be among us and always sustain us sinners. Christmas is not about a baby born long, long ago. It is about Jesus Christ, the Risen Savior who is with us today to be 'good news to all the people.'

Christmas Day

Why on Christmas Day don't we hear the story of the birth of Jesus?

Let's think about stories. There are bedtime stories. There is prime-time television in our homes. Story telling is something we do at night.

Daytime requires something different. Daytime is when we take the message of the story and act upon it. So, on Christmas Eve we had the story; on Christmas Day we have the meaning: 'the Word became flesh and lived among us.'

One advantage of learning new languages is that we learn new words and through them learn new things about the world and ourselves. Like every human being, I have a poignant, and in English inexpressible, feeling of mourning, longing, nostalgia and peace regarding people, places and things in my past that can never be regained. But, until I learned that there is a single Japanese word for that feeling, *natsukashii*, I couldn't really grasp it for myself, nor could I be sure that it was anything more than a personal neurosis.

In English, we use the word 'word' in an interesting way. One of the highest forms of praise we can give is 'He's a man of his word.' On the other hand, 'She doesn't keep her word,' is one of the worst condemnations we can make. If I say, 'You can take my word for it,' I expect to be believed and am insulted if I am not. My word is equivalent to my self. If I give my word, a violation of that word is a selling out of my self, my soul.

And today we celebrate the fact that 'the Word became flesh and lived among us.' What might that mean?

The Word whose story we told last night tells us something about the universe in which we live: 'God so loved the world that he sent the Son to be our savior.' We live in a world loved by God. And not only a world loved by God—we, each of us, is loved beyond measure by God. It is a world of pain, confusion, suffering and death, but it is also the world where we meet God.

Like realizing new ways to see myself, the coming of the Word made flesh shows me that I am called to be more than I might otherwise think. The Son became one of us that we might become sons and daughters of God. And the coming of the Word affirms that the deepest longings of our hearts for love, life and peace are not empty dreams. Those longings have a divine answer, and therefore are precious.

This is the meaning of Christmas. The decorations, the gifts, the songs, the food and all the rest are good, but the reason for them all is not simply the birth of a baby a couple of thousand years ago. Today we remember and celebrate the fact that we can know God's glory and power not as some sort of information, but as a person.

Knowing him, we shape our lives in accord with that Word, hearing the words of the Son and obeying them. Even more, it means living in such a way that we, too, become the word of God for the world.

So, on Christmas Day we move from the story to the program, from what happened long ago to our vocation today.

It's a big order. Can we be the word of God for the world? Can we be the means for others to understand who God is and what our destiny is as the beloved ones of God? Can we speak words that will make real for them the love of God, the forgiveness of God, the hope of God?

Yes, we can. We have God's Word for it.

Holy Family (A)

I saw a picture of the Holy Family that showed Joseph doing carpentry while Jesus held a tool and Mary watched at the door, doing nothing. Not like any family I know.

We know what real families are like. In a real family, Jesus would have been getting in his father's way or been off somewhere else when Joseph wanted help. Mary would have been working at keeping the house livable and the family fed.

If that picture of Joseph's workshop is of a holy family, we're all out of luck. All we can do is look on wistfully, and think how nice it would be if our families were perfect. If family holiness is some impossible situation of goodness, harmony, cleanliness, comeliness and industry, there is no reason for us to celebrate this day.

Perhaps the picture was wrong. Maybe Jesus was a pest around the house. Maybe Mary shouted herself hoarse calling him to meals. Maybe Joseph got so caught up in his work that Mary and Jesus stood at the workshop door, ignored. Maybe Mary sometimes burned the bread.

We have just celebrated the birth of Jesus. The mystery of the Incarnation is that Jesus was not God's play-acting at being human (that's a heresy called 'docetism'). Jesus really was human. He really needed to be toilet trained, he really got bumps and bruises roughhousing with friends. He really could be a pest. He really could be a precious son. The family we call the Holy Family was not all that much different from other families.

Are we wrong, then, to call it a *holy* family if it was no more 'holy' than our own?

Because of the Incarnation, holiness cannot be other-worldliness. The place where God is met, the place where God loves us, is here, now. A truly holy man or woman lives in the here-and-now, is a sign here and now that God's love is real and at work.

The word 'holy' comes from the word 'healthy.' Holiness is a kind of health, and health may be the means for us to understand holiness and, therefore, what we celebrate on this feast of the Holy Family.

When I am healthy, I am able to move through life with a certain confidence. I feel that nothing the world brings me by way of challenge can overwhelm me.

Holiness, too, is a kind of confidence, a conviction that God's love embraces me. God's love is stronger than sin, stronger than death, and so I can live with confidence. I need not fear to love others or be loved by them. I need not fear the world and what it may do to those who serve. I need not fear the power of sin or death.

Think of people who make health an object of life. Besides annoying the rest of us, they are neither happy nor truly healthy. That is because health is a by-product of a certain kind of life. One who walks, runs, dances, or climbs for the joy of it is healthy. One who walks, runs, dances, or climbs for the sake of health is unhealthy.

Holiness, too, is a result, not an objective. When I am filled with amazement at God's great love, when I share that love with all I meet, I become holy. I pray with joy, with gusto. If I turn prayer into some sort of spiritual calisthenics, I will be neither happy nor holy. I will not be a sign of heaven to the world.

That brings us back to the Holy Family. It was holy not because it lived an exalted life unavailable to the rest of us. It was holy because it was a group of people not unlike ourselves who loved, who lived, who wept, who laughed. Theirs was a home in which a boy could 'grow in size and strength, filled with wisdom, (with) the grace of God on him.'

Our homes can be the same. Perhaps more than we realize, they are. They have their problems. No family is without them. Every mother feels swords pierce her heart at some time or other. Yet, our homes are where we learn to love, where we learn of God's love. It is in our families that we practice the sharing, openness and patience that enable us to show the glorious love of God to the world.

Holy Family (B)

Matthew and Luke (the only New Testament writers who present pictures—sometimes contradictory—of Jesus' infancy and childhood) did not intend to give a chronicle of the early life of Jesus.

They wrote introductions to their accounts of the life, death and resurrection of the man Jesus. So, they left out details of his teething, first steps, toilet training, weaning, puberty and all the other events of his early life that we must assume occurred. Their infancy and childhood narratives are meant to tell us about the adult, and only about him.

So, then, what does the story of Jesus in the temple tell us about the vocation of the adult Jesus?

Throughout his Gospel and the Acts of the Apostles, Luke lays stress upon the Jerusalem temple. It is Luke who tells of Jesus saying to his parents that the temple is his father's house. Luke shows us the infant Jesus being carried into the temple, not a usual practice in those days when Jews were scattered all over Israel and the rest of the world. The message is that Jesus is the One who from the moment of his coming really belongs in the temple because he is the real divine presence among the People of God.

When 'guided by the Spirit, Simeon came into the temple,' he was seeking the Lord. When he found him, he said a prayer that proclaims Jesus as the fulfillment of all the hopes of those who rely upon God's promise. Not only that, Simeon also praises God because Jesus is the fulfillment of the unspoken hopes and dreams of those who do not even know God. 'My eyes have seen your salvation which you have prepared in the presence of all peoples.'

Then Simeon tells Mary that Jesus is a sign that is opposed, and that she herself will be pierced with a sword. Traditionally, this is taken to refer to her pain at the crucifixion. However, it has a broader meaning, one that includes all of us. We believers, like Mary, are faced over and over again with Jesus forcing us to make a decision to follow him, a decision that can be heart-rending because it is ultimately an embrace of the cross.

Then comes Anna. Luke does not put any words into her mouth, but in a sense, she is a more important speaker than Simeon. He talks to Mary and Joseph. Anna spoke 'about the child to all who were looking for the redemption of Jerusalem.' In other words, Anna is a model of the Church, the community that speaks of Jesus to all who are looking for redemption.

We are all seekers. Some of us may say we are looking for God. More of us, probably, put it in different terms. We are looking for love, for happiness, for peace, for some sort of answer to a deep-down unease we feel but cannot put into words. This searching is one of the things that appears to distinguish us from other animals.

In our seeking, we sometimes settle for answers that eventually show themselves to be no answers at all. Sadly, many of us then decide there either is no answer or that the very quest is a neurosis rather than one of the God-given glories of humanity.

If there were no answer to our search and longing, then, indeed, our lives would be futile. What use is there for a hunger that cannot be filled? What sense can there be to an existence defined in part by something that is meaningless?

But, there is an answer. That is what the temple was all about. It was a proclamation in stone that God was present among the people and that their search leads to a real place. That real place is not merely a building; it is the presence of God.

That presence is not limited to a particular building or location or people or even a religion. It is a person who can come to us and be with us anywhere, any time. It is Jesus in what he said, what he did, what he was and what he is.

So, Simeon and Anna went to the temple and met the Lord, the answer to their search and ours that God has 'prepared in the presence of all peoples,' including us.

Holy Family (C)

What sort of parents could mislay their child for three days? And, what about the teachers in the temple? Didn't they ask Jesus where he was staying, where his parents were? Were they stupid? Did he lie to them?

Is the account of the boy Jesus in the temple about careless adults and a footloose though precocious 12-year-old? No, it is about the man he grew up to be.

The hint comes from the fact that it was on the 'third day' that his parents found Jesus. For any Christian, that phrase brings to mind the Resurrection.

Luke presents this story not to tell us about the childhood of Jesus, but to give a synopsis of his Gospel, a summary that begins with the birth of John and ends with the discovery on the third day of Jesus who had been lost.

The synopsis presented as the infancy and childhood of Jesus is followed immediately by a shift to the future, to the prophetic ministry of John. It then moves through the activity of Jesus to his death and the disciples' encounter on the third day with the Risen One everyone thought was lost forever in death.

What can we learn about the life and mission of Jesus from the part of the summary that we hear today? It might be helpful to turn off our imagination for a few minutes, to drive from our minds the pictures we've seen of a boy sitting with bearded old men, looked at by a surprised lady in blue and a bearded man with a staff in his hand. Let's just look at the words of the account and see what they remind us of in the life of Jesus.

Luke's story takes place in Jerusalem at Passover, the feast of the liberation of the Hebrew people by an extraordinary work of God, the Exodus. Years later, at another Passover in Jerusalem, God freed all people from the power of sin and death through another extraordinary work, the Passion, Death and Resurrection of Jesus.

At the end of the celebration, the parents of Jesus think he is lost, though he is exactly where he belongs. After that Passover years later, the Emmaus story puts a pair of disciples on the road, thinking that Jesus is lost though he is exactly where he belongs—with them.

Then, Luke tells of finding of the child in the temple on the third day. The temple is the place of God in the world, the chief point of worship, the place where people could expect to experience the holiness of God. Jesus is there, because Jesus has become the new temple. (Remember that Luke tells us the old temple's veil was torn apart when Jesus died).

In the temple, Jesus is among the teachers, because he is a teacher. Luke intends to share Jesus's teaching, so from the start he is among the teachers. However, Jesus is much more than a teacher. He is the Son of God. Therefore, he says, 'Did you not know I had to be in my Father's house?'

The mystification of his parents, who 'did not grasp what he said to them' is paralleled by people in every age who are mystified by Jesus. However, mystification does not mean separation. Jesus stayed with his parents as he stays with his Church. As the boy Jesus 'increased in wisdom and in years and in divine and human favor, ' so, too, the Church grows in wisdom, years and favor.

This Gospel story, then, is not a story about the child Jesus. It is a story of the Gospel as Luke plans to present it to us. In this liturgical year, we will reflect upon that Gospel of Luke. We will re-affirm our commitment to follow the teachings of Jesus, to recognize him as the true Son of God, the temple where God dwells among us. We will struggle as a community of faith and as individuals to grow in wisdom and favor with God and the world.

Epiphany (A)

Those astrologers or wise men from the East have picked up a lot of baggage on their journey through the centuries. First, they got a number—three—though Matthew says nothing about how many there were. As time went on, they got kingships because the psalm we pray today as a responsorial speaks of kings bearing gifts. They got races and even, eventually, names: Melchior, Balthasar and Gaspar. In 1248, construction began on one of the world's most beautiful buildings, Germany's Cologne cathedral, to house a gold casket that supposedly contains their relics. Sometimes, it seems they have so much baggage that we can no longer see who they are.

So, who are they? What is this special celebration today all about? Literally, an epiphany is a showing. That's a hint of what this day is. Epiphany is a celebration of the showing of Christ to some very fortunate people: us.

Jesus was born of Jewish parents in a Jewish town, a Jewish boy who grew to be a Jewish man. Why would the birth of Jesus mean anything more to the greater world than the birth of any other Jew? Even granting him to be the incarnate presence of God on earth, of what significance would that be to those who are not themselves members of the chosen people, the Jews? Other great acts of God for that people did not particularly help others. Moses lead the Hebrews through the sea, but it was not the best thing that ever happened to the Egyptian chariot corps. The good news promised to the Jewish people and fulfilled in the coming of Jesus could have been exclusively theirs.

What we celebrate today is the wonderful love of God that did not limit itself to a single people. Jesus came to and for the Jewish people. But he also came for all of us who have no natural ties to that people.

Were that not the case, most of us would not be followers of Christ. Most Catholics, most Christians, are not Jews by descent. We are Chinese and Cheyenne, Maoris and Magyars, Americans and Armenians, Thais and Tlingits, Indonesians and Ibos. We are everybody, and we all bring to the Church our own ways of being Christian, our own colors, to add to the caravan.

That is what we celebrate today, what we give thanks for today. God has chosen to love us, the unchosen people.

The centuries God spent, the prophets God sent, were all meant to build a people within whom a savior could be born for all of us. On the Epiphany we celebrate the fact that Christmas was not just for one people, Christmas is for all.

So, who are the wise astrologers? They are all of us. We are the strangers who come from afar, from outside the chosen people, to worship the king of the Jews. We come to Christ, conscious that we have no right to him, and grateful that God's love is not hemmed in.

We, like the astrologers, come to worship. We have seen the signs and wonders of Christ, and recognize and worship him as God among us. We don't bring the gold of a king, the frankincense of a god or the myrrh of the dead, but we worship him nonetheless as our ruler, our God, the One who died and rose. We bring the gifts of our personalities, our cultures, our histories, our traditions and even our sins. We also show the way and invite others to join us as we go to worship the Lord.

On Epiphany, we thank God for the gift of Jesus Christ, a gift given to all of us throughout the world, throughout time. Like the wise astrologers, we respond by bringing our gifts to the Lord: our ways of praying, our ways of singing, our ways of thinking, our ways of acting. Let us give thanks today, too, for each other, for the variety of gifts our fellow travelers bring as 'bearing gifts we travel afar.'

Epiphany (B)

The schoolboy sitting in front of me on the bus was carrying a textbook titled *Advanced Physics for Hong Kong*. I presume the title of the book referred not to some supposed uniqueness of physical laws in Hong Kong, but to the fact that the text was written for students whose first language is not English, or that it used examples familiar to people in Hong Kong. In other words, there was probably a perfectly logical explanation for the title.

However, that title started me thinking about the ways we sometimes think that a particular place, race, nationality or whatever is somehow special. In fact, everyone is special, since every single person is a child of God, made in the image of God and given a special vocation that no other living being will ever share.

Epiphany is the feast on which we celebrate the fact that all people are sons and daughters of God. The wise men who pay homage to Jesus stand for all the people of the world. That is symbolized in the custom of representing them as members of different races.

Throughout history, we humans have been exclusionists. Sometimes we have gone beyond exclusion to outright persecution. For some reason or other, or no reason at all, we view people who differ from us as remote from us. The less we know about them, the more we believe stereotypes and fictions, and then act upon those misconceptions.

Today, the Church says that Christians cannot follow the way of the world in this matter. Today we see that God's offer of salvation in Christ, God's love, is not limited by colored shapes on a map. Anyone and everyone is welcome.

It need not have been that way. After all, Jesus is the Messiah promised to Israel. He came to a particular people in a particular time. He may not have been what they were expecting, but he was certainly theirs. All of theology could have been taught from a book titled *Advanced Salvation for the Jews*, and the rest of us would have had no right to complain.

But, God issued an invitation to the whole world to join the new People of God. That is what today's Gospel story tells us. Easterners, that is, strangers and pagans, came to worship. Not only did they come, but they were led by a star of God. God not only welcomed them, God wanted them there.

It's unfortunate that we have settled on three as the number of those who came. The Gospel does not give any number. I think that we should represent today's feast with a long procession of people stretching beyond our sight and time. It should include all the wise men and women whom God has called to see the divine glory present among us in a man born some two thousand years ago to a Jewish mother. In other words, everybody.

So, should we go running out to buy more statuettes for our Christmas creches? Should we add airplanes and autos to the camels, and men and women of all ages and places to our three kings? Perhaps we should, since what we see influences what and how we believe. But, we are called to more by today's feast.

We are called to be Stars of Bethlehem, leading men and women to Christ. The chief vocation of the Church is to proclaim the Good News to all nations. How do I share in that great vocation?

All of us are called to be missionary in our day-to-day lives. Our neighbors should be able to see the light of Christ shining in our words and deeds. Is my life such as to attract others to journey to meet the Lord?

I hope that at least on occasion, it is. But, I have to admit that there is much in me and in my life that would not draw others to look to Christ whose name I claim when I call myself 'Christian.'

Today, I am especially called to root out from my speech, my thoughts and my deeds all prejudice toward other races, religions, cultures, and so forth. I am called to be as welcoming in my life as God, who welcomed strangers to share the wonder of knowing Jesus. God, who sent a star once upon a time and sends us today to lead others to worship him. I could call it *Advanced Christianity for All the World*.

Epiphany (C)

Scholars tell us the earliest feasts of the Church were Easter, Pentecost and Epiphany. The Annunciation (the original feast of the Incarnation), Christmas and all the others came later.

Originally, Epiphany celebrated several events in the life of Christ, including his birth, the adoration of the magi, the hidden years of Jesus' youth, his baptism by John and his first miracle at the wedding in Cana. What all those events have in common is that they were 'introductions' of Jesus to the world.

In the Western Church, Epiphany eventually developed into three feasts: Christmas, the Epiphany feast as we celebrate it today and the Baptism of the Lord. Each of them commemorates and celebrates some aspect of the manifestation or appearing of the Lord, his introduction to the world.

While there is something to be said for the later development of three feasts from one, let's look at them together, seeing what unified message they might have for us today.

First, the Christmas aspect, the manifestation of Jesus as one of us. We can get so caught up with Mary and Joseph, the baby, the manger, the angels, the shepherds, the wise men and so on, that we can forget that the feast is not about birth so much as about a manifestation, the showing of God as one of us, born to live, grow, learn, love, die and rise.

Think about that. If we want to see God, we need not spend years doing spiritual calisthenics or wait until we die. God has come among us as one of us. If you wish to see God, look at Jesus, the manifestation of God among us.

And not simply among us. The second aspect of this feast is the fact that Jesus is one of us for us. The wise men from the east who come to adore Jesus symbolize the wise men and women of all times and places who are invited to come to Jesus. In welcoming those worshipers from pagan lands, Christ shows that his coming is not limited to a particular time or place or even religion. He is here for us all, and the salvation he brings is meant for all, including even those who do not know him.

The third aspect of the original Epiphany feast now celebrated separately is the Baptism of the Lord, next Sunday's feast. When the Father proclaims, 'This is my beloved son,' it is obviously a manifestation of Jesus as the Christ, the Messiah.

But, there is more to the Lord's baptism than that proclamation. His baptism marks the end of his 'hidden years' and the beginning of Jesus' public ministry. The Lord is among us and for us with a purpose.

That purpose is the proclamation to all the world of the love of God. That love is the reason for the Incarnation and Jesus shows that love to us in his teaching, his healing and above all in his cross.

In our own baptism, we are united with Christ. So, what we say about him is, in some way, something we say about ourselves. In that case, what does looking at the three aspects of Epiphany teach us about our own vocation as Christians?

The Christmas aspect certainly applies to me. After all, I am a born-and-bred human being, as was Jesus. But, it's not so simple as that. I too often try to avoid the implications of being human. I pile up goods, run after fads, and give myself over to idols of wealth, status, nation, culture and even religion to hide from myself the fact that I am weak, mortal. I allow myself to forget that real human life is lived in community with others, a community of shared love and concern. Like Jesus, I must manifest the presence of God who is love.

And my showing that love of God must not be limited. It is easy to love those whom I like, those similar to myself. But the wise men were not like Jesus. They were foreigners. They were pagans. Our own community must be as open to the world, accepting those children of our Father who are different from us, whether in race, nation, gender, sexuality, religion, politics or physical or mental abilities and disabilities.

Finally, we must, like Jesus, accept that vocation to manifest God to the world. We must make that a part of our lives, shaping who we are and what we do.

When we do that, we become an epiphany, an introduction of God and the world.

Sacred Seasons:

Lent and Easter,

Trinity and Corpus Christi

Ash Wednesday

Remember the story of Cinderella? Her father loved her, but she became the victim of a wicked stepmother and stepsisters. They made her a slave, forced to sleep in the ashes. One of her stepsisters gave her a new name, Cinderella, 'ash girl'.

Eventually, Cinderella's godmother, a fairy who had been her mother's friend, rescues her, turning degradation into glory and freeing her to become the bride of the prince.

Sounds a lot like us, doesn't it?

We are children of a Father who loves us. Yet, we are enslaved. It is clear that I am not living as a child of God. I am enslaved to evil, to selfishness, to laziness, to fear. I am controlled by advertizing, by social expectations, by wrong notions of what constitutes health, wealth or happiness. I spout 'ideas' and prejudices that come from ignorance—my own and that of the world in which I live. I and those I love suffer and die. I am called to eternal joy, but crouch in the debris of burnt-out hopes and dreams. I live in ashes.

So, today, we smear ashes on ourselves as a reminder of who we are. 'Remember that you are dust, and to dust you will return.' That means of course, that I will die and decay or be burnt up, but it also describes my whole life till then. We are all Cinderella.

Is that where the similarity ends? Are ashes my whole story? Is there a godmother who will save me?

Welcome to Lent, a time to reflect on our ashiness and our salvation. From now till the start of the Sacred Triduum we will remember that we are Cinderella sitting in sin.

Even though we may wash today's ashes off, we must not forget our need to wash away the separation from God, others and our true selves that the ashes symbolize. That is the reason we also hear the words of Jesus, 'Turn away from sin and be faithful to the gospel.'

Jesus warns us to 'beware of practicing your piety before others.' Yet this is probably the one day in all the year when Christian piety is most noticeable. But, are we parading our piety or, rather, proclaiming our problems? Ashes on my forehead are no guarantee of goodness in my heart. All they declare is the fact that I am not all-good. The real test of piety comes in the day-to-day conversion that the ashes remind me I need.

Perhaps the real reason we wear our ashes today is to let everyone else who lives on the ash heap know that they are not alone. There is a community of people who are with them, but who believe there is more to our lives than the ashes.

So, we have forty days to get ready for the Easter Vigil, the great ball when we celebrate the fact that we, like Cinderella, are invited to glory. And not in some make-believe, but in the reality of God, the most real.

However, in Lent we do well to not allow ourselves to anticipate Easter. God's saving love always embraces us, and at the same time our ashiness is always with us. But, if we are to experience the heights of Easter joy, we should probe the depths from which we are drawn.

That is the reason we fast during Lent. We are not punishing ourselves. In fact, one of the Prefaces for Lent speaks of 'this joyful season.' By not tasting the foods we like, we give ourselves a taste of life in the ashes, life without the hope of resurrection. In a sense, it is make-believe, this playing at being Cinderella.

But, it also gives us an idea of the horrible reality that life could be if God had not chosen to give us more. Not an empty stomach, but an empty life. 'Remember that you are dust' could be the whole story.

Thanks to the Baptism we will renew at Easter, we know that ashes are not the whole story. Many of our brothers and sisters think they are. Lent gives us a chance to taste the emptiness of their lives so that we will be better motivated to share the good news with them that they, like we, are invited to leave our ashes behind and take part in a glorious dance of joy and an unlimited future in God's love.

We can and will live happily ever after.

First Sunday of Lent (A)

The Lenten readings for the first year of the three-year cycle of readings we use in the liturgy emphasize the fact that Lent is a season of preparation for catechumens who will be baptized at Easter and a season of renewal for the already-baptized who will reaffirm their own baptismal commitment. Some of the readings are unique in that they should be used in any year that there are catechumens in the community.

In the course of five weeks, we reflect upon the temptation of Christ, his transfiguration, his meeting with a woman at a well, his healing of a man born blind and his raising of Lazarus. Each teaches a different aspect of Baptism.

So, what has today's Gospel passage got to do with Baptism? More specifically, what has it to do with *my* Baptism, whether past or pending?

Is the Christian life easy or difficult? Considering that it entails a life-long struggle against temptation, it is difficult. Considering that it entails a life-giving awareness of the forgiving love of God, it is easy. If God has created me to live a certain way, why do I find it difficult to live the kind of life God calls me to?

Something is very wrong. I continually make choices that seem based upon the mistaken belief that what is bad for me is better, or at least easier, than my true good.

The temptation that Jesus faced is, in fact, the temptation I face. It was a temptation to take the easy way out. Jesus was hungry and tired after his fast. To go for the 'quick fix,' to take no responsibility for his actions and leave everything up to God, to grab for power—we all face similar temptations. We disguise laziness as faith. We disguise irresponsibility as hope. We disguise lust for power as love.

Basically, there is only one temptation, the temptation to betray my vocation. The vocation of Jesus was to face rejection and the cross. The devil offered him a way out, tempting Jesus with ways to avoid the suffering that his vocation entailed: 'You face hunger, danger and ineffective powerlessness? Come to me!'

What is my vocation? Paradoxically, temptation may help me find it. If the basic temptation I face is to betray the very purpose God has given to my existence, then looking at my temptations may give me hints of God's will for me.

One of the values of the Sacrament of Penance is that it gives me opportunities to reflect upon temptations in my life and take an honest look at those to which I give in. If I do more than merely compile a list of sins, but look for the underlying reasons for my sin, I may come to see patterns in my life, patterns that show the paths by which I try to get away from or get around the vocation God has given me. If I trace those paths back, I may find out the kind of person the devil would rather not have me be.

A broad hint of that vocation can be found in the Renunciations we make at our Baptism and when renewing our Baptismal commitment: 'Do you reject sin so as to live in the freedom of God's children?'

Baptism is a rejection of sin in our lives. It is uniting ourselves with Christ who sent the devil on its way when he refused to give in to temptation. What we reject is anything that prevents our living in the freedom of God's children.

That is my basic vocation, to be a child of God, free to grow, to love, to serve. Free to reject the glamour of evil, refusing to be mastered by sin. I will have a unique way to live that vocation, just as you will.

This, then, is the aspect of Baptism that the Gospel tells us of today. When we accept Christ's call to union with him in the Church, we commit ourselves to spurning the enticements of evil that would lessen our freedom as sons and daughters of God.

Lent is, then, among other things, an opportunity to prepare to make that renunciation at Easter by examining myself to find out where in my life temptation finds it easy to take root. Then, through prayer, fasting, reflection and works of mercy that break down my self-centeredness, I make in deeds the renunciation I will make in words as we celebrate the Resurrection.

First Sunday of Lent (B)

Whether it be giving up sweets for Lent, giving up marriage for life, giving up chances at wealth to serve others, or whatever else, Christian asceticism does not arise from a belief that the pleasures of life are evil or that we must punish ourselves for our sins. Neither is it religious athleticism, an attempt to turn ourselves into spiritual superheroes who earn, deserve or wrest God's grace.

Asceticism is an act of faith, a chance to remind ourselves and proclaim to others that we need fear no loss so long as we are embraced by God's love. In a sense, it is a preparation for death, when we give up everything except the undying love of God.

During Lent, we 'give up' various things. Kids give up sweets, adults give up alcohol or meals. Some individuals and families engage in what may be the most drastic form of modern self-abnegation, putting aside various electronic devices from Ash Wednesday until Easter.

What happens when I give something up? Well, the first thing is that I notice it's missing. My stomach rumbles, my eyes stare at a blank screen. I go through withdrawal. If I don't panic and give in right away, pouring a drink, opening a bag of snacks and grabbing for some electronic device or the TV remote, I realize a few things.

The first is that my life has depended upon things that are not actually essential. After all, I'm not dying of my Lenten practice. I can live without.

The second is that by voluntarily doing without I understand a bit of what many of my brothers and sisters must experience and endure involuntarily every day. I feel communion with the rest of the world.

Third, I realize I'm turning a profit. Each day I do without something, I reduce my expenditures. I can lose weight and make money by doing nothing! I also turn a profit of time. Time I spent on what I've given up is now available for new things. I may decide to use those profits for the sake of others.

Fourth, I am reminded that I can indeed 'do without' because no matter what I lose, God is with me. I can go hungry, I can even starve. I will die. But, nothing can separate me from the love of God. And so, I pray in gratitude, in awe, in hope. My growling stomach can be a call to prayer.

Ultimately, our Lenten practices are an opportunity to renew faith in God's love that went to the Cross for us and showed that the love of God is stronger than evil, stronger than death.

But why now? Why spend our penitential 40 days before the Sacred Triduum of Holy Thursday, Good Friday and the Easter Vigil instead of, for instance, before Christmas or Pentecost?

It's tied to something very important that happens at the Easter Vigil and at Mass on Easter Sunday. The Easter Vigil is when catechumens are baptized. Lent was originally the season of their preparation. At Easter, those of us who are already baptized renew our own baptismal commitment.

Because it is primarily a time for catechumens, Lent is a time for the Church to prepare to welcome them. Are we worthy to lead these men and women to Christ? Are we dedicated enough to encourage them on the way? Are we examples to them of what their new life in Christ will mean? Lent is a time for our conversion.

Mark's Gospel gives us a summary of Jesus' message: 'This is the time of fulfillment. The reign of God is at hand! Reform your lives and believe in the good news.' The Lord has come among us, and God is with us. Easter, with its promise that life is unconquered by suffering and death and in fact comes through them, is near.

The Lord calls us to a change of life, a change we exercise in some small way in Lent as a means of recommitting ourselves at Easter to the big reform we accepted in our baptismal commitment.

That reform is a life free from enslavement to the things around me, free of the need to find my value in the things I own or use. It is sharing my time, talents and treasures with my brothers and sisters. It is joyful, grateful hope that in my death I am not lost to God.

In other words, it is Lent.

First Sunday of Lent (C)

I have never gone 40 days without eating. I've never seen the devil in an immediately recognizable form. I cannot turn stones into bread. I've never been offered power over the whole world. I doubt that if I jumped from some pinnacle angels would come to my rescue; I certainly will not try.

And yet, I face the same temptations Jesus faced.

'The devil said to him, "If you are the Son of God, command this stone to become a loaf of bread". In other words, the devil tempted Jesus to take care of himself as if even in the face of starvation he were not cared for by God. Not only that, but to look out for himself first by taking the easy way, the quick fix.

I know that temptation. I also know something Jesus did not know. I know about giving in to it. Many times I let my needs and wants become the focus of my attention and action. I think I live by the things of this world, rather than by the ever-present, ever-vigilant love of God. And I am not always careful that the way I meet those needs and wants is in accord with the life I should live as a Christian. I choose to forget that my commitment to Christ is not simply about what I do in church; it is about what I do outside of church. So, rather than trust in God, I act as if God were not part of my life. I look after myself and will do whatever I think necessary to do so.

'Then the devil led him up and showed him in an instant all the kingdoms of the world. And the devil said to him, "To you I will give their glory and all this authority; for it has been given over to me, and I give it over to anyone I please".

Jesus does not contradict the tempter. He does not say that worldly power does not belong to the devil. Nor does he deny that the road to power is devil worship. Instead, he says what the devil offers is not worth the price. Better to be a powerless worshiper of the Lord than a powerful worshiper of evil.

The thirst for power is stronger, perhaps, in the schoolyard, in the workplace or in the family than in politics. Even in the Church we often see power at work rather than humble service. And every time we see it, we see a case where the devil has won.

I may not be in a position to rule the world, but there are areas of my own little world where I like to be in charge. I am willing to be a servant, but on my own terms and only as suits my convenience. Otherwise, I will do whatever is necessary to stay in charge, to have some degree of power over myself or others.

'Then the devil took him to Jerusalem, and placed him on the pinnacle of the temple, saying to him, "If you are the Son of God, throw yourself down from here".' If Jesus were to do so, the tempter continued, he would force God to rescue him. This is the temptation to make God into a tool.

In my prayer especially, I try to run God, as if God must do certain things because I want them done. Often, those things are good. A mother's prayer for her dying child is certainly no sin. Neither is her anguish and anger when the prayer is not answered as she wished.

The temptation is in the move from 'even so, your will and not mine be done' to 'my will be done, and you must do it'. We must accept the most basic fact of the universe, that God alone is God and the divine will is not ours to control. We live in trust of God's love, confident that whatever else may happen, that love will never desert us.

It is Lent. It is good to begin the season by reflecting upon the temptations that Jesus faced and that we face that hinder us in living the Baptism commitment we renew at Easter.

Easter is God's triumph over sin. It is another point at which we are like Jesus. We are tempted like him, but in our Baptism into his death and resurrection, we are conquerors with him. Jesus faced temptation and refused it. We can be like him in that as well.

Second Sunday of Lent (A)

In his classic work of theology, *The Idea of the Holy*, Rudolf Otto says that the basis of religion is an experience of spiritual power that overwhelms our day-to-day understanding and life. Otto speaks of our reaction to such encounters with holiness with the Latin phrase *mysterium tremendum et fascinans*. That is, we find divinity to be something beyond our understanding that is awe-inspiring yet attractive.

Today's Gospel passage illustrates Otto's point. Peter, James and John go with Jesus 'up on a high mountain by themselves.' This brings to mind Moses, who went up on Mount Sinai to meet with God. While atop the mountain, the disciples see Jesus, the carpenter-turned-preacher whom they have been following, revealed to them in glory. 'He was transfigured before them, and his face shone like the sun, and his clothes became dazzling white.'

Moses and Elijah, epitomes of the Law and the Prophets and therefore of the whole of Scripture, join Jesus. He is the fulfilment of the will and promise of God.

Peter's first reaction is fascinated attraction. 'Lord, it is good for us to be here.' But, when the full import of what he is experiencing dawns upon him, things change.

A bright cloud overshadows them. The voice of God comes from the cloud and 'when the disciples heard this, they fell to the ground and were overcome with fear'. Fear is a common reaction in the Bible to encounters with God's presence. Isaiah, Zechariah, Mary, the shepherds at Bethlehem and the women at the tomb of Jesus are just a few more of the many people who experience fear.

Fear is different from fright or terror. Fear as we understand it from Scripture is a sense of awe, of our weakness and insignificance. CS Lewis likens it to the feeling someone might have when standing at the base of a tall cliff. It is basically an honest appraisal of ourselves when faced with the overwhelming power and goodness of God. Our prayer, 'Lord, I am not worthy', before receiving the Eucharist is an example of it.

We have gone to the moon. We have turned the atom into a power source as we once did with fire and the horse. We have killed millions. We are driving species to extinction. There seems to be little or nothing before which we need kneel in awe. We are hard to impress. If we had been with Jesus at the mountain of the Transfiguration, we would have been too busy taking selfies or tweeting to either feel attraction or fear.

What has this to do with Lent and our preparation for baptisms and the renewal of baptismal commitments at Easter?

Like Peter, James and John, we have been invited by Christ to know him as he truly is, the Lord, the Son of God. Others may consider him a notable teacher, someone to be admired and, perhaps, emulated. We, however, have been called to see his glory, his holiness.

In our Baptismal profession of faith, we are asked if we 'believe in God, the Father almighty,' the *mysterium tremendum*. We answer, 'I do'. Then, we are asked to declare our belief in 'Jesus Christ, his only son,' the *mysterium fascinans*. Again, we answer, 'I do'.

My faith in Christ is more than a commitment to certain teachings or membership in a group that carries on various 'religious activities'. It is a relationship with God, a grateful response to the fact that the all-powerful ruler of the universe has invited me to kneel in awe at a love that embraces me and leads me in a fascinating man, Jesus Christ.

The Transfiguration reminds me of the mystery that Jesus, the fully human one, is also God. If I would know what it is to be truly human, I must look to Jesus. If I would know God, I must look to Jesus.

And to the Church. Not the Church as an institution, but to the Church as the People of God, the community of those who have been invited by Jesus to join him on the mountain, who have been united with Christ in Baptism and made sharers in his glory.

In every Christian the *mysterium tremendum et fascinans* is present. We hide it by our sin. We fail to see it because we fail to seek it. But, it is there because Christ is there. It is even present in myself. In our Baptism, we become signs of God to the world. We are the Transfiguration today.

Second Sunday of Lent (B)

One evening at a parish Bible group's discussion of Abraham's willingness to sacrifice his son Isaac, the first few speakers were nuns who lived in the parish.

Each made observations about how Abraham's faith challenges us to deeper trust in God. They spoke of how Abraham's example called them to recognize their attachment to things of this world.

When the last sister had spoken, Mr. M's turn came to give his reflections. I always envied his ability to get to the heart of a passage of Scripture without intellectualizing it or making it so abstract that it sounded uncomfortably like some of the worst homilies I had ever preached.

'Maybe I'm a bad Christian, but I'll tell you right now: I don't care if God himself told me to do it, there's no way I'd ever hurt a hair of my boy's head, let alone be willing to kill him! If God wants that, I don't want God!'

The issue of child sacrifice was not an abstraction for Mr M. He had a son and a daughter whom he loved no less than Abraham loved Isaac. Mr M knew what Abraham had to face in order to obey. And Mr M, unlike Abraham, knew he had to disobey.

How often when I hear the readings at Mass, or when I read the Bible or pray words of Scripture do I look upon them as beautiful phrases, as food for thought, as points for reflection? Most of the time. Sometimes, the words seem merely ants crawling across a page or bees droning in the sanctuary.

How often do I allow the Word of God to be a real message addressed to me, comforting me, challenging me, calling me? Oh, I like to think I do. Like the sisters that evening or like me had I not been able to swallow my words while still unsaid, I can make reflections upon the Word. But they come from my head. The Word doesn't get mixed up in my real day-to-day thoughts, emotions and activities.

Lent is a special time to hear the word of God. Lenten practices, including, perhaps, a renewed familiarity with Scripture, free me to some extent from what distracts me from attending to the Lord. During Lent, I can grow to be more like Mr M, ready to not merely hear the Word of God, but to hear it as something addressed to me here and now.

In today's Gospel passage, three disciples hear the Word of God addressed to them. The voice from heaven confirms the vocation of Jesus announced at his Baptism: 'This is my Son, my beloved.'

The voice spoke at the beginning of Jesus' ministry. Now, as that ministry reaches its culmination, the glory that will be Christ's through the Cross is shown to the disciples. The baptismal call to start off on the road to the Cross is the same as the proclamation of Jesus in glory.

It may seem strange that early in Lent, a season we tend to see as gloomy, we are presented with a picture of the Lord in glory. However, if we look at the Transfiguration with the sort of heart that Mr M had, we may find it appropriate, comforting and encouraging for ourselves.

The Transfiguration is not just a story about Jesus on a mountain once upon a time in a land far away. It is my story. As I prepare to renew my baptismal commitment at Easter, I remember that at my own Baptism, God said, 'This is my beloved child.'

God loves me as Abraham loved Isaac, or as Mr M loved his son. In fact, as St Paul reminds me in the second reading, God went so far as to actually sacrifice the Son for me. 'Is it possible that he who did not spare his own Son but handed him over for the sake of us all will not grant us all things besides?'

Today's Gospel is a Lenten reminder that the gift of being a beloved child of God that I received in Baptism leads to my own transfiguration. I walk the way of the Cross in this world, but it is a way that leads to incomparable glory.

Sometimes, the word of God can be a threatening challenge. Today, it is 'tidings of comfort and joy.' Let's hear these words like Abraham and Mr M, ready to hear the word of God as personally addressed to me, to us.

Second Sunday of Lent (C)

Is heaven a definite time and place? No. Place and time are within our universe, and heaven is beyond creation. Is heaven, then, totally unconnected with place and time? No. In Christ heaven has come to earth. Is heaven, then, something that was once here, but is here no longer? Is it something that will come?

Those are not idle questions. Saint Paul tells us, 'As you well know, we have our citizenship in heaven.' Someone's this-world citizenship can tell a lot about him or her. If that be so about political citizenship, how much more important is what can be learned from my heavenly citizenship? Curiosity about heaven is not mere speculation. It is an attempt to know who I really am.

Jesus takes three of his followers up a mountain. As he is praying there, he changes somehow. He becomes glorified. What Peter, James and John experienced on that mountain was heaven. It was Jesus in glory, with saints of heaven. We call it 'transfiguration.' Peter was not sure what to call it, or even what to say.

That is the difficulty with heaven. We do not know what to say. That is not because we are totally inexperienced. The problem is that words just do not suffice. So, we use images. The Gospel uses the image of brightness, of light. We sometimes visualize that by using rays or halos. Sometimes we use the image of freedom that flight symbolizes. So, we put wings on those in heaven. For many, music is the best image of heaven. It cannot be seen, it cannot be touched. Yet it moves us. So, we put harps and horns into our picture of heaven, and we make music an important part of our worship of God who cannot be seen and cannot be touched, but who moves us.

I said we are not totally inexperienced when it comes to heaven. How can that be? Isn't heaven what happens to us, God willing, after we die? Yes. And no. Heaven is yet to come, but it is also present.

I live today as a citizen of heaven, looking forward in hope for full residence in my real homeland. I am on a journey, a life-long journey, toward it. That is heaven yet to come.

Christians have been criticized for being so concentrated upon heaven as a goal that we ignore the world through which we journey. Though there may be some Christians who live that way, the criticism is not fair. The real Christian life is indeed in heaven, but it does not begin when life in this world ends. Heavenly life begins with the death we call Baptism. Heaven is all around me today.

Heaven was present to Peter, James and John on the mountain. Where Jesus is, there is heaven. So, if I wish to experience heaven, I should come to know Jesus better. That means growing in friendship with the Word of God in Scripture. It means prayer.

Another experience of heaven, one that is hard to believe, perhaps, but which is true nonetheless, is the Church, the People of God. Look around at the people with whom you worship. It is an unlikely looking heaven, no doubt, but those are the chosen People of God, the citizens of heaven. When you are together, you are all experiencing heaven. One day beyond all days, you'll experience the fullness of heaven together.

Finally, we share the Eucharist. Christ unites ourselves to him in the most intimate way. That is the fullest experience of heaven.

Why all this in Lent? Lent is a chance to live our true citizenship. In prayer, fasting and sacrifice, we weaken our ties to the world. We withdraw from our citizenship in this world in order to focus upon our true home, our true citizenship. As we journey toward Easter, we move along in our journey toward heaven.

We spend more time in prayer, in reflection on the Word of God and on Jesus Christ. We gather more often, perhaps, with the People of God for prayer. We share the Eucharist. We spend the season in heaven as we move toward it.

Third Sunday of Lent (A)

Christians engage in many activities. We build places of worship. We conduct rituals. We pray. We theologize and teach. We have commandments and customs. We go on pilgrimages. We use various objects and images. We have publicly recognized leaders in the community. We have monasticism and mysticism. We have fund raising and do works of charity. We pray. We fast. We dance. We sing.

In other words, we do the same things as followers of other religions. Obviously, what makes Christianity unique is not to be found in such activities.

The basic difference between Christianity and other religions is an acknowledged relationship with God in and through Jesus Christ. Certainly, all people and all creation have a relationship with God in and through Jesus Christ, but Christians have accepted God's invitation to live in the knowledge of that relationship.

Some theologians would say that Christianity is not even a religion. They feel it is more accurate to say that Christianity has religious elements attached to it, but because of the relationship upon which it is based, it is basically so different as to be in a separate class from religions. That position makes sense, but whether we consider Christianity to be a religion or to merely have religious-looking aspects, let us look at what makes it look like a religion to outsiders.

So, what activity is unique to Christianity when viewed as one among many religions?

To be baptized, to be a Christian, means that one not only does 'religious' things—worship, meditation, study, service etc—but that one is first and foremost united with Christ and is therefore an evangelizer, a missionary as he was and is.

Today's Gospel passage is the one of this year's Lenten readings that brings the relationship between Baptism and mission to the fore.

The first evangelizer at the well as in our lives is Jesus. When he meets the woman, he does not hesitate to speak with her. Rabbis avoided contact with women. Jews avoided dealing with Samaritans and to accept food or drink from one was to risk impurity. John later presents even more reason for Jesus to avoid this particular woman—she is a notorious sinner.

The woman is shocked: 'How is it that you, a Jew, ask a drink of me, a woman of Samaria?' So are his disciples: 'They were astonished that he was talking with a woman.' But, this is the heart of evangelization. Jesus showed that God's love has no limits by breaking the limits of custom, propriety and even religious purity.

This is the source of the missionary vocation that each Christian shares with Christ by reason of Baptism. Mission comes from being known by Christ and accepted by him regardless of who we are.

The way in which he does this in the case of the woman is important. He invites her to break the same limits of custom that he has broken. When he asks her for water, he is giving her her first chance to evangelize, to share God's caring love. He is willing to share his vocation with her. (This is the reason evangelization includes the call to Baptism, to membership in the Church—we wish to share the missionary essence our vocation with all.)

The woman does not stop with giving Jesus some water to drink. As she comes to realize the extent to which Jesus has loved her, she leaves him to evangelize others. 'Then the woman left her water jar and went back to the city. She said to the people, "Come and see a man who told me everything I have ever done!"' He knew her, yet loved her.

Christ has not called me to be a disciple because of any goodness I have to offer or because I have talents that might be useful to the Kingdom. As St Paul tells us in the Epistle to the Romans, 'God proves his love for us in that while we were still sinners Christ died for us.'

To accept that love and to be baptized is to accept as well the vocation that Christ has from the Father, a vocation he chooses to share with me. That is, the vocation to be an evangelizer, a missionary.

I do not have to wander the world looking for opportunities to fulfill that vocation. I can find them even over a glass of water.

Third Sunday of Lent (B)

Jesus swung a whip at sheep and oxen that would soon be sacrificed, terrorizing them a bit more before they faced the knife. He attacked people making a living by providing a service to worshipers who needed animals to sacrifice. Dove sellers served the poor who could not afford bigger sacrifices. The commandment against graven images meant that people who wanted to contribute to the temple had to change coins bearing images of pagan gods or rulers into temple money. So, why does Jesus go after them in a way so alien to our view of 'gentle Jesus, meek and mild'?

The layout of the temple tells us. There were sections of the temple for different people. The high priest could go where no one else could, into the Holy of Holies. There were sections for priests and Levites, for men, for women. The outermost courtyard was open to non–Jews who wished to associate themselves with the prayers and sacrifices going on in the temple. It was here that the needs of those entering the temple for worship were met.

Imagine yourself as a gentile coming to the temple to pray. You know you're not allowed inside, but you're willing to settle for any place that allows you to be close to the temple of God. You climb the steps to the courtyard reserved for you, and what do you find?

The courtyard is full of cattle, tables and crowds carrying on business. There's no room for you! The needs of temple worshipers have crowded you out from being a worshiper yourself.

That is the source of the Lord's anger. All people have the right to come to God, but the religiosity of some was blocking others. So, Jesus drove out those who had usurped the prayer place of the outsiders. His problem was not with the temple, but with the fact that the very temple of God had somehow become an obstacle to men and women who were seeking God.

One reason we read this passage in Lent is that the attack on the vendors and money changers was one of the reasons that leaders in Jerusalem brought about Jesus' death. As we draw closer to our commemoration of the death of Jesus, we trace some of his steps to the Cross.

However, there is another reason to reflect upon this event during the season of repentance and conversion. The situation that enraged Jesus continues.

There are no animal vendors in our churches, and any parish struggling to pay expenses will accept contributions no matter whose picture is on them. However, we, like the temple vendors, block men and women who seek God.

Imagine once again that you are that non-believer hoping to draw closer to God. You look at those who claim to show the presence of God in the world. What do you see?

One thing is a history of Christians killing, exploiting and abusing each other and the rest of the world. You turn to the news, and see injustice and violence in the part of the world with the longest, most sustained Christian presence. You see the Church divided into denominations and sects, considering what may or may not have been said centuries ago more important than a shared vocation to be a sign of God's unifying love.

Somehow you find your way through those obstacles, and encounter an actual community of Christians.

You find yourself in a mob of people who neither know nor care about the so-called brothers or sisters worshiping with them. You see worship that leaves you wondering if God, the creator of beauty, could have anything to do with something so dead.

In sadness, you turn away, because Christians have blocked your meeting God just as the temple vendors blocked the gentiles' access to their place of prayer.

Mid-way to our celebration of the Cross and Easter, we reflect on how we are like the animals, tables and vendors in the temple, interfering with others' finding the Lord. As individuals and as a community, we must repent. But, we are called to more than guilt feelings.

Lent is a time to commit myself to living in such a way that a world looking for God will find in me and the Church a welcome, an example and a guide.

Considering how Christ dealt with those who interfered with others' search for God in the temple, I dare not fail to purge from my life or from our community anything that may provoke his anger at me.

Third Sunday of Lent (C)

The Galileans murdered by Pilate may have gotten off easy in public opinion. After all, Roman rule was not popular. It is easy, though, to imagine the tongue wagging that went on in Jerusalem when the tower at Siloam collapsed. 'Well, those 18 must have been big sinners. It was God's punishment, sure enough.'

The same sort of talk goes on today. Some people claim to have a clear idea of God's will. They have an advantage, perhaps, because they have discovered that God thinks just as they do. I am certain that God's thoughts are not my thoughts, nor are God's ways my ways. So, I am less certain of what God thinks in specific situations.

I cannot agree that God devises cruel punishments for people so beloved as to be worth the crucifixion of Jesus. If we could be forgiven nailing him to the cross, what sin is beyond forgiveness? Jesus says there is only one, the refusal to accept forgiveness. Not AIDS nor the rain that ruins a picnic nor any other tragedy or mishap, whether big or small, is God's torturing us.

However, I agree on one point with people who are sure they see God's will in the misfortunes that befall others or even themselves. They believe that God is involved in the matter. They are right.

But, what is the nature of that involvement? What could God be doing besides causing the situations from which we suffer?

We are getting ready for our Good Friday commemoration of what God does with suffering. God undergoes it.

The mystery of the cross of Christ is that God suffers. The suffering of Jesus was not deserved—legally, morally and in every way, Jesus was innocent. Jesus suffered because there is something about God's relationship with us that entails the suffering of God.

We feel farthest from God and God seems farthest from us when we suffer. The pain may be physical as in injury or illness, it may be psychological as in depression or rejection, it may be spiritual as when we feel sinful or that God is far off. Whatever the source or sources, we feel that God has abandoned us.

That is, then, when we most feel the need for God. And God is there. Not that God takes the pain away. That is not the message of the cross. Jesus was not removed from the cross until he was dead. He did not rise to new life until he had suffered fully.

God is with us in our pain, doing what anyone who loves us does when we are in pain: God suffers with us. Some religions may talk of the power of God. Christians should proclaim the pain of God, an infinite pain that comes of infinite love.

Much of God's pain (and our own) is caused by us. The things we do to one another, the things we do to ourselves—everything that goes against the will of God breaks God's heart because it goes against our own good. We call it sin.

We are celebrating Lent, the season of repentance. We reflect upon our sinfulness and do what we can with God's help to change our lives. Rather than punishing us, God gives us chance after chance to stop causing divine and human suffering.

That is the point of the parable of the fig tree. That does not mean that we can postpone our conversion. Let us not cause God who loves us and whom we love any more pain.

Fourth Sunday of Lent (A)

Insight means being clear-sighted enough to see the obvious. The man healed by Jesus in today's gospel has it: 'I know this much: I was blind before; now I can see.'

Being united with Christ through Baptism is to receive the gift of insight. We know we have insight because we know what the world is really all about. It is the place where God does wonders of love. Not the least of those wonders is healing the blindness that keeps us from seeing the truth.

The man who was blind since birth is a model of a Christian. When he stands before his judges, he is an example of the Christian standing before the world, proclaiming Jesus, light of the world, at the risk of ostracism.

Until we meet Christ, we are like that man was in that we have not known light. We may think we see, as the Pharisees did, but we do not really see.

The man's vision of Jesus develops. This parallels the process by which someone moves from being an inquirer to a catechumen and eventually comes to Baptism. Even those who have been baptized in infancy probably go through much the same development in the course of their catechesis and life.

At first, he speaks of 'that man they call Jesus.' At his next interrogation, he declares that Jesus is a man 'from God'. Finally, when he has been driven out because of his growing insight, he calls Jesus 'Lord'.

Coming to see who Jesus is constitutes true enlightenment. Knowing who he is, we finally know the true story of the creation into which he came. We can see what is in front of us, and recognize it.

What do we see? What is it that should be so obvious to the followers of Christ yet is missed by others?

God.

All people have the possibility of seeing something of God. However, without seeing Jesus Christ, one cannot know God in the fullest revelation. To see Jesus is to see God and to know something of God that can be known in no other way.

The call to Baptism is an invitation to be cured of the blindness that afflicts the world. But, why us? Why should I be chosen to know the Lord when billions of better people than I will never have that chance?

Perhaps I need it more than others. Perhaps without the eye-opening experience of knowing Christ my blindness would be worse than that of the Pharisees. In the First Book of Samuel, it is not the strong and good-looking older sons of Jesse who are chosen. It is the runt of the pack, the youngest boy who is not even important enough to be under consideration. He is as unlikely to be a king as a blind man is to be a teacher of true sight to the religious experts.

Yet, it is David who is chosen. It is the man blind since birth who becomes the teacher. It is I who am called to see God in Christ. Unlikely, but God's ways are not ours.

How can I respond to this choice? The man in the Gospel can enlighten me here. He does the two things that define a Christian.

First, he proclaims Christ, standing up for him before the world, arguing his case and suffering on his behalf. In other words, the man says what he sees. This may help others realize their blindness and lead them to the eye-opening experience of knowing Christ. On the other hand, it may confirm some in their complacency.

Second, 'he said, 'I do believe, Lord,' and bowed down to worship him.' The healed man not only told others what he believed, he said it to Christ as well and adored.

Grateful courage is what underlies his actions. He knows that he needed to be cured and has been cured, and he knows who did it. He is not afraid to state that obvious truth.

Proclamation and worship are the essence of the Christian life.

When I reflect upon my call as one who has undeservedly been healed of the blindness that prevents our knowing God, I, too, should be moved to that same sort of grateful courage. I, too, should be a worshiping proclaimer.

Fourth Sunday of Lent (B)

The heart of what Christians celebrate and proclaim is a verse from John that deserves memorization and frequent recitation and meditation: 'God so loved the world that he gave his only Son, so that everyone who believes in him may not perish but may have eternal life.'

What is the world that God so loved? Is it an ideal place where everyone lives in justice and peace? Is it an Eden where sin is absent and humankind lives in harmony with itself and nature? God would certainly love such a world, but unfortunately it doesn't exist.

Does God love the good things that happen in our world? Justice and peace really do occur. God's beautiful creation is appreciated, is protected and has its harmful effects softened or prevented. This is a world where love among peoples and worship of God actually happen. Perhaps God so loves the good things about our world as to send the Son as a reward to those responsible for that goodness.

However, that is not what the passage says. It says 'the world' without modification. The world God loves is this world, the one in which we actually spend our lives. It is a world of injustice and discord as well as of love and cooperation. It is a world where there seems to never be good unmarred by pain, stupidity, selfishness, weakness, hatred, sin and death. The good news is that God loves the world as it is, not as it could be or should be.

What makes this good news is the fact that we are part of that world so loved by God. We do not have to earn God's love. We have it, bad as we can be, to the extent of God's sending the Son to save us from whatever keeps us from experiencing that love in its fullness.

Does this seem a strange message for Lent, a season to reflect upon repentance and our need for salvation? Shouldn't we be gloomy in order to set off the joy of Easter? Isn't it a few weeks too early to be hearing such incredibly good news?

Later in the passage, there seems to be an opening for a bit of gloom: 'Whoever does not believe is already condemned for not believing in the name of God's only Son.' Does this mean that we are saved by believing in a single word and damned for not believing in it? Are all those who do not know the word 'Jesus' doomed?

A pitfall for those who look to Scripture (and other Church teachings) for knowledge of God is what theologians call 'objectification'. It is the tendency to treat the words of Scripture as if they were a checklist rather like instructions for flying a plane or baking a cake. However, they are more like poetry and should be read that way.

In the Bible, one's name is the equivalent of one's self. To believe in the name of Jesus is not to make declarations regarding how the neighbors called him; it is to accept what he really is, perhaps without ever hearing the word 'Jesus' (the condition of most men and women alive today and throughout history).

What is he, then? That brings us back to the overall theme of his words to Nicodemus. He is the love of God made present among us. He is the source of eternal life, offered to the whole world because God loves the whole world. To accept his name is to live in the love of God, not refusing any of the gifts God offers us, whether we know the donor or not.

Lent is the season when we prepare to renew our baptismal commitment in solidarity with those being baptized at Easter. It is a time of preparation to re-dedicate ourselves to proclaiming to the world the good news that God indeed loves us now, here, as we really are.

God's love will not wait or depend upon my repentance. That love will not make any demand upon me except that I accept it. That love will not even be overcome by my death, and so is the source of eternal life.

Can I really believe that? I can easily believe that I must repent, but it's harder for me to believe that God loves me whether or not I do anything to earn it. God loves me not as I could be or should be, but as I am. Even I don't do that.

Fourth Sunday of Lent (C)

When we hear 'A man had two sons', don't we stop listening? Instead, we think, 'Oh, yeah—the Prodigal Son'. We think about the son. However, the parable is not about a prodigal son. It is about a prodigal father.

The first thing he does is to give away one third of his possessions, the share that would eventually be inherited by the younger of two sons. Right from the start of the story, then, the one who is 'extremely generous, perhaps to the point of wastefulness'—the definition of 'prodigal'—is not the son, but the father.

The next thing that happens is that the son leaves home and wastes his fortune. Or, is it? It is time to ask when the forgiving happens in this story.

Can it be when the son faces facts? No, it cannot be then, because no one at home can hear him come to his senses.

Can it be when he turns and begins his journey home? No, it cannot be then because he is too far off for the father to know.

Can it be when he falls at his father's feet? No, it is not then, because the father does not let him finish his confession.

So, when is the son forgiven? The Gospel tells us that the father saw his son while he was still far off. The reason is clear. The father was standing outside looking into the distance for his son's return.

In other words, when the son walked out the door, his father went out, too. He stood there, waiting for his son to come to his senses and return. The father forgave the son's sin as soon as it was committed. All that remained was for the son to come home and accept forgiveness.

So, what follows the son's receiving his portion is not his departure, but the stepping outside of father and son.

That is the point of Jesus' parable. The father, of course, is God, God whose love is so prodigal that no matter what foolishness I commit, forgiveness is there from the start. Jesus is saying that all I need do is come to my senses, turn around and accept the gift God always offers.

The Pharisees and scribes did not like that. They saw Jesus welcome sinners and eat with them. Eating with them was especially offensive. One description of the Reign of God is of a banquet for all God's people. There might, perhaps, be space at the feast for sinners, but that would depend upon repentance and forgiveness at the coming of the messiah.

By welcoming sinners to the table already, Jesus was claiming that God's reign had begun, and that he himself was the host at the banquet. No wonder the Pharisees and religious teachers acted like the elder brother in the parable. They weren't merely jealous of the folks with whom Jesus ate; they felt that the whole meal was premature and presumptuous.

But, Jesus was telling them by what he did and the story he told that God does not wait to forgive us. We are not doomed to remain in our sin until some special time. We don't have to start being good. All we have to be is loved by God, and that is always, whether we know it or not or whether we accept it or not or whether some like it or not.

Lent is a time for me to come to my senses and return to my Father. I do not need fancy words. I do not need to buy forgiveness with good deeds or intentions. All I need is to say, 'Father, I have flunked'.

Then, we go out to share the Good News that God is waiting for the whole world to come to its senses, waiting to embrace it with the love that is always there for it.

Fifth Sunday of Lent (A)

The story of Lazarus is our story. The Lord says to all of us, 'Come to me!'

Today the catechumens take the last liturgical steps before their Baptism at the Easter Vigil. They have prepared themselves for a new life with Christ in the Church, and the Church is preparing itself to welcome them and renew our own baptismal commitment.

The raising of Lazarus is a reminder that to be a Christian is not just to live in a certain way. Christians do have customs and commands that we obey and disobey, the chief among them being to love God and all those whom God loves. But, the Christian life is not based upon those laws or defined by them; those laws are based upon something else that we are called to reflect upon today.

We love God because God loves us. Our love is a response. That is the reason that the mission of the Church is to show others the love of God. Only when they have experienced God's love can they come to love God themselves.

God's love is not limited in any way. I can sin, and God forgives me, saying, 'Come to me!' I can wander off, and God goes with me, saying 'Come to me!' I can suffer, and God suffers with me, saying, 'Come to me!' I can die, and God, who died with me in Christ, says, 'Come to me!'

We started Lent with the Ash Wednesday reminder, 'Remember, you are dust, and to dust you will return'. Death is the most powerful force we know. It comes to all, and puts an end to all. It makes a mockery of our plans, our achievements and even our virtues and good deeds. They will not survive.

But, in Christ, we will. St. Paul tells us that 'if for this life only we have hoped in Christ, we are of all people most to be pitied'. We are dust, but remember, though dust is our end, it is also the material of life-giving creation.

In John's Gospel, the raising of Lazarus is the seventh of the 'signs', starting with the wedding feast at Cana, that Jesus gives to show who he is. Seven is a biblical number for wholeness, since God's creation of the world reached its fulfilment on the seventh day. The fulfilment of Jesus' mission is found in the raising of the dead. That is really what the Lord is all about.

'I am the resurrection and the life', says Jesus to Martha and to us. 'Those who believe in me, even though they die, will live, and everyone who lives and believes in me will never die. Do you believe this?' When we make or renew our baptismal commitment, we are asked the same question: 'Do you believe in . . . . the resurrection of the body and life everlasting?'

What is my answer? I say, 'I do', but is that merely a gesture on my part? Do I really live as if I were convinced that nothing, not even death, need terrify me with the threat of abandonment by God? Am I convinced that death, fearsome though it be, is a 'sleep' for one who has been baptized into the life of the risen Lord?

We will soon celebrate the resurrection of Christ. That is our joy and our hope. Today, before we are overwhelmed with that celebration, we recall that his resurrection involves us as well. Just as Lazarus was called from the tomb, we know that in some way or other we, too, will be called by the Lord to new life.

All we know about Lazarus is that his sisters loved him and that he had friends. One of those friends was Jesus. In our Baptism, I accept the Lord's offer to be that kind of loving friend to me. He will do for me what he did for Lazarus. I will return to dust, but I believe that one day I will be called: 'Come to me!'

Fifth Sunday of Lent (B)

When Jesus speaks in John's Gospel, he often makes it easy to misunderstand him. Nicodemus, for example, gets mocked by Jesus for having difficulty figuring out how a grown man can be born again. Today Jesus does it again, saying one thing, but meaning more than folks would catch at first hearing.

When Jesus says he will be lifted up, the expectation is that he is describing some sort of glorification. 'I—once I am lifted up from the earth—will draw all to myself.' After all, the passage begins with his declaration that 'the hour has come for the Son of Man to be glorified.' It sounds encouraging. Jesus will be lifted up from this earth to something better and we will be drawn to him there. Good news, but the wrong message.

John 'lets the beans out of the bag' by telling us that Jesus is actually talking about the way he will die, lifted up from the earth on a cross. Do I really want to be drawn to him there?

The paradox is that both understandings of what Jesus says are correct. For John, the Crucifixion is the glorification of Christ and his glorification is inseparable from the Cross. How can that be? How can death by torture be glory?

As we approach Holy Week, it is time to think about the puzzle of John's equating death and glory. Theoretically, Jesus could have saved us by doing something other than dying. Sharing intellectual or spiritual enlightenment would have been easier for us to handle.

Let's start by thinking about glory. We may not be sure what it is, but (aside from John's equating it with the Cross), we think that, on the whole, it's more pleasant than being tortured.

It's hard to describe glory, since we have not experienced it fully. However, we have all had moments that have seemed close enough to the real thing to give us a hint of what glory is. Over the centuries, we have used light, halos, trumpets, anthems, dances and ecstasies to describe it. To put it prosaically, glory is the experience of being embraced by God's overwhelming love.

That love has no limit. Time, sin and death cannot overcome it. It is a love by which God gives life in all its richness. When I intuit it or, like a contemplative, experience it directly, I am transformed, transported by a joy so great it can feel like pain.

But, can I trust it? How can I be sure of it? After all, I will die. Even before that happens, I feel the love of God less often and less intensely than I feel its seeming absence. Believing in it doesn't make my life any easier. It certainly doesn't make me a nicer person. So, is the love of God that the Church proclaims real?

This is where John's insight that the Cross is the glorification of Christ gives comforting assurance. Even in his death that seemed as far as possible from the love of God or anyone else, Jesus was in glory because he was embraced by God's love and showing the nature of God's love.

God's is a crucified love. It is so completely self-giving as to be a self-immolation, the death of God. In John's account of the Last Supper, Jesus says there is no greater love than to lay down one's life for one's friends. On the Cross, that is what God does. The eternal God dies of love.

The ultimate example of the presence of God's love, the ultimate glory, is indeed the Cross. So, Jesus can say that in being lifted up on the Cross he will draw all to himself in glory.

And what of us? At Easter, we will renew our baptismal union with the death of Christ. Jesus says that unless a grain of wheat fall to the earth and die, it remains merely a grain. I will certainly die. In various ways, I have suffered and will suffer. Can I believe that even in these experiences, I am embraced by the love of God, that I am in glory?

That is one of the things Lenten practices should be teaching me in a low-key way. In deprivation, privation, suffering and death I am embraced by God. In those experiences I am, in fact, most closely embraced by God, because they are the times I can myself be most like God whose love is a suffering love.

Fifth Sunday of Lent (C)

The scribes and the Pharisees should get credit for honesty. After all, in the case of the woman caught in adultery they could have made believe they were virtuous and started throwing stones. Instead, when Jesus said, 'Let anyone among you who is without sin be the first to throw a stone,' they 'went away, one by one, beginning with the elders'.

As we get older, we have more experience of our weakness, so perhaps the oldest realized soonest that they were not sinless. Their honesty and courage in admitting they were little different from the woman gave courage to their juniors to be as honest. So, three cheers for the scribes and Pharisees!

Jesus, on the other hand, is something of a disappointment. There are many things he could have done but did not do. Is doodling in the dirt what we want him to do when a woman's life is in danger? Why didn't he try to rescue her? How did the poor woman feel when he entrusted her fate to a mob of religious fanatics?

Then, after the mob melted away, where was Jesus the teacher? After all, the woman had been caught in serious sin. Was it right to just say, 'Run along now, and, by the way, try not to do it again'? Faced with the sin of the woman and the self-righteous violent inclinations of the scribes and Pharisees, Jesus seems rather too nonchalant.

The English Jesuit priest-poet Gerard Manley Hopkins wrote a sonnet that begins,
> My own heart let me have more pity on; let
> Me live to my sad self hereafter kind.

Hopkins apparently treated his own heart much as the scribes and Pharisees treated the woman—rigorous, demanding and unforgiving. At least some of the time, we all do that. I am my own strictest judge. I look on my sins and refuse to temper my judgement with mercy. Much of my reflection on my life as a Christian consists of enumerating my faults and then either feeling miserable about them or feeling miserable that I don't feel miserable about them.

But, if we concentrate solely upon our sins (or the sins of others), we are in danger of becoming so self-absorbed that we will be unable to notice, let alone accept the loving, forgiving embrace of God. We must leave room for comfort to put down roots.

In Lent it is easy to become obsessed with my sinfulness. After all, it is a season of penitential reflection. I'm supposed to engage in at least some ascetic practice. The season lends itself to concentrating upon my weakness.

Perhaps that is why as we near the end of Lent we take a look at Jesus refusing to get excited about sin. He does not say it is alright to sin. When the crowd pushes the woman forward, he does not deny her sinfulness. His attitude seems to be, 'So? She's a sinner. Who isn't? If any of you aren't, then do what you wish with her'.

Of course, there was not one of them who was not a sinner. There is not one of us who is not a sinner. That is not, however, the most important thing about us.

Sin is serious, but the most important thing in the world is the love of God that forgives our sins. The scribes and Pharisees had forgotten that.

So, Jesus says that we have to see sin in the proper perspective. He refused to get excited about the woman's sin. Instead, he accepted her sinfulness (and that of the scribes and Pharisees) as a normal part of life. He told her to avoid it, but did not let her sin become the sole description of her existence.

Does that mean that we need not avoid sin? No. I am a child of God. Therefore, there is a certain kind of life that I should live if I am to be true to who I really am. Like the scribes and Pharisees, I should be brave and honest enough to admit that I am a sinner. Then, like the woman going on her way after meeting Jesus, I should get on with my life as a beloved child, a forgiven child, of God.

Passion or Palm Sunday (A)

The night I saw the film *Schindler's List* about a man who schemed to save Jews from the Nazis, I did not sleep well. I kept wondering what I would have done if I had been there. Would I have done evil? Would I have cooperated with it? Would I have tried to not be involved? Would I have resisted quietly with low-grade subversion or at least disloyal, though unspoken, thoughts? Would I have opposed it, even if it meant death?

Today we involve ourselves in the events of the week in which Jesus was executed. In the Palm Sunday liturgy, we identify with various ways of responding to Jesus on his journey to the Cross.

We begin the liturgy as supporters, bearing palm branches and singing hymns. Within 15 minutes or so, we join the cry, 'Crucify him!'

Perhaps some of the people who demanded Jesus' death at the end of the week had begun the week singing hosannas. Who knows how or why they changed? Perhaps their 'Hosanna' was not sincere. Perhaps their 'Crucify him!' was not sincere. Perhaps both were sincere.

What would I have done? Would I have gone along with the crowd? Would I have stayed a silent spectator to 'Jesus' Joyride' as well his Way of the Cross? Would I have opposed either the praise or the punishment? Like my dilemma over the Nazis, I don't know or fear to know the answer.

It is fairly easy for most of us to say we are Christians, especially if we do so in moderation. Sunday Mass? Generally okay. Renouncing a promising career because of what it does to the world or to my spirit? Crazy, but somehow admirable. Denouncing the values of my family or society because they have become life-destroying idols? 'Crucify him!'

Today, I am forced to take both sides, to 'try them on for size.' I cannot avoid a decision, saying it only applied to people in Jerusalem long ago. I wave the palms and cry out for the death here and now.

Of course, in the liturgy, we are only play-acting. Or, are we? The choice to be an open follower of Christ or a Sunday-morning Christian or a betrayer is before me all the time.

Most of the choices I make are not life and death issues. They are compromises and corner-cutting that getting through life entails, like crying 'Hosanna' or 'Crucify' because everyone else is doing it or the script calls for it. No major decision, no major commitment.

That's frightening. Could it be that the 'little' betrayals that define my life are, when combined with the 'little' betrayals of others enough to send Jesus to the Cross? One small voice saying 'Crucify' would not have done much. A crowd of small voices brought Jesus to Golgotha.

When we meditate upon the Cross, we must look upon our sinfulness without providing excuses for ourselves. I am a sinner who needs redemption. I may not think of myself as a great sinner, but even my 'little' sins, my *ad hoc* refusals to live as a child of God, my momentary inattentiveness to the consequences of my actions or inactions toward God and my neighbor are sin.

In Holy Week we recall that God's love does not merely redeem the world from its sin, but even redeems me from my own 'Crucify him!'

Passion or Palm Sunday (B)

Is God some kind of monster?

Before you say 'NO!' too quickly, think about what we commemorate and even celebrate this week, the torture to death of Jesus. We say that the death by crucifixion of Jesus, the Son of God, was in accord with the will of God the Father.

Doesn't that sound like some form of child abuse? What kind of father would expect such a death of his child? And what kind of people are we who celebrate it? Let's face it, it all looks rather ghoulish.

We might try to avoid the issue by saying that the crucifixion of Jesus was some sort of accident that was not part of God's plan. Or, that it was the inevitable result of Jesus' confrontation with the religious and political authorities of his day.

But, the New Testament does not let us use those sorts of comforting evasions. The entire message of the Scriptures is that in going to the Cross, Jesus was fulfilling the Father's will. His whole life was a Way of the Cross to Calvary. Jesus is not the good teacher and healer who was murdered; he is the crucified one who taught and healed. That is the reason the Cross is the symbol of Christianity. Ours is the religion of the Cross.

But why? Why do we say that the death of Jesus rather than, for example, his healing the sick is the source of salvation? Wasn't the Incarnation, the coming of God the Son among us as one of us, enough? What is the link between his death and our liberation from sin?

Perhaps the place to begin thinking about it is to see if there might be some sort of link between death and sin. We often say that death is a result of sin, a punishment for the basic estrangement we have from God, each other and our true self that we call Original Sin.

But, what if it were the other way around? What if sin were a result of death? Clearly, death is a part of life. All living beings die, even those that do not sin. Death is built into creation. It is the engine that drives evolution, with species and individuals dying to make room for yet others.

However, most of creation does not know that it will die. A few animals seem to have some idea of death, but none besides ourselves seem to understand that death is not just something 'out there.' For us humans, death is very 'up close and personal'. In fact, it is something that will happen to me one day. And I know it.

The engagingly lively dead in Tim Burton's film, *The Corpse Bride* sing: 'Die, die, we all pass away/But don't wear a frown/Because it's really okay/You might try and hide/And you might try and pray/But we all end up/The remains of the day.'

They say 'it's really okay,' but is it? The comedian Woody Allen said, 'I'm not afraid of death; I just don't want to be there when it happens'. That sort of sums up our situation. We know we will die, and we don't like that.

So, we do all sorts of things to hide from death and all the limitations that remind us of it in various ways. We become obsessed with looking after Number One. We grab for power because if we are powerful, we can make believe death has no power over us. We look for fame and acclaim because we want to believe that we are too important to die. In fact, those were the temptations Jesus faced in the desert. He resisted and went to the Cross.

Throughout history, we have given in to the temptations. We have allowed death to estrange us from God, one another and our own true self. Our refusal to face, accept, and perhaps even in some sense embrace death is the ultimate source of sin.

And so, Jesus comes among us to do what we do not do, cannot do. He goes to death with all the fear and disgust that we have. But, he goes with confidence in the love of God that is stronger than death.

Because we are aware of death, we can try to avoid it out of fear. But, in the Cross of Jesus, we now know that because we are aware of death, we can face it with hope because by his death and resurrection Jesus has shown us that God's life–giving love does not die. That love is not overcome by death, neither the death of Jesus nor the death of each of us.

And so we mark this Holy Week with solemn joy. Death is real. But this week we know that love is even more real.

Passion or Palm Sunday (C)

Though Jesus said that people would recognize his disciples by their love for one another, it is certain that they are more likely to know us by the sign of the cross.

We mark our churches with a cross. We hang it on our walls and around our necks. We mark ourselves with the sign of the cross as a blessing. We even turn the cross into fancy jewelry.

The cross is so common that we often fail to reflect on what it actually is. We go through the motions of making the sign of the cross without thinking about it.

The Roman way of doing it may have been especially cruel, but in any form, crucifixion is a painful torture. The word 'excruciating' ultimately derives from the Latin word for a cross, *crux*. Not only was it an extremely painful way of dying, it was humiliating. Our crucifixes and art show Jesus in a loincloth, but in fact, people were hung up on display stark naked before crowds of people. Dying on a cross was the ultimate in shame. It was repulsive.

Revulsion at the cross was so strong that even a century after the Roman emperor Constantine outlawed crucifixion, Christians apparently still could not bring themselves to depict Jesus on a cross. Possibly the earliest surviving Christian representation of the crucifixion of Jesus (there is a much earlier anti-Christian one) is a carving on a wooden door of the basilica of Santa Sabina in Rome, dating back to about the year 430. It depicts Jesus and the two men crucified with him, but leaves out their crosses. In the background are some buildings with architectural details that merely hint at crosses.

In Holy Week, we reflect upon the cross as what it really is: a horrible torture device. And, we are forced to reflect upon Jesus as abandoned, degraded, tortured and defeated. It is an image that draws a sympathetic response even from nonbelievers.

If the murder of Jesus were all there is to Holy Week, there would still be plenty of matter for reflection. What is it about us humans that makes us able to devise such horrible ways of mistreating one another? Why do we turn to violence in order to deal with those who differ from, challenge or merely annoy us? What can we do to break humankind's addiction to violence?

But, Holy Week calls us to more than just sympathy for the agony of another or guilt feelings over our propensity to violence and cruelty.

For Christians, the cross is, indeed, a horror. But, it is also the means and sign of salvation. So, while shuddering at its ghastliness, we at the same time 'glory in the cross of our Lord Jesus Christ in whom is our salvation, life and resurrection'.

Holy Week is, more than anything else, a call to what we commemorate on Thursday: Eucharist, another word for thanksgiving.

We give thanks for what Christ has done for our salvation. The New Testament makes it clear that what he went through was something he did willingly, though certainly not cheerfully. He knew that faithfulness to the Father's love and to his own love for us would ultimately lead through his fear, pain, humiliation and death to a deeper experience of that love.

We give thanks to Christ for uniting with us, embracing the fear, pain and death that are an ineradicable part of our lives. At the worst times of my life, Christ crucified is there with me.

We give thanks to Christ for taking upon himself the worst of what we do to one another, entering into our sinfulness and violence. And forgiving it. The worst that we can do, the worst that we have done, has been embraced by God's forgiving love. And so, I can have the courage to turn from sin, knowing that God's love for me is stronger than my sin.

And finally, we give thanks because this Holy Week leads to Easter, the celebration of our baptismal union with Christ in the life-giving love of the Father. Like Jesus, we will die. We will endure our personal way of the cross. And, as for Jesus, that way of the cross will lead us to the fullness of life in God.

Holy Thursday Mass of the Lord's Supper

The foot-washing ceremony we enact in today's liturgy is not complicated, and in many churches the majority of the congregation cannot even see what is going on. Yet, we find the simple re-enactment of Jesus' washing of his disciples' feet a vivid reminder of who we are called to be.

The Eucharist is the 'source and summit of the Christian life'. Our communion with Christ and his people, united in Jesus' sacrificial offering to the Father, is the basis of our life as Christians. At the same time, our union with the risen Lord is a foretaste of heaven.

Yet John leaves out an account of Jesus speaking of the bread and wine as his body and blood. Why?

John knows how important the Eucharist is to the followers of Christ, but he puts his major reflection on the Eucharist earlier in his gospel, connected with the miracle of the loaves and fishes. So, he did not replace the bread and wine with a basin of water because he did not understand.

Actually, he made the switch because he deeply understood the mystery of the Eucharist. Apparently, as far as John is concerned foot-washing is the equivalent of the Eucharist. Of course, the point is not just a literal washing of people's feet. Foot washing is a symbol of all the acts of humble service that we disciples of Jesus should be willing to give to one another—and not just willing, but actively doing.

In our usual manner of speaking, service is something we *do* while the Eucharist is something we *receive*. Today, however, we are reminded that, in addition to being something which we receive, the Eucharist is something we do to and for the world. It is a form of service.

Of course, the Eucharist is primarily something that God does. The transformation of bread and wine into Christ's body and blood is impossible for us. God works through the Church to make the change.

Yet, God does not act alone. We are essential to the transformation. The bread and wine we bring to the altar are fruits of God's creation, but they are not natural. Human activity, 'the work of human hands,' has changed them from the wheat and grapes that are their source. We make the essential elements of the Eucharist. Then, there are the words of Jesus spoken by the priest who in that moment is speaking for Christ and acting for the community. So, there is a lot of our doing involved in the Eucharist.

When we bring bread and wine to the altar, they are not merely bread and wine. They are symbols of all the fruits of the earth and all the work of human hands—cows and computers, woodlands and woodwork, poppies and poetry, seahorses and service. So, there is a close link between our service and the Eucharist we celebrate in the liturgy.

When I receive the Eucharist or when I offer service, I am like the bread and wine. Just as they symbolize the fruits of the earth and the work of human hands, I symbolize humanity. In my communion with the Lord, the whole world is drawn into communion with him. When I receive the Eucharist, I serve the people of the world by receiving on their behalf, as their agent.

From the other side, is there Eucharist-izing going on when we serve? Yes, there is. The Eucharist is the transformation of the things of this world into the body of Christ, the fullness of creation. When we offer service to God or another person, we are turning the world a little more toward being what God intends it to be. 'God has made known to us the mystery of his will, according to his good pleasure that he set forth in Christ, as a plan for the fullness of time, to gather up all things in heaven and on earth' (Ephesians 1:9–10). The transformation of our service into the Reign of God parallels the transformation of bread and wine.

John wants to emphasize that such service is essential to our life of faith. Just as the Eucharist is the source and summit of the Christian life, so, too, is humble service. We cannot have one without the other.

Our sharing Eucharist is a service--a service to the world. We can wash its feet, and we can bring it with us as we share union with Christ. It's all one and the same.

Good Friday

The earliest surviving representation of the crucifixion of Jesus is a third century graffito that someone scratched into the plaster of a wall of the residence for imperial pages in Rome at a time when Christians were being persecuted. It is not much more than a stick drawing.

The Greek caption reads, 'Alexamenos worships his God'. On the left stands a figure of a young man with one hand raised in a gesture of salute or worship to a figure on a cross. The crucified one has an ass's head.

The Cross makes no sense. In a world where winning is so important, it is asinine to worship a loser who was tortured to death.

We can offer no rational explanation for the Cross. Over the centuries, we have tried, but our explanations always fall short. Some of them cause more harm than help when, for example, they show God the Father as some cruel monster who demands and delights in the unjust death of Jesus.

The only sense the Cross makes is the sense of love. God loves us so much as to join us in the worst of all human experiences, death. Like a mother who looks on her suffering child and wishes she could take the pain into herself, God looks at us and does what that mother would do.

Whether we try to explain the Cross or merely reflect in awed silence, we have never wavered in our faith that the Cross is the ultimate sign and source of God's saving love for us.

Good Friday is not a day for explanations. It is a day for love. My best friend, the one who loves me more than anyone else, the one who loves me more than even I could love myself, has died.

This is a day, then, for sorrow. I know that the cruelty inflicted on Jesus has something to do with my relationship with God and especially its inadequacy without his suffering. It is a day for repentance.

But, today is also a day of thanksgiving. I have no desire to die at all, let alone for another. 'But God proves his love for us in that while we were still sinners Christ died for us.' So, we give thanks for that love.

Today is also a day of commitment to be a sign of God's love. God felt it worthwhile for Jesus to die in order that I might know love. My life is worth giving in the day-to-day as well as, if necessary, in death so that others may know that love.

Finally, today is a day of witness to the world. Alexamenos was not afraid to let others know that he followed Christ, the crucified God. We know that many died for that profession of faith. We know that at the very least the boy Alexamenos was ridiculed for it.

Through the centuries, others have made that same profession of faith: I believe that the death of Jesus on the Cross is the most important event in the history of the world, and I worship him and give thanks to him for the love he showed on that Good Friday. Many who have made that profession have suffered for it. Many do so even today.

In other languages, today is 'Holy Friday'. The 'Good' we use in English actually originates in 'God's', so at its root, it does mean 'Holy Friday'. Yet, it is right that though the meaning of the word changed, we keep it for this day. Today is a Friday of sorrow, a Friday of thanksgiving, a Friday of commitment, a Friday of proclamation. It is the Friday of love that goes beyond all we could expect to receive and the Friday that invites us to love beyond all we could expect to give.

Today is, indeed, a good Friday.

The Easter Vigil

We have reached the liturgical high point of our night of vigil for the Lord—the proclamation of the Resurrection. Now, at the hinge connecting the presence of Christ in word and his presence in sacrament, it is time to reflect on what we have been doing.

We began our night of prayer in the outer darkness. Not in the ease-giving darkness of early evening, but in the dead dark of night. Not in the warm, intimate darkness of a bedroom, but in the infinite darkness of the universe. The place of fears, of terror, of lonely, silent foreboding.

This is a description of our world, of ourselves. It and we can be cold, forbidding, foreboding. The world can be unfriendly to us, and we to it. The indifference of nature to us is a sign of our estrangement from one another.

I, too, can be cold, dark and forbidding. It may even be my natural state. If I doubt it, all I need do is see myself as I walk the streets, indifferent to the people around me, as they are to me, in the cold, dark loneliness of the crowd.

Is it true that much of my sin is an attempt to escape loneliness? We are made in and for togetherness. That is the mystery of which sex is the most basic symbol. And yet, we are alone, somehow carrying our isolation like a tumor at even our most intimate moments. Our friendships are real sources of comfort and joy, yet we sense that they do not heal the radical separation from others and from God that we know lurks in our hearts. Friends, lovers, we huddle together in the cold darkness, sharing our meager warmth and hoping for the dawn.

Then, the ultimate cold, the final darkness—death.

Underlying all our fears, all our separation, all our sin is the reality of death, the inescapable cold and dark.

And so, we began our liturgy as we seem to begin our existence, in the cold darkness, the way the world lives unless the light come.

AND LIGHT HAS COME!

Before we could begin to understand God's work in history, before we could celebrate, we had to remind ourselves of the reason we need that work of God. We needed to be reminded that 'the light shines in the darkness, and the darkness has not overcome it.'

And so, we began with the celebration of light, of Christ, the Light of the World. Not Christ the fluorescent light, cold and efficient, but Christ the Flame, the living, moving, warming, fascinating, hypnotic light of God. Not Christ the neon light, the flashing, momentary come-on, but Christ the steady, the dependable. The one with us always, to the close of the age.

There is a warming light to break the cold darkness of our isolation from God, from the world, from one another, from our true selves. There is a warming light that overcomes the darkness of death. 'The light shines in the darkness and the darkness has not overcome it.'

Christ is our light. Knowing that, we can face our history—the history of God's people, and the history of one of God's persons—with confidence, knowing that those histories are enlightened and warmed by Christ.

And so, we moved on to hear the story of how God has enlightened the world through the history of a people.

Genesis assured us that neither our universe nor we who inhabit it are random concatenations of electrons, warps in the space-time continuum. We are not accidents. The universe with all its mysteries is itself a reflection of the light who is Christ.

Abraham's willingness to believe in God in the midst of an incomprehensible demand called us to reflect on God's willingness to sacrifice the Son for us, and calls us to examine our own willingness to trust God in the midst of doubt and pain.

The Exodus account describes how God freed a people in order that they might be signs of God's loving, liberating care for all people. By passing through the waters of the sea, the people of Israel accepted God's offer of salvation, just as in Baptism we have accepted God's offer of salvation.

However, that acceptance requires a growing faithfulness. Neither God's first chosen people nor we are entirely faithful. We are called continually to renew our faithfulness, to reaffirm our belief in the light even when all we see is darkness. Isaiah assured us that God is with us in our groping toward faithfulness.

'To be true in the darkness to what we have seen in the light' is our vocation. We need true wisdom, a true knowledge of the works of God in order not only to be true to the light ourselves, but to be as well signs of that light, to be through Baptism in Christ that very light itself in a darkened world.

In our Baptism, we have indeed been united with Christ who overcame the darkness, the light that is not overcome. We have died already, and have begun to live eternal life with him, the Risen One.

The Japanese greeting for this feast has always been for me a great comfort and challenge. *Gofukkatsu omedetoh gozaimasu! Omedetoh gozaimasu* means 'congratulations!' 'You passed your exam, *omedetoh gozaimasu!*' 'You had a baby, *omedetoh gozaimasu!*' 'It's your birthday, *omedetoh gozaimasu!*' The phrase is used to congratulate someone on some even that directly concerns that person.

Yet, we say, *gofukkatsu omedetoh gozaimasu*, 'Resurrection, congratulations!' The reason, very simply, is that the Resurrection of Christ is our affair, too. In Christ all of us who were baptized into his death have already been raised to a new life, a never-ending life that will not be overcome by death, by the seeming triumph of the darkness.

That sounds very good, but do we have any evidence upon which we can rely? As the saying goes, 'faith is a short blanket on a cold night'. And there are cold nights. There are times of darkness when we forget the light we have seen, the warmth we have felt. Is there nothing that can renew us in our commitment to live as children of light?

There is a very strong reminder of the truth of the Resurrection of Christ. It is right here tonight. It is ourselves, the Church gathered to remember and give thanks. This night, we are the proof of God's love for us. We are the proof that the darkness has not overcome the light. We are the proof that Christ is risen from the dead and calls us to share that new life. The fact that with all our weakness and unfaithfulness we have not forgotten the light is proof that the light has not been overcome.

Every Sunday, we gather to remember Christ, to re-member Christ. We share the bread and wine he left us as his everlasting covenant. We commit ourselves to be what we proclaim ourselves to be, the Body of Christ for the world—the Body of Christ freed from the darkness of fear, sin and death, the Body of Christ who shines in the darkness.

Many years ago during the sign of peace at Mass in the seminary, a murmur ran through the chapel. When it reached me, the message was, 'Christ is risen, pass it on.' Actually, that was the message of the angel at the tomb. It is, in fact, the definition of the Church. We are the community of those who believe in and proclaim the triumph of Christ our Light over our darkness.

Just as each of us earlier held a candle against the darkness, we are called to live as light in the darkness. We have, in fact, promised to do so in our Baptism, and will soon renew that promise.

We have declared to the world that we will be light-bearers. We have thrown down the gauntlet before darkness, renouncing it, and challenging it with our Abraham-like willingness to trust that we will not be bereft of God.

Christ our light is indeed risen, and in him we, too, live the fullness of life. Let us now renew our commitment to that life, give thanks for it in the Eucharist, and go forth into the dark daylight of the world bearing and being the light of Christ.

Easter Sunday (A)

Japanese Christians have a wonderful greeting for this day. They say *gofukkatsu omedetoh gozaimasu*. The phrase means 'Resurrection, congratulations!'

When do we congratulate others? Obviously, when something wonderful has happened in their lives.

By saying 'congratulations', I say I share the other's joy. It's an unselfish greeting. 'Congratulations' refers to the other person and the event's meaning for him or her, not so much to the event itself.

What is it for which Japanese Christians congratulate one another? 'Resurrection'. But, why should we congratulate each other for what happened to Jesus? Isn't it he who deserves the congratulations? He is the one whose rising we celebrate. What have you or I to do with that?

A lot, as it turns out. On Easter we do not celebrate the Resurrection of Christ as a once-upon-a-time event. It is our feast as well as Christ's. You should be congratulated on Easter and should congratulate your fellow Christians as well because in Christ's Resurrection, we, too, are raised to new life.

That is the reason that during the Easter Mass we renew our Baptismal commitment. As St. Paul reminds us, in Baptism we enter the grave with Jesus in order to be raised with him to new life. So, on the day we celebrate Jesus' rising to new life, we reconfirm our union with him.

This day new life began for all of us when Jesus rose from the dead. Easter is our birthday in eternal life.

When does eternal life begin? When we die? Yes, but not at the death we usually think of, our physical death. Eternal life began for us when we died with Christ in Baptism and entered into union with the risen Lord. So, the day we renew our Baptismal promises is in a real sense a celebration of our birthday. Resurrection, congratulations!

Christ is risen, and we are risen through him, with him and in him. So what? Is my life really all that different from that of others because I'm baptized? Am I more moral than others? Nicer than others? Better than others? Not particularly.

So, what's the point?

My biological life does not, for the most part, depend upon my conscious choices. I do not control the way my organs work. My life in Christ, however, requires some response on my part.

On Easter, we recommit ourselves to that response. We renounce a life apart from God and declare our desire to live as sons and daughters of God. We make a choice to live eternal life here and now. That, too is cause for rejoicing. Resurrection, congratulations!

What will this commitment mean to me and the world? It should mean freedom from the fear that prevents my accepting and sharing the love of God. If I am already living eternal life, why fear anything that can happen to me in this world?

I am united with the risen Lord. So, I can be a servant to God and my neighbor. I can be the sign of the new creation begun in the Resurrection of Jesus. Resurrection, congratulations!

Easter is the anniversary celebration of your new birth in Christ through Baptism. It is the day on which eternal life became available to you through his Resurrection. It is the day you renew your commitment to living that new life for God and the world.

Resurrection, congratulations!

Easter Sunday (B)

Construction workers in New York City found an Eighteenth Century graveyard for African slaves. One set of bones were those of a six-year-old boy. Scientists found that the lad had been malnourished, diseased, anemic and had broken bones from carrying loads too heavy for his little body.

What was his name? Did anyone weep over his life or death? Did anyone know or care about his pain? When he shivered in the snow or sweltered in the heat, did anyone comfort him? When he whimpered in confusion, loneliness or agony, did someone hug him? The boy lived miserably and died anonymously. What kind of people could inflict such a life and death on a child? Where was humanity?

Where was God?

I need not go back centuries to face that same question. If I look around, how much suffering and loss do I see?

Where is God?

I need not even look beyond myself. I have suffered and will suffer. I will die and even if people weep over that, I will be forgotten, as will those who wept over me.

Where is God?

The good and the bad, the rich and the poor, the wise and the foolish, the beautiful and the ugly—we all go into oblivion.

Where is God?

Easter answers that question. When that boy suffered and died, God was with him. When those I love suffer and die, God is with them. When I suffer and die, God is with me. God is not a spectator. God is a fellow sufferer.

He suffers as we suffer, he weeps as we weep, he despairs as we despair, he dies as we die. He cries out 'Where is God?' as we cry out. Jesus' cry on the cross, 'My God, my God, why have you abandoned me?' is one with our cries.

That is some comfort. Quite a big comfort, actually. When I have most reason to think that God is lost, that God does not care, that

God does not even exist, then God is most present with me, present with me in the same confused, pained way I am present to myself.

But, Easter says there is more. Christ rose from the dead. His suffering and his death, his confusion and his fear, his doubt and his hope were all embraced by God's love that is stronger than death. His rising from his death is a promise that we, too, will rise from ours.

We do not know what that means. Our statements are poetry more than prediction, and are true as poetry is true, not as almanacs are true. We know that God's love for each of us goes far beyond what we can imagine. Heaven will not fit into our imaginations, into our concepts, into our words.

What can fit into my head and my heart is a conviction. Christ has suffered, has died and has risen. That is the guarantee that we will share his life. He loves me enough to join me in death; he loves me enough to have me join him in life.

And what of that boy in New York or the billions of others who have died, most of them never knowing of Christ?

The place to look for an answer is my own case. On Easter I renew my baptismal commitment. I confirm my belief not only in the resurrection of Christ, but also in my own share in 'the resurrection of the body and life everlasting.'

Because my death is not apart from Christ's, what happens to me after death is not separate from what followed Christ's death—resurrection. I rejoice and sing 'Alleluia!' for Christ and for myself.

And for others. The love of God that is stronger than death knows no limit except, perhaps, our refusal to be embraced by it. All who have suffered have been united with Christ on his cross, whether they have known it or not. God's love will not be cramped by our knowledge or be held off by our ignorance. Those same people, then, are also united in his resurrection.

Our Christian vocation comes from this knowledge. All our brothers and sisters have the right to know the good news that Christ dies and rises for them and with them.

On Easter we celebrate on behalf of all the world God's love that embraces all the world. We celebrate for that boy, for all the dead and for ourselves, the living who are promised a share in the life of Christ who rose.

Easter Sunday (C)

Today celebrates Sunday at least as much as it does the Resurrection.

Easter is the feast with no date. It is the first Sunday after the first full moon after the vernal equinox. So, it can be any Sunday between March 22 and April 25.

In 1923, the Vatican declared there would be no problem in setting the feast at a particular Sunday every year and forty years later, the Second Vatican Council repeated that willingness so long as the other Christian Churches agree. So, at some time in the future, Easter may always be, for example, on the first Sunday of April. It does not matter when we celebrate, so long as it is on a Sunday.

The date on which Jesus rose is unknown. The date of the crucifixion on the Jewish calendar was either the 14th or 15th of the month of Nisan, but no one knows for sure how the first-century Jewish calendar matches up with others, and in any case, we don't know the year of the crucifixion. The date was apparently so unimportant that no one bothered to keep track of it.

However, we have never forgotten that Resurrection day was a Sunday, because there is something about Sunday that would not allow it to be forgotten and would not allow the Resurrection to be celebrated on any other day of the week. We even moved the Sabbath from Saturday to Sunday.

What is so special about Sunday? The answer comes in the first of the two creation stories in the Book of Genesis, when God began creating on the first day of the week, Sunday. 'God said, 'Let there be light'; and there was light.' Sunday is the day of creation, the day of light.

This is where the link between the Resurrection and Sunday comes in. In the Resurrection of Christ, a new creation has begun. 'So if anyone is in Christ, there is a new creation: everything old has passed away; see, everything has become new!' (2 Corinthians 5:17). We now see the world and our lives in a new light, the light of Christ that we symbolize by our Easter candle and proclaim in our Easter Vigil liturgy.

Based upon the story of the creation as a week's work, there is another way to view Sunday. It is not only the first day; it is also the eighth day, the start of the first full week for all creation. The work of God has been completed, and now we live with that completed product. Christ is that completion of creation, the first case of creation being all that God's love calls it to be. In our Baptism, we are united with Christ and are 'second week' people.

Compared to the proclamation that we live in a new creation and as a new creation, a date on a calendar does not matter. So, we celebrate the beginning of that new life on the feast of creation, the first day and eighth day, Sunday.

Therefore, every Sunday is a special day, a day like no other. That is why we gather to celebrate the Eucharist on this day. We share a foretaste of the banquet that is full union with God and one another in the fulfilment of God's creative will.

Sunday is special for more than being a day off from weekday duties. It is a day outside of usual time. That is the reason people traditionally wear their good clothes on Sunday (reminder of our baptismal robes) and share the best meal of the week (reminder of the heavenly banquet). It should be a day of prayer, but also a day of play and of creativity in union with God who set the lights to play upon the world this day and gave us the joy of the Resurrection.

Every Sunday we re-experience our baptismal union with Christ and his Church. Every Sunday we rejoice that the Lord has risen and has given us a new life. Every Sunday we recommit ourselves to living as a new creation. Every Sunday, we begin a new week of showing to the world what it means to live as children of the light, citizens of the Kingdom of God.

On this Sunday, this Easter Sunday, we remember what every Sunday is because of what happened one Sunday long ago when the mission of the Church was born in the proclamation, 'The Lord is risen!'

So, today we say 'Happy Easter!' But, we can say as well, 'Happy Sunday!'

Second Sunday of Easter (A)

Years of living on the streets of Tokyo had taken their toll and the man needed hospital care. The doctor at the voluntary clinic asked me to accompany the patient to the welfare center to ensure that they would arrange hospitalization for him. It was only a few blocks away, and he could walk that far.

As we took a shortcut through an alley, the man suddenly started frantically brushing his body with his hands and screaming, 'BUTTERFLIES!' He was hallucinating, and saw and felt that his whole body was covered with butterflies.

'There are no butterflies here,' I said.

'Can't you see them? They're even all over you!' he said.

'No, there are no butterflies on either of us.'

'Are you sure?'

'Yes.'

Then, that man paid me possibly the greatest compliment I have ever received. He believed me. He still saw butterflies, he still felt butterflies. But, in spite of all the evidence, he decided to trust me when I said there were no butterflies.

Some fools like Thomas in the Gospel say that seeing is believing. 'Unless I see . . . I will not believe.'

There is a bit of Thomas in all of us, but I think that man in Tokyo is a better example of what we are like. To believe in Christ is to trust in spite of a lot of what we see and feel.

This is Easter time. We proclaim that Christ is risen. We say that God's love has overcome the power of sin and death. We say that the power of evil is broken.

Yet, when we check the news we see that evil seems to have survived the breaking of its power. Whenever I look into my own heart, I see very clearly that sin remains alive and well there. Injustice continues, and suffering is universal. Disease, disaster and death destroy without regard for the innocent or sinner, the believer or nonbeliever. The same liturgical books that contain the prayers of

Easter contain funeral Masses as well. No sane person I know has met Jesus walking down the street.

There can be no doubt about it. The evidence that Jesus was God, killed yet now alive, is hard to find. Rather, the evidence makes a good case that either there is no God, or if there be one, God does not or cannot care for us.

And yet, we Christians keep singing alleluia. Are we crazy?

That is possible, and an honest Christian should from time to time face the question of our sanity. Facing it will help us to have a faith that can live in the real world, rather than in some realm of self-created make-believe.

In addition, since our vocation is to proclaim Christ as the answer to the world's doubts, fears and woes, we had better be ready to honestly face those doubts, fears and woes ourselves. If we don't, our proclamation will be unbelievable to those who live with the bad, rather than the Good News.

But, let us assume for the moment that we are not crazy. Let us assume that we are like that man in Tokyo, turning from craziness to reality in spite of what we see and feel.

He believed my vision of reality because he was willing to trust someone of a different nation and race. He made a decision about me and about how he would understand reality.

Is that similar to my faith in Christ? What I know of him has been told me by a community of his disciples called Church. And, I choose to trust that community and the One of whom it speaks. I choose to accept their vision of reality in spite of all the evidence that says that we are alone in this world without any loving God caring for us.

Thomas did not trust that community. Not believing the Church, he could not see reality.

In the final analysis, it becomes a matter of choice. I can choose to trust the Church and Him of whom it speaks. That choice, like that of the man in Tokyo, will be based upon an inkling that this community is interested in my good and will accompany me on my journey, risking the fact that it may, in fact, be mistaken and covered in butterflies itself.

Second Sunday of Easter (B)

Often when we hear or read familiar passages of Scripture we put a label on them. We hear, 'It happened that one of the Twelve, Thomas, was absent'. We think, 'Oh, yes, Doubting Thomas'. Then we stop paying attention because if familiarity doesn't breed contempt, it certainly breeds inattention. Yet, in this Gospel passage, attention to an easily overlooked detail is essential if we are to know what the story has to tell us.

When we wish to emphasize something, we repeat ourselves. Scripture does so, too. Today's repetition is barely noticeable. The passage begins, 'On the evening of that first day of the week . . .' That day, of course, is Sunday. The repetition is in slightly different words, but says the same thing: 'A week later . . .' The next Sunday. The Evangelist begins each part of the passage emphasizing that whatever is going on has to do with the fact that it is Sunday.

Well, what is going on? For one thing, the disciples are gathered. On the first Sunday, these followers of Jesus come together and the Lord appears among them, greets them, blesses them and empowers them.

But Thomas was not there. We don't know why. All we know is that on that particular Sunday he was not gathered with the rest of the followers of Jesus and so did not meet the Lord. And so, he did not, could not, believe.

The next Sunday, the disciples were again gathered, and this time Thomas was with them. Again, the Lord appeared before them, greeted them and invited Thomas to believe. And Thomas did believe.

The Sunday gathering of the followers of Jesus is the place where the risen Lord approaches us in a special way, offers us peace, blesses us and empowers us. He can, and does, work elsewhere, but this Sunday gathering of his people is a special place for meeting the Lord. Therefore, for twenty centuries we have gathered each Sunday as his followers. It is so important that for Catholics it is an essential part of our life as Christians; we have an obligation to be with the community on Sunday.

Does it always work? Does my being gathered with the followers of Jesus on a Sunday guarantee that I will encounter the risen Lord, that he will say to me, 'Peace be with you'?

That certainly has not been the case in all my years of going to Sunday Mass. In fact, more often than not, Sunday Mass is a somewhat neutral experience for me. Sometimes the gathered people, the presiding priest, the music, the church decoration, the weather, my own sinful weakness or whatever can 'turn me off'.

But, there are Sundays when, like Thomas's, I suddenly know the Lord is with me. A prayer, a word of Scripture or the homily, a hymn, the presence of my brothers and sisters, the Eucharist—something puts me in the presence of the Lord or makes me notice him. I go to Mass for those times, and that is where the risk comes in.

Meeting the Lord is a risky business. Legend has it that Thomas's meeting the Lord in that Sunday gathering resulted in eventual martyrdom in India. Others who were in that gathering did not fare better. Often when we meet the Lord in our private prayers, he is a comforter. But, I think when we meet him in the Sunday gathering of disciples he more often than not comes to commission us as he did the disciples on those Sundays long ago when he sent them out to confront the sin of the world.

For, to forgive the sins of the world is to face the sin of the world with the same powerlessness that Jesus had on the Cross. We are sent by him with his powerful weakness to meet the evil of the world with God's love.

Considering that whenever I join my fellow Christians on Sunday, I am putting myself at that kind of risk, going to church must be one of the bravest or most foolhardy things I can do. Who knows where it will lead?

Living a Christian life takes courage. However, we need not search for it. We have it. Each Sunday when we join the community of disciples we take the greatest risk, that of meeting the Lord. If we can, and do, take that risk, the other risks of the Christian life should be easy by comparison.

Second Sunday of Easter (C)

'I'm angry at my mother', said the boy with all the seriousness and solemnity a five-year-old can muster.

'Why is that?' I asked.

He wrinkled his forehead, and pronouncing each word firmly, clearly and slowly, he answered. 'She cleaned my room. I didn't want her to clean my room. I didn't ask her to clean my room. She didn't ask me if she could clean my room. She just went in and cleaned it.'

'Can you forgive her for cleaning your room?'

'No!' Then, silence. 'Maybe.' A bit more silence. Then, finally, 'Yes—after it's messed up again'.

That boy was not different from the rest of us. When I have been hurt or insulted, I am not ready to forgive right away. Sometimes, I never get around to forgiving at all. Usually, if I do forgive, it is because I have received at least an apology and perhaps some restitution.

In other words, I set conditions on my forgiveness. That boy was willing to forgive his mother once his precondition—restoration of the mess—was met. Once my conditions are met, I, too, will consider forgiveness.

That is usual, isn't it? First comes repentance and apology, then forgiveness. However, in the Gospel, the Lord seems to forget part of the process. He does not say, 'If you forgive the sins of anyone who repents, they are forgiven'. He says, 'If you forgive the sins of any, they are forgiven'. Apparently, there are no preconditions.

That is what we celebrate at this Easter time, unearned forgiveness. God will forgive us without waiting for us to fulfill preconditions. It's only a week since we recalled how Christ forgave those who crucified him even while they were doing it.

It does not take much reflection to realize that there are many things I have done or failed to do that need forgiveness. I have repented of some of them. For whatever reasons, I refuse or am unable to repent of others. I am unaware of yet others. I am forgiven of them all.

That means that Easter joy is not just about something that happened 'once upon a time in a land far, far away'. It is about something that has happened to me, still happens to me, and will always happen to me—God's forgiving love.

With all that Easter means, and all that his appearance to the disciples could be, why did Jesus make forgiveness the point of his message? He could have reminisced about the past or told them about death. Instead, he told them to go out and forgive. Why?

The Resurrection of Jesus is the beginning of a new kind of life not only for him, but for his disciples as well. Those who are united with him—and that means all his followers—now share the life of God in a new way. In our Baptism, we are one with the risen Lord; we are the Body of Christ. Because of that, we share the power of God.

When we think of the power of God, we may think of images that provoke awe, or even terror—thunder, lightning, galaxies hurtling through space. But, what God shares with us is not that sort of power. What God shares is the power of God's selfhood, the power to forgive out of love, the power to overcome evil by not letting it limit love.

So, Jesus tell us that the power to forgive is ours. It is the ultimate weapon against evil. That is the reason for not setting conditions, not waiting for evil to somehow weaken before we forgive. We confront it in its strength and overwhelm it with love.

Does that mean that we condone evil, that we look upon the sin of the world (including our own) and say, 'That's alright'? No. Such an attitude would not be a confrontation with evil, but a bowing to it. To forgive evil we must first say, 'This is evil; it can have no place in God's world; this needs forgiveness in order to be overwhelmed by God's love'.

God entrusts us with a great gift. Overcoming evil depends upon our willingness to forgive. It is up to us. We can forgive, or we can refuse to forgive. God will accept our decision. Of course, if we refuse to forgive, refuse to confront sin with the power of God, we may need some forgiveness ourselves for desertion in the face of God's and our enemy, evil.

Third Sunday of Easter (A)

Luke's Gospel only names one of the disciples on the road to Emmaus, Cleopas. There is no reason, then, to assume, as artists and others invariably do, that the second disciple was another man. Perhaps the disciple was a woman— Cleopas's wife Mary, for example, who was, as John's Gospel tells us, at Calvary for the crucifixion of Jesus.

It would be suitable for the second disciple to be a woman, because theirs is not a 'once-upon-a-time-in-a-land-far-away' tale. It is about us, men and women who struggle to understand and believe in Christ.

The first notable thing about the disciples is that they are not paralyzed by the frustration of their hopes about Jesus. It is the third day since those events, but already they are on the road, getting on with their lives. That does not mean that they have forgotten Jesus, or that they ignore reports that he has risen. As they walk along, they keep him in mind and in their talk.

We, too, carry on our day-to-day lives. Sometimes we feel disappointed in our hopes. Sometimes we wonder about the value of our commitment to Christ. But, we still get up in the morning and go through our day. We must, because just as the disciples met Jesus on the road, we, too, will meet him on the road. Our daily lives are the place where faith is explored, questioned and ultimately confirmed.

The disciples talk with each other about Jesus. When the stranger joined them, they continued to talk about him. They talked about Scripture. They talked about what Jesus had said and done. That was not enough.

Some Christians think it is sufficient to hand Bibles to people. The experience of the two disciples should be a caution for such believers. Information about Jesus, conversation about Jesus, theological statements about Jesus, or even the best explanations of Scripture will not bring people to faith. Something more is needed.

So, the disciples continue on the road to Emmaus, still talking about Jesus and through his explanation coming to a deeper understanding of Scripture. But, they still do not, cannot, really believe. Faith does not depend upon information.

The basis of faith is an encounter with Jesus Christ. Understanding the Scriptures and the teachings of the Church can and should help us toward that encounter, and we should continually grow in our understanding of them, but they cannot replace the encounter.

Where does the encounter take place? Here we come to the core of Luke's message today, in what the two disciples say about their experience. 'They told about how he had been made known to them in the breaking of the bread.'

They had walked with him, but could not believe. They had talked with him, but could not believe. They had listened to him, but could not believe. But, 'when he was at the table with them, he took bread, blessed and broke it, and gave it to them. Then their eyes were opened, and they recognized him.'

From that Sunday to this, we followers of Jesus break bread and in that action know that the Lord is risen and is with us. The Eucharist proclaims the Resurrection.

When the disciples recognize the Lord and realize that the rumors of a 'vision of angels who said that he was alive' are true, 'He vanished from their sight'. Once they realized that the Lord had been with them all along, they no longer needed to see him with eyes of flesh; the eyes of faith see better.

'That same hour they got up and returned to Jerusalem' where they told the others of their encounter. They became missionaries, proclaiming the Resurrection of the Lord. That is the only appropriate response to their encounter with Jesus.

That, too, is our story. We share the Eucharist, and in that sacrament we know that the Lord is with us on all our roads, at all our tables. Then, we go to share that Good News with all. A Christian's encounter with Jesus is always meant for the sake of others.

The way we share that Good News is the same way that Jesus shared it with those disciples. Just as he walked with them in their sorrow and confusion, we walk with our brothers and sisters in their sorrow and confusion. Just as he joined them in their meal, we join others in their everyday lives. Just as he shared with them the Word of God and the Bread of Life, we offer them not only the fruits of our encounters with Jesus, but the opportunity to experience that encounter themselves.

Third Sunday of Easter (B)

Exuberant joy is the proper way to live the Easter season. Easter is 50 days long precisely because our joy in knowing that Christ is risen and we share his new life cannot be confined to or used up in just one day.

Yet, the joy is paradoxical. In Luke's Gospel, the disciples talking about the Resurrection are terrified when they see that what they are talking about and hoping for is really true. When Jesus appears and gives them a greeting of peace, everyone panics. He has to prove to them he is no ghost by having them touch him and by eating some fish.

What would my reaction be to meeting someone I knew to be dead, someone whose corpse I had seen, someone whose grave I knew? Living in an age more inclined to psychological rather than spiritual explanations, I would probably think I was hallucinating rather than that I was seeing a ghost. Like the disciples, though, I would panic: 'Am I cracking up?'

Let's face it—the Resurrection is unbelievable. Even seeing the risen Lord is not going to convince us otherwise. It's easier to believe in ghosts or to doubt one's own sanity. Actually, we don't have to do the doubting ourselves; others do it for us. The wisdom of the world assures us that we're at least deluded and probably crazy in our belief that Jesus, once dead, is now alive.

To understand the joy of this season, we must remind ourselves of the impossibility of what we celebrate. We know as well as the disciples did that Jesus really died. There was, and is, no doubt about it. Even if he had not been tortured to death on a cross 2,000 years ago, he'd be dead by now.

We can be so used to the idea of the Resurrection that we can forget its basis, the death of Jesus. Unless we remember that, we cannot fully celebrate this season. It becomes mere good feelings and folklore.

However, if we remember the fearsome reality of death, we are ready to rejoice over a piece of cooked fish. In the Resurrection, the impossible has happened. A dead man has returned to his friends, spoken with them, shown his fatal wounds to them, eaten with them.

And we are those friends. The best friend I can ever have, because he knows me in every detail, in all my weakness, yet loves me without limit is Jesus Christ. His earlier friends, our forerunners, were 'incredulous for sheer joy and wonder.' In our own sheer joy and wonder, we remember how impossible it is that our friend is alive after being dead.

He was dead; he is alive. That in itself is cause enough to whistle, whoop and dance. Yet, there is more to our joy.

I will one day die. There is no doubt about it. The one statistic that never changes is the death rate. It is, and always will be, 100 percent. No medical technology, no cloning, no wonder drug, no diet, no exercise, no prayers, no nothing will ever change that. One day, I will be as dead as Jesus was. Dead. Done. Full stop.

And yet, through my really dying, I have a promise of new life in Christ's rising from death. United with Christ's death by the Baptism I renewed on Easter Sunday, I am united with his Resurrection. In some way, though I will really die, I will also really live. That's as impossible for me as it was for Jesus. Incredible.

Incredible, but true. Those men and women 2,000 years ago were incredulous in joy and wonder. So can we be. They saw Jesus, spoke with him, were taught by him, ate with him. The impossible, his living again, is real. The impossible, my living again, is real. What else can I do but jauntily, joyfully stride through life?

Well, actually, there is one more thing I can do. The end of today's gospel reading tells us Jesus said that 'penance for the remission of sins is to be preached to all the nations.' I can be a preacher. Not someone standing on a street corner haranguing the passing crowds, but someone whose jaunty walk through life, whose bewildered joy and wonder proclaim to all who see me the incredible, unbelievable good news that a dead man has eaten some fish. My dead friend is alive. I, like him, will also die. And I too will live.

Third Sunday of Easter (C)

Even though there are 153 fish flopping around on the beach, I don't think the gospel story is about that particular animal. No, if there are animals in the story of Jesus and Peter at the lake, they are cats and dogs.

Think of a cat entering a room. First, the nose, whiskers and eyes slowly enter. A look to the left. A look to the right. A look up. A look down. A look back. Then, a paw glides in. A look to the left. A look to the right. A look up. A look down. A look back. Then, another paw. A look to the left. A look to the right. A look up. A look down. A look back. It goes on and on.

Now, think of a dog entering, a big dog with a big tail. Thump! Thump! Bound! Bound! Tail wagging, drool dripping, tongue lolling. Furniture bumped, tabletops tail-swept.

People have a lot in common with cats and dogs. Perhaps that is why they are our favorite pets. There are cat people who like to plan things out. I am one of them, though I prefer dogs. We check out the possibilities and options before carefully committing ourselves. We are also the ones who frequently have to clean up the mess left by dog people.

Dog people rush in, not giving much thought to consequences. They think that problems need not be headed off, since if they happen they can be fixed later, usually by cat people.

Peter was a dog person. Who else when surrounded in the Garden of Gethsemane would pull out a sword and try fighting a gang of professional swordsmen? Who else would *put on* his clothes to jump in a lake for a 100-meter swim?

The others in the boat, cat people for sure, realized that rowing would be more efficient than swimming, so they rowed ashore. 'One, two, three, stroke! One, two, three, stroke!' Peter just jumped overboard. If he had possessed a tail, he probably would have swamped the boat with its wagging.

Throughout the Gospels, Peter is always jumping into things. Often, he goes wrong. If he had that tail, it would often be between his legs. Peter has the distinction of being the biggest jerk in the New Testament. And yet, the Lord chose him to be the leader.

In day-to-day life, I prefer dealing with other cat people. We are careful and canny. Dog people exasperate us. However, when it comes to my life of faith, I wish I were a dog like Peter.

John's Gospel talks of the disciple whom Jesus loved. But, when today Jesus asks Peter, 'Do you love me more than these?' The answer is an immediate doggy 'Yes!' Peter doesn't think about consequences, Peter doesn't plan, Peter doesn't prepare a way out because Peter has only one thing in his mind and heart—his love for Jesus. Peter may not have been 'the disciple Jesus loved', but he was the disciple who loved Jesus most.

I wish I could love the Lord in that way—no calculation, no holding back, no double-guessing, no doubts.

Can a cat become a dog? No, but I think and hope cat people can become dog people. It is not easy. Compared to it, bioengineering is child's play. How can it happen?

It takes effort on our part. We have to grow in love of the Lord to the point where we one day find we are getting doggy. The first step is prayer. We must come to know the Lord as one who loves us as a dog. (After all, going to the cross is a dog person's act.) Reflection on our experience and upon the Word of God will deepen our awareness of Christ's love. Gathering with our fellow Christians to share the sacraments, especially the Eucharist, is essential. Perhaps most important is to imitate the Lord's dog-like love. We must begin to lay aside our calculations and considerations and start loving others in deed as well as in speculation.

When we do that, we will see the love of God working through us. We will know that God's love is surrounding us, using us. And we will begin to find the courage to love in return.

Peter was chosen to lead the disciples, to lead the Church, not because he was bright or well-spoken or a deep thinker. He was appointed to look after the Lord's flock because he loved the Lord.

Heaven is full of dog-people. The place is probably a messy chaos, with no order, no calm. Just lots of song and dance (the human equivalent of yelping tail-wagging) because of the joy of those who are with the one they love.

I sometimes fear that even if cunning, calculating, considering, careful cats get there, we will miss half the fun.

Fourth Sunday of Easter (A)

In ancient Palestine, shepherds frequently kept the village sheep penned together at night. That way, the shepherds could take turns on guard and all could get some rest. In the morning, each shepherd would call his own sheep, and they would come to him, following him to the pastures.

There is a special relationship between a sheep and its shepherd. The sheep knows the shepherd. On his part, the shepherd knows the sheep, even recognizing them as individuals to whom he gives names.

Our relationship with Christ is similar. He knows each of us as individuals, not merely as part of a flock. He addresses us each by name. He knows me because he loves me. Because of that love, he watches me because, like a shepherd, he wants to protect me and lead me to good pastures.

There is one true shepherd, Jesus, and many false ones. In John's Gospel, this section is presented as an attack upon Jewish leaders of his day. If that were all it were, it would have little meaning for us today.

However, it is likely that the evangelist included this passage in his Gospel because the Christian community for which he wrote was experiencing problems with false shepherds, those who would lead the community astray. That problem is not limited to the Christians of long ago.

We use the word 'shepherd' in the Church quite often. However, since we use it in a Latin form, we might not recall that we are speaking of a shepherd when we say 'pastor.' Those who care for the Church and have responsibility for leading it exercise a 'pastoral' ministry. They are shepherds, responsible for protecting and leading the community.

In the fullest sense, pastors are not solely bishops and the priests who are appointed by them. All who lead, heal and nurture the faith of a Christian community exercise, in various ways, a pastoral role.

Theirs is a heavy responsibility, since they must imitate the Good Shepherd who knows his sheep and loves them. It is a responsibility with great temptations to exercise power rather than service, to receive special treatment rather than to give without seeking return and to seek fulfillment of one's own physical, psychological or spiritual needs at the expense of others.

We probably all know men and women who have turned away from the flock of Christ because of the actions or inactions of some 'shepherd.' Sometimes, these men and women merely use a shepherd as an excuse. But, sometimes, they really have been driven off by someone who acts more like a wolf than a shepherd. Others do not leave the flock, but carry wounds inflicted by bad shepherds, wounds which they may have forgiven, but which leave scars anyway.

We must pray for those bad shepherds. We must pray for those who have been hurt or driven off by them. And, in our prayer, we must be willing to be used by God to be the instrument of healing for shepherds and sheep alike.

We must also encourage and thank good shepherds with our words, prayers and actions, and be examples of willing cooperation with them for the sake of the entire flock.

Often, however, we sheep are to blame for being led astray by bad shepherds. The sheep of whom Jesus speaks in the Gospel can tell the difference between their own good shepherd and a bad one. We are not always so discerning.

We follow shepherds merely because they hold some title. We follow shepherds who tell us what we want to hear. We follow shepherds who make us feel good. We follow shepherds who will relieve us of the responsibility to make choices for ourselves. Sometimes we even choose men or women as our shepherds who do not want to be so in the first place.

The solution to both problems—unworthy shepherds and willingly misguided sheep—is to know the true shepherd, to 'know his voice.' If we know the Lord, we will recognize false shepherds and will also know when we are searching for false shepherds.

And how will we learn to recognize his voice?—by knowing Scripture, by deepening our understanding of his Church, by prayer, by gathering in his name, by sharing the Eucharist and by imitating him in his love of God and people. If we do that, we will recognize his voice and follow when he speaks through real shepherds.

Fourth Sunday of Easter (B)

I don't know much about sheep, but I have the impression that they are dirty, smelly and stupid. It's no compliment to say someone is a sheep. It implies cowardice, a lack of conviction, a willingness to follow without thought or responsibility. Someone who is sheep-headed is stupid. I don't want to be a sheep.

But, I must admit that in many ways I am one. Compared to the splendor of the life to which God calls me and for which I was created, I am dirty, smelly and stupid. I lack the courage and conviction to live as a child of God, imitating the Lord in loving without stint, without fear. I follow where the world leads. Left on my own, I will wander through life, losing my way, following whatever or whoever attracts me at the moment, but never really getting anywhere. I need a shepherd.

What do shepherds do? They protect sheep from their sheepishness. Shepherds ward off dangers that threaten the sheep, who are helpless otherwise. A shepherd also leads sheep from place to place for their own good. Left on their own, sheep might denude a pasture of all its grass and then stand around staring at each other as they starve. The shepherd knows where to take them for more food and knows how to force them to move on. Sheep need a shepherd.

Jesus announces himself not merely as a shepherd, but as the Good Shepherd. He is the one shepherd we can trust because he is the one shepherd who is not a sheep himself.

What is the sheep–idity from which he guards us? There are many things in our lives from which we need saving. One of the most dangerous is, perhaps, our tendency to follow false shepherds. We do not usually notice it, because all the other sheep around us are walking in the same direction we are. We go along with the crowd, the flock.

We do not consciously decide to live lives that go counter to our own real best interests, lives that go against what our creator intends them to be. We just go along. We stretch the truth from time to time.

We swallow whole the prejudices against people, races, religions and nations that our society tells us are 'normal.' We commit many minor mindless insensitivities toward others. We forget God.

It is from all this that the Lord, the Good Shepherd, leads us, but in an interesting way. He saves us from sheep-idity by turning us into shepherds.

In today's second reading, John tells us that in Christ, we have been made children of God. This brings us to the heart of what we celebrate in this Easter season, the immeasurable, incredible love of God. We recall that God's response to humanity's murder of the Son is undeserved forgiveness and more. We kill the Son, and God offers us eternal life, the eternal life of the risen Good Shepherd.

It's hard to believe, because it doesn't always seem to myself or others that I am a child of God, that I am one who has received a promise of a new kind of life. John says that the world does not recognize us as children of God. I don't recognize myself as such, either.

John says that in our resurrected life, we will become more like the Lord because we will see him as he is. Jesus says much the same. We know the shepherd, recognize him and follow him. In so doing, we become more and more like the shepherd.

That means we need not be sheep. We can dare to live in freedom. We can take the risk of loving others and God. We can, by the way we live, show others the way God has set for the world. All we need do is keep our eyes on Christ, following him whom we meet in prayer, Scripture, sacrament and the community of his followers.

That is important because a world full of sheep needs real shepherds who by their lives can lead others to the Good Shepherd, Jesus Christ. In our baptism, we have received the vocation to be Christ for the world.

So, perhaps it's not all that bad that I am a sheep. For some reason or other, God has called me to follow the Good Shepherd, who will turn my sheep-idity into discipleship by showing himself to me and reshaping me into a shepherd myself.

Fourth Sunday of Easter (C)

We often make the mistake of thinking that being a Christian means living in a certain way, doing certain things. Simply put, it means 'being nice'. At times, it may mean being extraordinarily 'nice' or even heroically 'nice'. In any case, we think it means obeying certain rules, particularly one that says we should love our neighbors.

That is certainly part of our Christian life, but it is not the core of that life. Living a certain kind of life that involves doing good for our neighbor must be a result of our faith, but is not the faith itself. The core of our faith is in a short passage—only four verses—from the Gospel of John that is this Sunday's reading.

Faith is, first and foremost, a response to a call from the Lord. We are his sheep who hear his voice. And that voice is not some generalized invitation, a 'Hey, guys, come with me'. The Lord addresses each of us individually, inviting us one by one to follow him. That is what he means when he says he knows his sheep. Sheep may all look alike to the unpracticed, uncaring eye; however, the shepherd can tell them apart.

The two billion or so Christians in the world also look generally alike. There are, of course, variations of gender, build or race, but to some hypothetical visitor from outer space who did not love us, we would probably seem pretty much the same.

But Jesus is not some unloving visitor from outer space. He loves us. So, he calls and cares for us one by one. He knows who I am and calls me by name.

What he calls me to is eternal life. For whatever reasons of his own, in his love Christ has called me to be one who 'shall never perish.' Or, more accurately—since that infinite love is given to all people—he calls me to know that gift and the love that gives it.

I have seen enough corpses of Christians (and expect to be one myself some day) to know that whatever this promise of eternal, imperishable life means, it does not mean an escape from death.

Christ died in order to rise. I, too, must die in order to fully experience the eternal life to which he calls me.

Jesus gives us reason to be hopeful in the face of death. 'No one shall snatch them out of my hand . . . there is no snatching out of the Father's hand.' Jesus affirms his identity with the Father in the context of a guarantee. Death shall certainly take us, but it can never snatch us away from the loving care of God, the life-giving love of God. So, we will live as long as that love lives—eternally.

What then of my day-to-day life? Should I just drift along, every so often (an hour each Sunday, for example) remembering that I have been promised eternal life, but otherwise being indistinguishable from my neighbors who do not know that promise?

If I do so, it is a sign that I probably do not really believe what the Lord says. It is, after all, hard for anyone after adolescence to really believe that he or she is going to live forever. I mouth the Creed, saying I believe in 'life everlasting,' but that declaration does not shape my life.

A Christian is not basically someone who does nice things. A Christian is someone who has been chosen to know God's promise of eternal life. Knowing it, really knowing it in the depths of my being, means that I will live a particular sort of life.

I will not fear the tongues or opinions or other weapons of the world, because I know that they are nothing compared to the eternity I am living. I can take the risk of loving other people, sacrificing my time, talents and treasure in their service because I know I have all eternity.

I do good not because that is what makes me a Christian, but because what makes me a Christian—the promise of eternal life—frees me to do good.

It is still Easter time. It is still the season of resurrection. It is still the season to recall that my life is not a matter of the merely day-to-day, but of eternity.

Fifth Sunday of Easter (A)

My sympathies are with Philip: 'Lord, show us the Father; stop the fine words and give us something we can understand. Make it easy for us to believe and we will believe.'

The disciples two thousand years ago had trouble understanding. We disciples today still have that problem.

Actually, as is so often the case, the evidence we seek is under our noses. In fact, the evidence follows our noses wherever they go. We are the evidence that there is reason for faithful confidence in Christ.

Obviously, the basic place where I dwell is myself. It is also the place where Christ dwells, because in Baptism I have become one with him. Jesus has gone to the Cross and returned to us, as he promised. In the Father's house called the People of God, there are many dwelling places. Since the Father and Jesus are one, wherever he is, there is heaven.

However, looking at the world, at the Church or at myself, can I actually say, 'Here is heaven'?

Yes, I think I can. The words of Jesus that we hear today are from his discourse at the Last Supper. So, as Jesus headed to torture and death, he spoke of being 'the way, the truth and the life.' Apparently, the presence of heaven on earth does not preclude the possibility of evil, of suffering or of death.

To understand this, it is necessary to understand something about the theology of the evangelist we call John. Something that takes place for Luke in the Ascension happens on Calvary for John. For him, the Cross is Christ's glorification. So, in preparation for his Passion, Jesus says, 'The hour has come for the Son of Man to be glorified'.

It is impossible for me to understand how God allows suffering in the world. I can admit that generally my 'suffering' is rather less than terrible when compared to that of others. But, no one's suffering is insignificant to that person.

Much of what I undergo in life is, in fact, my own fault. If that were the only sort of suffering, I could see some sense in it, a sort of therapy for my weakness and sin. However, there is much undeserved suffering in the world.

In fact, suffering seems to be one of the basic realities of life where so much of life depends upon the ingestion of other creatures. We kill and eat to live.

So, suffering in its many forms is the story of the world. (Not the whole story, of course—there are also love, friendship, good humor and other graces.) Perhaps what Jesus tells us today is that in the midst of this story, God is with us, sharing divine power with us that helps us not only endure but also to turn our disaster into triumph. 'I tell you, the one who believes in me will also do the works that I do and, in fact, will do greater works than these.'

We do this through the Spirit, the Spirit that is present with us no matter where we may be, no matter who we may be and no matter how many of us there may be. Jesus was limited in his ability to be with his disciples. Only a small number could see him at any time because he could only be with a small number at any time. The limitations of time and place that hem us in hemmed him in as well. But, his going to the Father means that the Spirit of God is among us. Wherever we go, whatever we endure, God's Spirit is with us. Heaven is with us.

That should be enough, but there is more. Jesus was the presence of the Kingdom in the world, and the Holy Spirit is the continuation of that presence among us. But, our story here has an ending. We all die. The world itself will die.

Saint Paul reminds us that 'If for this life only we have hoped in Christ, we are of all people most to be pitied.' We are citizens of the Kingdom of God, united with Christ in Baptism. But, we also pray for the coming of that Kingdom, for its fullness. The Kingdom is something in store for the world, but also something in store for you and me.

Jesus tells us today that the place where we live with God is not only this world we live in now. He has prepared another place for us, one with 'many dwelling places,' enough dwelling places for each of us to live with him in his Father's house.

Fifth Sunday of Easter (B)

Jesus said, 'My Father has been glorified in your bearing much fruit and becoming my disciples.' That's not fair. Shouldn't we get the credit for bearing fruit and being disciples?

Though God owes me nothing, part of me wants God to be beholden to me. After all, I try to avoid evil. I even do good. In fact, sometimes I do good or avoid evil precisely because I want some reward from God.

God has given me life and all that comes with it—love, friends, beauty, opportunity and faith. I have already received in abundance. Beyond that, in the Resurrection, God has given me the promise of eternal life. My saying 'Yes' to such generosity may be prudent, but it is certainly no credit to me. God should be glorified, not because of what I have done in responding to those gifts, but because of the offer of those gifts in the first place.

The source of the gift is my union with Christ, a union described in the parable of the vine. In Baptism, I am as intimately united with Christ as branches are with the trunk and roots. This is not biological life which I have by virtue of being a breathing human, but the Christian life, a special form of human life.

Today's second reading summarizes Christian life. 'We are to believe in the name of (God's) Son, Jesus Christ, and are to love one another as he commanded us.' The passage continues, saying that this is the way that we will remain united with Christ, remain part of the vine.

But, what is it to believe, what is it to love? There is really no difference. The word 'believe' comes from an old way of saying 'be in love.' To believe is to love. And love is not just an emotion. True, feelings are part of love, but at its most basic, love is a decision, a decision to act in a certain way toward another, toward others.

That is the reason the second reading starts by calling us to action rather than nice words or good feelings. 'Let us love one another in deed and in truth and not merely talk about it.'

In the Acts of the Apostles Saul shows what love calls for. He continues to proclaim the fact that he has met the Lord though no one trusts him and some even want to kill him. That is the basic vocation to which all followers of Jesus are called. We must show the world through our confidence in the face of frustration, threat and death that we are united to the true vine, the Risen Lord.

We do this by public proclamation of our faith, uniting in prayer and worship with the community of those who follow Jesus. We do it by unselfish service of our neighbor. We do it by making our faith in Jesus the measure by which we make the day-to-day as well as the major decisions of our lives.

Our objective is to draw others to union with Christ, so that they, too, may share his vocation of showing his Father's love to the world.

We have a tendency to think that living like St Paul means that we have to be super-human. We feel guilty about not being like him, but at the same time, a bit relieved by the thought that we need not live lives that proclaim the Lord because we are not super-saints.

However, we are too hard on ourselves. God knows us, loves us and calls us just as we are. As John's letter says, we 'are at peace before him no matter what our consciences may charge us with; for God is greater than our hearts and all is known to him'.

We need not be superior beings in order to live every moment of our lives as Christians. Neither does leading such a life make us into superior beings. When all is said and done, we are merely shoots from the true vine. Whatever we have comes from him, and without him, we are nothing.

That is why God is blessed in whatever we do. It is the work of Christ in us, giving us his life, challenging us with his teaching. So, we move through life, being as faithful as we can, bearing what fruit we can, and rejoicing that God deserves the credit, but has chosen us to be the means by which the divine will is made real for the world.

Fifth Sunday of Easter (C)

Jesus says, 'This is how all will know you for my disciples: your love for one another'.

Our record of loving one another is not good. In the fourth century, we started killing one another for holding different theological opinions. We've stopped the physical torture and killing, but the Vatican office that ran the Inquisition still exists (with a name change) and its methods still shock those who see it in action against fellow Christians.

Saint Robert Bellarmine was instrumental in having the philosopher Giordano Bruno burned alive in part for saying that there might be life on other planets, and in getting Galileo imprisoned. *Saint* Joan of Arc led troops who ravaged the countryside when not killing fellow Catholics for the sake of the Kingdom of Charles VII, not the Kingdom of God. Then, her Catholic rivals burned her alive.

The wars between Catholics and Protestants in sixteenth-century Europe were among the most vicious in history. In Ireland, Lebanon, Serbia and many other places, we've killed one another using the names of Christian communities—Catholic, Orthodox, Protestant—as our labels and war cries. A poster rightly says that a major step toward world peace would be for Christians to stop killing one another.

In the past century, we experienced two world wars, both occurring in large measure in the so-called Christian part of the world. The wars fought elsewhere and the other violence perpetrated around the globe today use weapons and techniques developed in what is left of 'Christendom'.

Majority Christian societies are no more loving than other societies. Even in nations dotted with churches we find lies, cruelty, injustice, racism, oppression and the treatment of men, women and children as economic, social, sexual or political tools.

Our Christian homes are no less prone to violence, coldness and hatred than those of any other families. My own Christian heart cannot show the world the unadulterated love of God.

Our love for one another? It's little wonder that after two thousand years we have not converted the world to Christ. The problem is not with the world's vision. The problem is with us. We Christians have not even converted ourselves to Christ.

The place to begin looking for an answer is in the case I know best, my own. Why do I not love as I know I should, as I know I could?

The problem is that the love of God has too small a place in my belief. I find it hard to really believe deep-down that the creation and sanctification of the world is done out of love for me. I don't think I'm worth that kind of love, and I am not. No one is, but God gives it anyway.

Because I find it hard to believe that God can love me, I fail to make love the source of all my life and action.

The cross and resurrection of Jesus mean many things, but one of the chief messages of our redemption is that God's love for us is unbounded, uninhibited. We can sin, and God loves us. We can run away, and God loves us. We can spend two thousand years claiming to be disciples with our words while denying it with our deeds, and God loves us. We can die, and God loves us.

For those who are willing and unafraid to see that love (for love, especially that of God, can be frightening), the natural response is grateful love in return. God's overflowing love for me prompts overflowing love in me. I then love—not merely serve— my neighbour. I look like a disciple of Christ.

The task, then, is not to try harder to love my fellow Christians. I must reflect in prayer and stillness upon the love God really has for me. I should be constantly alert to see God's love at work in the events and people around me.

If I can believe in that love, then the world may see a new kind of Christian, a new kind of Church, one that lives as Jesus did, as Jesus does. When that happens, the world will know that I, that we, are companions of Jesus. The world will experience that love, be drawn by that love, and join in that love.

Bringing the world to Christ is our vocation. Loving one another is the way to live that vocation.

Sixth Sunday of Easter (A)

The Greek word 'paraklētos' that we translate 'Advocate' was a legal term meaning 'one called to stand beside'. The function of such a person was to support someone standing before a court— in other words, an attorney.

Why would Jesus speak of sending an attorney? Is following Jesus illegal, that we need fear being hauled into court? Well, that has happened, and for many Christians the thought of having the Spirit of God as an attorney beside them has been a source of courage and hope in the face of persecution.

But what of most of us Christians? Are we likely to stand before judges to defend our faith?

As a matter of fact, yes, even though the judges do not sit in a courtroom.

Peter's letter tells us, 'Always be ready to make your defense to anyone who demands from you an accounting for the hope that is in you'.

Why would anyone demand an accounting for my hope? Obviously, the reason would be that they had seen hope in me.

What does hope look like? How would someone recognize it, and how would it be enough of a characteristic of a Christian that others would want to ask about it?

The place to look is hopelessness. Hope in the midst of hopelessness raises eyebrows, questions, doubts and sometimes even ire.

In the Easter season we rejoice that the most hopeless situation, the death of God, is the way to eternal life. This hope in hopelessness is the reason the Cross is the symbol of our faith.

It is not hard to find hopelessness today. There are wars and violence. There is poverty, injustice and disease. Our environment is being altered in ways that may cause irreversible damage to the planet and life on it, including ours.

More real to me is hopelessness in my own life and the lives of those around me. Friendships fail. Dreams decay. Love is lost. Death awaits us all. Even my good desires and hopes are dashed 'for I do not do the good I want, but the evil I do not want'.

In the midst of all this, to talk and act as if there were reason to hope does raise questions, sometimes even in myself. I must stand before accusers who say, 'Get real; you are a deluded fool who refuses to live in the real world'.

What, exactly, is our hope? It is not that our little dreams will be fulfilled. Nor does it mean that our most desperate prayers will be answered as we wish. Christians' prayers at the bedside of a dying loved one do not seem to have a greater 'effectiveness' than prayers of those who are not disciples of Jesus.

Our hope is based upon the very same Spirit that Jesus promises to send to us. The Advocate who will give us the means of answering for our hope is itself our hope. 'You know him, because he abides in you, and he will be in you.'

Because the Spirit of the Risen Christ is in us we can face our own crosses with confidence that God is still at work, that God's will is done even when it is thwarted, as it so often is.

Since we have that hope, we can love the 'unlovable,' forgive the 'unforgivable' and do without the 'essential.' That provokes interrogation by the world: 'Why do you have such hope in you?'

The answer is that Christ the Lord is risen and with us so intimately as to be in us. 'On that day you will know that I am in my Father, and you in me, and I in you.'

The Lord is with me, so there is no reason to despair, to not hope. My own hopes and dreams may collapse around me, but compared to the fulfillment of the hopes and dreams of God, that collapse is a minor affair. Disappointing, but not crippling.

Hope does not mean that we assume in the face of the facts that all will be well with the world. It does mean having confidence that even when all is not well, we are not abandoned by God.

It also means committing ourselves to living as if we believe it, so that others may ask us to give a reason for the hope that is in us and thus give us an opportunity to proclaim the presence of God the Holy Spirit with us.

Sixth Sunday of Easter (B)

One the real saints I've met was a homeless man in Tokyo. He looked like what he was, one of life's casualties. He kept himself in food and drink by collecting scrap cardboard in a cart and selling it.

Every day, he came to a soup kitchen. Most of those who came ate and left. Many would offer thanks for their meal. This man made it a point to visit the volunteers in the kitchen, asking how far they had traveled and thanking them for their generosity. He was a gentleman.

One winter day, he came with a man who had been struck by a car. The center had a free clinic, and the doctor examined him. There was a broken bone in his foot, but the injured man refused to go to a hospital. The doctor agreed that complete rest outside a hospital bed would eventually work as well as rest in such a bed.

From that day on, the gentleman cared for the injured man. The cart became home for him. For six weeks, the gentleman gave his food to the patient. Since the cart was now a hospital bed, the gentleman could not work to earn even his usual poor living.

One cold morning, the injured man shook the gentleman to wake him. He was dead. Six weeks of giving up most of his food and six weeks of sleeping on the winter sidewalk in order that his friend might sleep in the cart had cost him his life.

In John's Gospel, Jesus says, 'There is no greater love than this: to lay down one's life for one's friends'.

When I learned of the gentleman's death, I was embarrassed. After all, I know these words of Jesus. I know the promise of eternal life. Yet, here was a man who may never have heard of Christ, but who did what I have never had the faith and courage to do.

Gradually, I realized that the gentleman and I had something in common. He was without doubt a saint. That's not what we have in common. What we have in common is imperfection. His problems and imperfections were obvious to anyone who looked. Mine might be better disguised, yet, even so, they are prominent to me, at least.

Isn't it true that we tend to see what is lacking in our lives, in our faith? The broken part of my life overshadows the child of God that I am. From childhood on, people point out our shortcomings. Ask anyone to make a list of his or her failings, and one sheet of paper will not be enough. Ask the same people to list their qualities that show them to be sons and daughters of God, and when the list finally appears after much hemming, hawing and crossing out, it will be short.

Today's continuation of our Easter celebration is a joyous proclamation of the great love God shows in calling us to be united with Christ. It is a day to look at our faults and failings and put them in perspective. Next to God's love, they are nothing. Can I give thanks today for God's love that does not look at my faults, failings and weaknesses?

In the Acts of the Apostles, Peter sees that God's love will not be limited. 'I begin to see how true it is that God shows no partiality.' God showed love through Cornelius and that gentleman in Tokyo. God can, and does, show that same love through me as well.

'Love, then, consists in this: not that we have loved God, but that God has loved us and has sent the Son as an offering for our sins', says John. All humankind is embraced by that love.

Throughout this week, let's make an effort to see the children of God hidden in our families, our friends, our foes, strangers and even ourselves. Let's look beyond the problems, sins and weakness that too often draw our attention and see how great God's love is.

Chosen to know and proclaim the Son, we Christians are especially blessed. Among our blessings is the knowledge of who it is that acts in men and women such as the Tokyo gentleman. Let us give thanks for that extra love that has called us to know Christ. Let us give thanks for God's love that overflows the Church and shows itself through saints beyond our community, saints we might not even recognize at first glance.

Sixth Sunday of Easter (C)

Throughout the history of God's relationship with us, there are many cases of people disappearing just when you would expect they would get some well-earned rest and glory. Moses leads the Hebrews out of Egypt and through the desert for 40 years to the edge of the Promised Land, but then dies without entering it. There are men and women in the Old Testament whose sole reason for appearing seems to be to ensure that there is a next generation.

Even in the New Testament, people disappear. Once Jesus is found by his parents in the Jerusalem Temple as a boy, Joseph disappears from the story. In the first chapter of The Acts of the Apostles, Luke mentions that Mary was among the women who gathered with the disciples following the resurrection. That is the last we hear of her in Scripture.

In John's Gospel, Jesus prepares his disciples for his own departure after his death and resurrection: 'I go away for a while, and I come back to you.'

God seems to work on the principle that people are to serve a function, then move on. We call it 'vocation.' Catholics often assume that 'vocation' refers solely to a call to the ordained or consecrated life. It is actually a call to spend a lifetime trying to live faithful to our growing understanding of what God hopes for us. That may mean ordination or vows, but they are not, in most cases, the way to live one's vocation.

In the Bible, men and women who have fulfilled their vocations have no more reason to stick around. Their task is done and they move off the stage. So, is the sopping paper towel the symbol of our lives? Used, used up, and tossed away when we no longer serve a purpose? Is the goal of our lives God's wastebasket?

The going away of Jesus proves that we are not bound to be God's trash. Jesus says that his going is not only linked to God's chief gifts to the disciples, but that his going is a necessary prerequisite to that giving.

There are two gifts that are linked to Jesus' leaving his disciples—peace and the Holy Spirit.

'Peace is my farewell to you', he says. In one sense, this is a trite statement. 'Peace—*shalom*', was the normal greeting and farewell in Jesus' world. Just as most of us do not intend to say 'God be with you' when we say 'goodbye', most people who gave 'Peace' as their farewell did not think of wishes for peace. It was a conventional greeting.

But Jesus means what he says and confirms that the peace he wishes upon his friends will indeed be theirs: 'My peace is my gift to you. I do not give it to you as the world gives peace.'

But, that gift of peace is a parting gift. It is when Jesus has fulfilled his vocation and is ready to move on that he can give peace. The man or woman who has found and lived the vocation God gives becomes a peace giver. That may already be true of ourselves at times, if not always.

The quest for peace takes a lifetime. It is not a political peace, nor just an absence of conflict. It is something much deeper. It is union with God, a union that will reach its fullness when we have lived our vocation fully and it is time to accept the reward of our journey.

The second gift of Christ is the Holy Spirit. Jesus fulfills his vocation and becomes a peace-giver. He also gives the means for us to be like him. The gift of the Spirit is essential to growing in our vocation. Without the action of God in us, we could never discern what God calls us to be and do.

The gift of peace would be glorious in itself, but as Christians we have a special vocation. We are called not merely to find peace, but to be the means of peace for others. We must find and live our own vocations, but also be guides and assistants to others in fulfilling their vocation to receive peace.

If by the time our turn has come to move offstage we have been the means of others' finding peace, we will have indeed lived our Christian vocation, served our purpose. We can then joyfully join Moses, Joseph, Mary and Jesus not in God's trash bin, but in God's glory.

Ascension (A)

People are fascinated by last words. There are even books that collect them. Among my personal favorite parting words are those spoken by a general during the American Civil War to soldiers who were taking cover from enemy snipers: 'They couldn't hit an elephant at this distance.' Perhaps not, but in the absence of elephants, they could hit a major general.

One reason for our fascination with parting words is that they sometimes summarize the life of the speaker, whether that speaker is dying or simply leaving for someplace new. That is especially true when the speaker has had time to think out the words ahead of time.

Sometimes, the words that are passed on are not actually those of the person to whom they are attributed. Others invent words after the fact to provide inspiration, entertainment or a fitting tribute to one who is gone. Such are the last words attributed to Mother Teresa, 'Jesus I love you. Jesus I love you', and some variants on that. According to an eyewitness, her actual last words were, 'I can't breathe'.

To conclude his Gospel Matthew gives us a version of the parting words of Jesus. Like parting words that summarize the speaker's life and work, Matthew has thought them out and intends them to summarize his Gospel.

He begins by having Jesus declare his credentials, reminding us that it is important to pay attention to what the Lord has to say. He says that all authority in heaven and on earth have been given to him. In other words, what he commands is not only trustworthy, it is to be obeyed.

And then, he gets to the important part of the message. 'Go, therefore, and make disciples of all nations.' The Lord does not command reflection, prayer or worship. He commands action. His disciples are to get moving. All else is secondary to that and is meant to aid that. Reflection, prayer and worship should help us better go to the nations.

In Scripture, 'the nations' are not countries like those whose flags are lined up in front of the United Nations headquarters in New York. The nations are Scripture's way of speaking of those who do not believe, those who are not yet part of the People of God. Jesus tells his followers to go to them, to make those people the focus of the Church's activity.

In fact, they are the reason the Church exists. Just as the Son was sent into the world by the Father, the Church is sent into the world. The reason we exist as Church is for the sake of those who do not know Christ, and to the extent that we focus our attention, service and concern toward ourselves, we are not really being Church.

Too many people do not know of the love of God. Most of them believe in some god or religion or other. Some even claim to be Christians. But, their understanding of God is not based upon a conviction that God is love, and therefore they still need to hear the Good News from true disciples. Others are doubtful about who God is. Yet others deny that there could be any God at all.

There is only one way that they are going to learn the truth about God who is a loving relationship among Father, Son and Holy Spirit that overflows as love for us. That way is for disciples of Christ to teach them what Christ has taught us, that God so loved the world as to send the Son to be our savior.

We are to do that in such a way that attracts followers just as Jesus did in his ministry. Our service to God and our sisters and brothers should be such as to draw others to join us through baptism into the death and resurrection of Christ. Then, they, too can proclaim the Gospel to all nations.

There are many obstacles to our doing that. The world often seems uninterested in hearing the Good News. Sometimes, like the disciples who were with Jesus on the mountain, we ourselves doubt. At other times, our sin and weakness interfere and make our proclamation seem more like bad news or empty words.

However, we must not give up hope nor must we give up the proclamation. The Lord assures us that in his glory he is no longer limited by time and place and is with us today and always. That assurance gives us the confidence we need to obey his great command.

Ascension (B)

The disciples stood around staring upward.

'Hey, Pete, how do you figure he did that?' asked Andrew.

'Beats me. What do you think, Jack?'

John answered, 'I dunno. Maybe he used a helicopter.'

James sneered, 'Don't be stupid. Helicopters won't be invented for almost two thousand years!'

John retorted, 'Alright, smartie, *you* say how he did it.'

Then, two men in white robes joined them and one of them asked, 'Men of Galilee, why do you stand looking up toward heaven?'

Peter pointed up to the sky and answered, 'Well, you see, Jesus sort of went up that way and we're wondering how he did it.'

'Oh? Did he say anything before he left? Did he tell you to wait here for him? To build a shrine on this spot? To organize meetings or pilgrimages? To go back to your fishing nets?'

'Well, no,' Peter replied. 'Actually, he told us to proclaim him to the ends of the earth.'

Puzzled, the man in white looked at the disciples and repeated, 'Men of Galilee, why do you stand looking up toward heaven?'

The Church exists to do one thing. Our vocation is to proclaim in word and deed the gospel of Jesus Christ, God's forgiving and life-giving love. Everything we do—worship, teaching, preaching, work for justice and peace—must be directed toward that. That is the reason the men in white asked the disciples why they were standing around rather than getting a move on.

The way Mass ends is a lesson for us. Once we have heard the Word of God, prayed our thanksgiving and shared the Eucharist, we do not hang around waiting to see what comes next. We are dismissed rather abruptly. 'The Mass is ended, get out of here', while not the actual words of the deacon or priest, are the import of the message.

Certainly the Church grew beyond the small group of disciples because Christians did not hesitate to go out and proclaim Christ. They invited others to join them. Peter and Paul did not found the

Church in Rome, they found it. There were already Christians there who welcomed them. Apparently Christian merchants, soldiers, slaves and travelers brought the Good News to Rome first and were not hesitant to proclaim it.

Evangelization includes a call to faith in Christ and an invitation to membership in his Church, but is not limited to them. Jesus called some people to follow him, but he showed the forgiving, healing love of God to all.

Instead of telling those he forgave and healed that they should follow him, he sent them home to tell others what God had done for them. Every follower of Christ must do as he did. If we do our part, many will not become Christians. Others will be drawn to Christ and join us in our proclamation. Their response is something between them and God.

What, then, is our part? It is right in front of us, if we stop gazing off into space and look around. There are people who are hopeless and confused. There are people trapped in sin. There are people suffering the effects of illness, poverty and injustice. There are people who are ignorant of God's love for them. Evangelization, the fulfilment of our Christian vocation, means finding practical ways to answer those needs.

Ascension (C)

The Gospel According to Luke and the Acts of the Apostles are two volumes of a single work by the same author. Each volume includes an account of the last encounter of the risen Lord with his disciples before he leaves them.

The first reading in the Mass for the feast of the Ascension is the opening of volume two, the Acts of the Apostles, and tells the familiar story of Jesus parting from his disciples after forty days. The reading from the Gospel are the final words of volume one, and so they immediately precede the words we hear at the beginning of the liturgy of the Word.

But, they contradict each other! Acts has Jesus appearing to the apostles for forty days after his resurrection and then being lifted up. However, the Gospel presents the event as taking place on the evening of Resurrection Sunday in the presence of many disciples and speaks simply of Jesus' parting from them.

If we assume that Luke is reporting facts about the life of Jesus and the Church, there is certainly a problem. Might it be that he had taken a break between writing the two volumes and had forgotten what he wrote in volume one before starting to write volume two? After all, we too have the experience of not paying close enough attention to readings at Mass and missing connections. But how could Luke forget such important facts? On the other hand, and more likely, the differences between the two accounts might give us an insight into how to read Scripture.

One of the mistakes that Biblical fundamentalists make is to assume that when people wrote and thought thousands of years ago, they did so in exactly the same way that we do. They did not. So, a fundamentalist might assume that something is literal reporting when it is actually an ancient writing style that introduces details not for the sake of accuracy, but as spurs to memory or thought.

So, unless we want to say that Luke did not know what he was doing as he moved from writing the Gospel to writing Acts, we must admit that some of his 'information' that we reflect upon today is meant to tell us truth rather than facts.

There is a difference between truth and fact. Something can be truthful without being factual. For example, the two accounts of creation in the book of Genesis tell us the truth that God creates and considers the world something good. It assures us that our existence is not absolutely divorced from the concern of God. However, if we want the facts about the universe, we must go to scientists.

On the other hand, something can be factual without being true. If truth be what is in accord with the will of God, then sin, injustice and violence are not true, merely factual. And, since we follow Christ who is the Truth, we confront, repudiate and combat such facts for the sake of truth.

So, if we admit that Luke is not trying to present facts in his different accounts, what is the truth he hopes to convey to us?

The Gospel account, by having Jesus ascend to glory as an immediate part of his Resurrection, stresses that the glorification of Jesus is an effect and part of the Resurrection, not something separate from it, an add-on. And, by having all the disciples there, men and women, Luke is affirming the missionary vocation of all the followers of Jesus.

In the Acts of the Apostles, Luke's placing the Ascension forty days after the Resurrection brings to mind the forty years that the Hebrews wandered in the desert on the way to the promised land. In Scripture, forty days, weeks or years are not exact measures of time, as if we can assume that there were 960 hours between the Resurrection and the Ascension. The number means a long time, long enough for people to become what God intends them to be.

And that is part of the truth that opens the Acts of the Apostles, the volume of Luke's work that presents the new community, the new people of God, going out into the world to proclaim the Good News. They are now ready to take up the mission of the Lord.

Acts tells a truth about us. We, the new people of God, have been prepared for our vocation. We are the apostles. Christ has stepped aside so that we might step forward. The Acts of the Apostles begins with the Ascension of Jesus; they continue with us.

Seventh Sunday of Easter (A)

There are many ways to keep the word of God. One is to get a Bible. We might even go so far as to read it instead of merely keeping it on a bookshelf.

The Church keeps the word by making Scripture a part of our worship. The Church also passes the Scriptures on from age to age. We study them, reflect upon them and quote them. We use them to guide our lives. Sadly, we sometimes abuse them to find individual texts that 'justify' what we, rather than God, might want.

All that is probably the most basic, and in many ways, the least demanding way to keep the Word of God. It is focused on the word of God as we find it written in Scripture.

But, when Jesus spoke, there was no such thing as the New Testament. Even the Jewish Scriptures that we Christians call the Old Testament were still not formally organized as they are today.

So, when Jesus prayed, 'they have kept your word', he was not referring to texts. He was speaking of the word as the will of God, a will that we learn in the pages of Scripture, but not solely there.

Scripture and the guidance of the Church can give us informed hearts in order that we might perceive the will of God as it is found in the two most important places. The first is, of course, in the teachings, actions and attitudes of the Word made flesh, Jesus Christ.

It is not enough to know *about* Jesus. In Scripture, prayer and reflection, we must come to know him as our teacher, our model, our companion and our savior. We must develop a sense of how he would live and act today in our circumstances.

The second important place to learn what it means to keep the word of God is our own experience. The Spirit of God is at work in the world, and we must do as Jesus did, using our faith, hope and love to discern the will of God.

We are in the world as the presence of Christ for today. 'I am in the world no more, but these are in the world as I come to you.' Since Jesus lived in a different age and culture, we cannot expect that imitation of his acts alone will be appropriate to us today. We trust in the Spirit that he has sent us for guidance and insight.

Saint John XXIII misused a phrase from Scripture but gave us keen advice when he told us that we must 'read the signs of the times' to see what God calls us to today.

What are those signs of the times? Some are positive. Many aspects of human life have improved greatly. The growing concern for human rights is a positive sign for those who believe that God's word calls for a communion of brothers and sisters, children of one God.

However, some signs of the times are not so positive. Yet, they give us an indication of the will of God. The history of the past century has been marked by unprecedented violence that has forced us to recognize the power of sin in our lives. We have been horrified into reflecting upon the kind of world God intends.

The world as it is has not yet become the world as God intends it to be. We are sent to show what it should be by being keepers of God's word.

In today's second reading, Christianity is contrasted with behaviors that we can assume in any age and any place do not keep the Father's word. Three—murder, theft and evildoing—are fairly straightforward.

The fourth is hard to translate, and the wide range of translations gives us a broad idea of the behavior that Christians and their societies should avoid: 'concealer of stolen goods', 'spy', 'informer', 'mischief maker', 'intriguer', 'busybody' and the one that may sum up all the others, 'destroyer of another's rights'.

However we translate, it is obvious that Christian behavior is contrasted not with sins 'against God', but sins against our neighbor. In the Incarnation of Christ, the place to obey the Word of God is, above all, in daily life.

So, we should examine our lives and commit ourselves to living as those who keep God's Word. That will often mean going against the ways of the world, including when those ways have found a home in our own hearts or in our own Church.

Seventh Sunday of Easter (B)

Jesus prays for his disciples, including us. In that prayer, there are three characteristics that Jesus seeks in his followers.

The first is unity, 'that they may be one, even as we are one'. Yet Church history is a story of divisions, heresies, schisms, mutual persecutions, excommunications, hatred, torture, intolerance and even warfare. The Church of Christ is divided among Catholics, Orthodox, Anglicans and others lumped under the title 'Protestants' who are themselves divided among themselves.

Within Churches, things are no better. To hear the way Catholics talk of one another or treat each other based upon differences of spirituality, structure, theology or mission, one would wonder if they follow the same Lord. Can we say that our parishes or families are models of how men and women can come together in spite of differences to build a community that praises God and proclaims his Good News?

Well, what of the second element of Jesus' prayer? 'I gave them your word, and the world has hated them for it; they do not belong to the world.'

Not only are we Christians very much of the world, but the predominantly Christian part of the world is the leader of the world's economic, military and political power. We are so much of the world that some people even join the Church to have a share in that worldliness. Even in the Church, the values of the world often determine policies and activities. Instead of the world hating us, we and the world get along very well.

Then, there is the third part of the Lord's ideal: 'As you have sent me into the world, so I have sent them into the world.' We are certainly in the world, but are we there in the same way that Jesus was? Are we a redemptive presence to our brothers and sisters living in fear of death, of sin, of God? We do not usually seem so to most of those outside the Church.

The evidence indicates that either God did not hear the prayer of Jesus or that our selfishness, laziness, fear and sin have prevented the fulfillment of the Lord's hopes. We have blocked the all-powerful God.

We have alleluia-ed our way through the weeks since Easter Sunday. Now, we must temper our rejoicing with repentance and a commitment to live the resurrection throughout the year.

What does that mean? Today's prayer of Jesus makes it clear, if not easy. If we wish to follow him faithfully and be the sort of people he desires, we need only begin to live and act as he prayed.

The first step is to build unity. Unity is not uniformity. It is a recognition of the different gifts and personalities God has given us for the sake of the world. In fact, it goes beyond recognition to rejoicing. We give thanks for our differences, and then strive to support each other's gifts in our common task of showing the world the forgiving, unifying love of God.

Living the second wish of the Lord, being free of the world's values and power, is the really difficult part of Christian life. After all, we depend upon the ways of the world to make a living for ourselves and others. From long experience, we know how to make our way in the world with some degree of comfort, confidence and success. Giving that up is hard. Maybe it's impossible for me.

The way out of our quandary is found in the Lord's third wish, that we go into the world as his heralds, proclaiming him and his message. If we commit ourselves to that, the world will, paradoxically, help us escape slavery to this world.

The reason is that the world itself at its deepest level seeks liberation from the power of sin. People hope that death and futility are not the whole story of their lives. When we go among our brothers and sisters proclaiming Christ's resurrection triumph, they scrutinize us to test our authenticity and the authenticity of our message.

When that happens, we are forced to start living the message we talk about. The expectations of non-believers make us act like the believers we claim to be. What God cannot get us to do, those who perhaps unknowingly seek God achieve.

So, the way to live as Jesus prayed we would live is to start doing it. From the action will come the reality in our hearts, a freedom to walk through this world as citizens of heaven, a unity with all creation that comes from the one God.

Seventh Sunday of Easter (C)

If John's community were living in harmony, there would have been no need to waste ink calling for it. By including Jesus' prayer 'that all may be one,' John is telling friends and foes in his community, 'Hey, gang, let's try to do what the Lord wants of us'.

Right from the start, followers of Christ have not been united. The epistles of St. Paul, the earliest writings in the New Testament, show that we have been contentious, pig-headed and fractured into factions right from the start.

There are obvious divisions in the Church. We talk of Anglicans, Catholics, Orthodox and Protestants. There are others who would be welcome in none of those groups. Even within these groups, there are divisions based upon politics, history, language, theology, selfishness and plain stupidity. We back-bite, bicker and sometimes even kill one another over our ways of following Christ. The ecumenical movement uses Jesus' prayer as its mandate and motto with good reason.

Though scholars point to hints in the Gospel of John of divisions between his community and others (particularly that which followed Peter), he was probably not thinking solely of divisions between communities when he decided to include Jesus' prayer for unity in his Gospel.

If the only divisions among Christians were among Churches, it would still be a scandal, but on the level that really matters—the lives of individual Christians—it would not necessarily hamper union in prayer, reflection and action.

The real problem is that even in our local communities we do not have unity. Anyone who has endured a meeting in any congregation knows that. One need not even go to a meeting to see it. Go to a church that has a parking lot, and as you watch the jockeying for spaces or the rush to the exit, you can see whether or not Christians are united in love as brothers and sisters. It's not a pretty sight.

Our lives outside the church grounds are no better signs that Jesus' prayer for unity has been fulfilled. In our day-to-day lives, we seldom, if ever, give thought to the fact that someone with whom we are dealing is a fellow Christian. If the thought crosses my mind, I decide it is irrelevant to the matter at hand. That matter may, in fact, be something I am doing to that fellow Christian that I eventually may have to confess as sin.

Obvious divisions are not, however, the worst sign that the prayer of Jesus has not been answered and that we have been the ones who have blocked the answer. Far worse than active divisions, rivalries and conflicts is plain indifference.

Jesus does not pray that we not be divided. He wants something positive, some quality of life and action called unity.

When I look at the average Christian community, I do not see division so much as I see indifference. We can sit next to one another on a Sunday, proclaiming one faith, hearing the one Word of God, partaking of the one Eucharist and sharing eternal life with one another, and yet not bother to say 'Good morning'. We do not know each other, and too often do not care to. We cannot welcome newcomers because we probably do not know the old-timers well enough to recognize who might be new. We are not divided, but we are certainly not united, not one in the love of Christ.

There are, of course, excuses for this. Many of our parishes are too big; too many of our leaders do not foster unity; modern society hinders our ability to form community. All of this can be true, but the fact remains that the Lord has prayed for unity, and no excuse should block that prayer's coming true.

What shall we do? Until we refuse to be satisfied with mere lack of division, and become dissatisfied with lack of unity, Jesus' prayer will be thwarted in our lives.

For the sake of unity, some divisiveness may be necessary. I may have to care enough to complain, to make demands. I may have to engage in activities that foster unity in our communities. I may have to become unpopular with those who are comfortable in avoiding the demands of community or who fear the unknown. I may have to overcome my own reluctance to be truly one with anyone whom Jesus has made one with him and me in Baptism.

It is a big challenge. But, it is also a chance for me to answer Jesus' prayer, a nice way to offer thanks for the prayers God has heard from me.

Pentecost (A)

What does it mean to say someone is 'at home'? If we are talking about sitting within the sound of their doorbell, we mean the person has not gone away. To be at home in this sense also means a readiness to welcome visitors.

It is possible to be 'at home' without being home. I can be at home at the address of a friend. I feel comfortable, welcomed and loved. My host is glad of my presence, but without fuss. The refrigerator door is mine to open.

If someone invites me to be at home, it is not the sort of 'at home' I enjoy or endure at my own place. I have moved, have gone away from my own home to enter another's. To be at home in this case means abandoning my own 'at home.' In other words, when someone makes me feel at home, I am not at home.

The two kinds of 'at home' are mutually exclusive. Either I am home at home, or at home away. I cannot be welcomed to my own house, nor can I be at home at another's without moving.

Pentecost is an 'at home' day, reminding us that God is at home with us and we with God.

In what sense of 'at home' is this true? Is God 'at home' at some divine residence, awaiting our visit, or has God entered our home? Are we 'at home' in our world, or are we welcomed in God's home? Who is the welcomer? Who is the welcomed?

God is separate from creation. In other words, God is not at home as a native of the universe. Yet, we celebrate the fact that God has 'moved in'. The Holy Spirit has taken up residence in our world. It is God's home.

So, we are invited to be at home in God's own home—not just a heaven beyond place and time, but in this world. We live in the house of God, God's welcome guests.

But, it is our home, too, and we can invite God to be at home. How? Well, what makes good hospitality? First, the welcome itself. We should be aware of God's coming to us and rejoice in it. Beyond that, like good hosts, we should do whatever it takes to make our guest comfortable. When that guest is God, hosting means not preparing favorite foods, but doing what Christ has told us is pleasing to God. That is, loving our Guest and all in the house—every child of God.

So, God hosts us and we host God. What about the guesting? When God joins us as guest, what happens? When guests come, they often bring a gift. In the Pentecost Gospel, Jesus presents a gift, the power to forgive sins. When God gives a gift, it is not like some of the gifts that guests bring, good only to be hidden away somewhere. God's gifts are meant to be used. We must be forgivers.

And what of ourselves as guests? What does it mean to be told by God to make ourselves at home? Feeling at home in the world is difficult. Very often, it seems like an unwelcoming place. It can be cold and threatening. Many men and women are fearful of the world. They feel unwelcome in it.

That is why this feast of the Holy Spirit's coming is so important. Since God is at home in our world, welcoming us as guests, we can live without undue anxiety. We have been invited to make ourselves comfortable here.

What does it mean to be comfortable in God's world? What are the spiritual equivalents of refrigerator privileges? One is the right and ability to pray. We can turn to our host and ask for what we need.

Even more basic is the right to feel at ease. When we make ourselves at home in another's house, we may hear all sorts of unfamiliar noises at night. But, knowing our host, we are confident and comfortable. In this house of God we call our world, there are many things that can disturb us, but we continue to live with confidence in our host.

Pentecost reminds us that God is at home in our world as our guest. It also reminds us that we can be at home in the world as God's guests.

Pentecost (B)

The miracle of Pentecost was not that people understood what the disciples said. The miracle was that they said it in the first place. Men and women who had been hiding, fearful that they would be discovered by the authorities who had killed their teacher, suddenly were making 'bold proclamations' to people from all over the world.

Pentecost was the Greek name for the Jewish feast of Shavuot that came 50 days after Passover. Though it was originally a harvest festival, by the time of Jesus it was (and still is) a feast celebrating God's covenant with Israel on Mt. Sinai. What happened there is a key to understanding the vocation of the Church that was born on that feast.

It was at Sinai that the people experienced the glorious presence of God. It was on Sinai that Moses received the law of God. It was at Sinai that the mob that had come out of Egypt became a people with a special relationship with God. It was at Sinai that the people accepted that relationship and committed themselves to a special kind of life in faithfulness to it.

The upper room was a latter-day Sinai. At Sinai, the power of God was shown in thunder and lightning. In the room, it was shown in 'tongues as of fire'. At Sinai, the people were made one by the law of the Lord. In the room, they became one Church by the power of the Spirit. At Sinai, the people learned the laws that would govern their lives and define them as a people. In the room, the disciples were given the vocation that would define the followers of Christ: they became proclaimers of the Good News.

So, the Church was born on the festival of the birth of God's chosen people. But, there was a difference. There was another high place in Scripture that must be kept in mind when looking at Pentecost. That is the Tower of Babel. That tower was built as a way to increase human power; it became the source and symbol of the linguistic and other divisions among people. In the upper room, the legacy of Babel was ended. The disciples spoke and people from around the world understood what they said. The way the world was created, with no divisions among people, was once again present. The new creation was born in the birth of the Church.

At Sinai, God formed a covenant relationship with one people, Israel. At Pentecost, the new covenant was made without borders, without limitations of language, nation or race. The new covenant is for all people. The whole world has become the chosen people.

The Church is Pentecost carried out through history. What happened to the disciples that day happens to us. The vocation they received is the vocation we receive. The bold proclamation they made to all nations is the bold proclamation we make.

That has implications for us today, the anniversary of our vocation to be Church. When the disciples became Church in the power of the Spirit, they did not immediately organize or figure out what to do among and for themselves. Getting the Good News out was more important than what went on inside the room or the community.

The Church exists not to be a club of the saved, but to be the herald of the Gospel. Our first concern must always be with those who are outside, for the men and women who have not yet come to know Christ. Whatever we do as Christians, whether as individuals or as a community, must be shaped by our vocation to tell the whole world the Good News that Christ is risen.

We do not do that as a mob, but as individuals who put our varied and necessary talents at the service of the proclamation. Each of us is essential to the mission of our Church. The gifts I have been given by God are meant to build up the body of Christ so that the world may know him. Seeing us, they should see him. They will see him if we do what he did: show the peace-giving, forgiving love of God.

We never do that perfectly. Our personal and communal fear, weakness and sin always interfere with our attempts. However, the Spirit who made the disciples understandable to people from around the world that Pentecost works through our stumbling, fumbling efforts to get the message across.

Pentecost (C)

'Peace be with you', was the greeting the risen Lord gave his fearful disciples. 'At the sight of the Lord the disciples rejoiced.' The first gift of the Kingdom is joy-giving peace and Pentecost is a feast of that peace.

The same spirit that swept over the waters at creation came over the disciples to make a new creation: 'From heaven there came a sound like the rush of a violent wind ... All of them were filled with the Holy Spirit.'

The next thing that happened was the birth of the Church in mission. The disciples who had been hiding in fear now praised God for all the world to hear. Peter, who had once denied even knowing Jesus, stood before a crowd and proclaimed that Jesus was risen. According to the Acts of the Apostles, three thousand people who heard him were baptized. This new creation meant to include those of 'every race and tongue, every people and nation'.

So, today's feast is a celebration of our mission as Church to proclaim to the whole world that Christ is risen. Since it is also a day on which we recall Christ's gift of forgiveness, we must reflect upon the sins that might hinder that proclamation.

There are, of course, many circumstances where hindrances to our proclamation come from outside ourselves. There are places in the world where Christians are forbidden to share the good news of the Resurrection.

However, probably the biggest obstacle to people's accepting the Gospel is we Christians. Our sin keeps people from hearing and accepting the call of God to know Christ. Today, we are challenged to examine ourselves for a terrible sin against creation and to recommit ourselves to fighting it.

When the new creation began, 'the crowd gathered and was bewildered, because each one heard them speaking in the native language of each'. Parthians, Medes, Elamites, Mesopotamians, Judeans, Cappadocians, Pontians, Asians, Phrygians, Pamphilians,

Egyptians, Libyans, Romans, Cretans and Arabs—a lector's nightmare of hard-to-read names—were able to hear the good news.

The Kingdom of God makes no distinctions. All hear the proclamation 'about the marvels God has accomplished'. The Kingdom of God, the new creation, has room for all. Yet, we make many distinctions in our personal and social lives, distinctions that betray what God has done. God created the world in variety, yet we refuse to accept God's creation.

The sin has many names because it takes many forms: racism, ethnocentrism, bigotry, prejudice, nationalism, tribalism, genderism, discrimination, snobbishness, intolerance. However, it is basically one sin, the refusal to accept the work of God's spirit in creating the world as the varied place it is.

Sometimes the sin is obvious in its enormity. 'Ethnic cleansing' is a new phrase, but not a new reality in our world. The refusal of so-called Christian nations to respond charitably to refugees can be called preemptive ethnic cleansing.

The persecution of Jews by Christians throughout history is our indelible shame. Christians have deprived others of their rights and even of life because they were of a different color. We have even killed each other because we have different ways of following Christ.

But, in some ways, the more terrible forms of this sin are harder to see, less stark. There are examples of prejudice in my life that are so much a part of me that I have to make an effort to even notice them.

We hope to spend eternity with men and women who are different from ourselves, but we balk at spending our short lives in this world with them, sharing our societies, our nations, our rights or our goods. Their difference, their God-given variety, is our only reason. All sin is idiotic, and since this sin is a great one it is greatly idiotic.

The people of many backgrounds who heard Peter 'were cut to the heart and said, "What are we to do?"'

Peter's answer was, 'Repent'. I must admit the sin, see how it manifests itself in my life, and then ask God's forgiveness for denying the creation. I must ask for the courage to confront my sin and not let it control my words or deeds.

That is our hope. Our sins are not unforgivable. God, who by our lights might have reason to discriminate against us, embraces us and offers peace. We who are sent to the world to continue the loving work of the incarnate Son must overcome our unreasoned fear and hatred of others so that we might share with them the joy-giving peace that is the Pentecost promise to all creation.

Trinity Sunday (A)

There is no way human minds can enclose the One who created them. Even so, it is good for us to reflect upon the mystery of the Trinity from time to time so that we can grow in knowledge and love of the One who loves us more than anyone else.

One meditation upon the mystery of the Trinity focuses upon that love. St John tells us God is love. In the Creation of the world and of each of us, in the Incarnation of Jesus, in the Cross and Resurrection of Christ, we see that confirmed. God is love without limit, love without prejudice, love without thought of return.

Love is something that gives of itself. A man's and a woman's love for one another is a nurturing, life-sharing gift. As fellow human beings, each is able to receive the fullness of the other's love and return it. The nature of love is mutual sharing.

Now, if God is love, where is that mutual sharing? The love God has for me and the rest of creation is so great that it gives us life, even eternal life. Yet, it is not mutual because there is no way I can love God as God loves me. If God is love, there must be something about God's self that makes the fullness of love, mutuality, really present. Otherwise, something is missing, inadequate, in the love of God. That mutuality is the relationship in the One God between the Father and the Son.

However, there is more to love than mutuality. There is creativity. When a man and a woman love one another, one expression of that love is in the creation of new life. Through the mystery of sex, two people bring a third into being. Mutual love finds its fulfillment when the lovers turn toward a third and share the mystery of their love for one another. This is a hint of the mystery of the Spirit, the third Person of the one God. The love of the Father and Son finds its completion in their sharing it with another who loves them in return, the Spirit.

The love of each Person in the Trinity is infinite, unstinting and absolute. It is infinitely equal in each, and therefore infinitely equal in all. So, the three are one.

These reflections may illuminate the mystery of the Trinity, and may even be an aid to prayer and faith. If they are not, forget them. The Trinity is true; the explanations are shadows of shadows of the truth.

But, if we grant that this meditation on the Trinity has some validity, we should look at it to see what implications it might have for our own lives. After all, if we are created in the image of God, then there must be something about us that at least parallels the mystery of the Trinity. A deeper appreciation of that mystery should teach us about what it means to be a human being.

So, where do I find the mystery of the Trinity in my life as a child of God?

Though my father was dead at the time, we celebrated my parents' 50th wedding anniversary because it was not only the anniversary of two people's marriage, but was the anniversary of the birth of a family. That man and woman eventually shared their love with children, making the one family a unity of several persons. One reason marriage is a sacrament is that it is in some ways an image of the life of God, the Three-in-One.

So, besides being a feast on which we reflect upon the mystery of God's love, perhaps this a day for all of us, especially those of us who are married, to reflect upon how our love for one another should be unselfish, unstinting and, within the limits imposed by our weakness and sin, unbounded.

Do I really share love with others, as the Father shares love with the Son? Is our mutual love a source of grace, life and love for others? Am I, are we, concerned for the well-being of all God's creatures? In other words, do I imitate the Trinity in my living and loving?

We are created in the image of God who is love. That love finds expression in a threeness in oneness in which the mystery of love overflows beyond the limitations imposed by mathematics and human understanding. So, Christians called to show God's love to the world should show a love that is so full as to overflow us, bringing unity to a world of many persons.

Trinity Sunday (B)

Ishmael, the narrator of Herman Melville's 1851 novel *Moby Dick*, describes the harpooner Queequeg unwrapping his god, putting it on the hearth of their room in an inn, praying to it and then putting it away.

Though the number of harpooners has declined since the nineteenth century, there has been no lessening of the tendency to like manageable gods who will do our bidding when we want them, but can be put away when we are not interested or don't want to be bothered by them. They are pocket-sized gods small enough to fit into our ideas, hopes and demands.

Christians say there is only one God. But, what we say and how we act do not always match. I have met people who would protest any suggestion that they are not Christian, but whose attitudes toward Mary and other saints go beyond veneration to idolatry, making them polytheists, worshipers of many gods.

Idolatry is not limited to religious figures like saints. Nations, races and even sports teams are handy pocket gods. Judging from the sacrifices we make for it and our obsessive devotion to it, can anyone deny that one of our pocket-sized gods fits nicely into our billfolds?

We even manage to turn the one true God into a pocket god. In every war, God is enlisted as a patron of the armed forces of whichever side happens to be 'Christian.' When Christian armies fight Christian armies, God is invoked as champion by chaplains on both sides.

In our day-to-day lives, our pocket-sized god is supposed to grant us winning lottery tickets, good weather and a general sense of well-being—the god in our pocket becomes a teddy bear.

More sophisticatedly, we try to fit God into our various philosophies and theologies, cramming God into our brains.

The dogma of the Trinity says 'NO!' to all that. Any god that can fit into my pocket, into my mind, into my concepts and into my expectations is too small to be the one true God. Any creation by my desires, hopes, prejudices, selfishness, dreams or intellect is not God, regardless of what I may call it.

Part of the mystery of the Trinity is the assurance that we can learn something about God by looking at beings who have personalities, ourselves. One of the surest things we know about ourselves is that every single one of us is beyond definition, though not beyond relationship. People are not predictable, they cannot be put into our pocket, and whenever we try to capture the essence of another, he or she shatters our neat ideas. I cannot even neatly categorize myself. Yet, we can hear, heed and love one another.

To say 'Trinity' is to declare that there is something about God that is, at its core, a relationship of love, love among the Father, the Son and the Holy Spirit. It is a love that overflows to include us and all creation.

From what we know of love among ourselves, we can guess, hope and intuit that the way to come to know God is to love. Love does not squeeze another into our ideas, but allows the other to remain other, just as the other allows me to be me.

It is here that God does for us what we could not do. God climbs into our pockets. The mystery of the Incarnation is that God whom we cannot capture comes into our lives in terms we can grasp. Not in intellectual terms, but in terms of love.

God does not cease to be God. God does not cease to be beyond all we can imagine. However, God shows us that we can be friends, lovers.

Trinity Sunday reminds us that God can 'get into our pocket' and become knowable and lovable not because of what I do, but because God chooses to be known and loved, chooses to be in my pocket.

That may be the most wonderful thing that God has done for us. One God in Three Persons is beyond us and would always be beyond us except by a divine decision to be known by us, known as truly other, yet truly loving.

Trinity Sunday (C)

What does the Trinity look like? Artists often portray the mystery by using images of a white-bearded old man, Jesus and a dove. I don't like those portrayals. The Old Testament very strongly forbids making images of God, a prohibition that Islam also takes seriously. That prohibition makes good sense.

The problem is that what we imagine can become or at least shape what we believe. By turning God the Father into a sort of Santa Claus figure, we are in danger of forgetting the absolute holiness and otherness of God. God the Father can become more like an indulgent uncle or a stern grandfather. In other words, we are in danger of making God in our image instead of recalling that it is the other way around. God has made us in the divine image.

However, for Christians, there is one exception to the rule, an exception that God has made. If we wish to portray God, we must portray Jesus, God's self-presentation in material form. In the Incarnation, God has said, 'If you want to know what I am like, look at me in Jesus.'

Of course, the New Testament does not tell us what Jesus looked like, and so we use our imagination to visualize him. Since until recently most Christian art has come from the West, many artistic portrayals of Jesus make him look like a European, though he was not one. Increasingly, artists now show him with Asian, African or other features.

But, more important than his looks is what Jesus did and does. We must look to his words and deeds if we want to know about God, want to know God. And his foremost deed and the clearest picture of the Trinity is the Cross.

The Cross is not merely something that happened to Jesus long ago. On the Cross, we see absolute love in action. That love is a self-giving that holds nothing back. Jesus offered himself to the Father totally on the Cross. That is the heart of the mystery of the Trinity, an absolutely unlimited self-giving love among the Father, Son and Holy

Spirit. On the Cross, God the Son shows what absolute self-giving looks like when it is enfleshed. It is a handing over of one's life, and through that a receiving of new life.

Scripture tells us that we are created in the image of God. In that case, there must be something about the mystery of the Trinity that tells us about the mystery of ourselves. Who am I really? Why do I exist? What is my destiny?

Because the unlimited and overflowing love in the Trinity undergirds all of creation, all that exists, including you and I, exists because the Triune God loves us. Because that absolutely self-giving love within the Trinity is the basis of our existence, that means that our own lives find their fullest meaning in self-giving, even to death.

In addition, if we are created in the image of the Triune God, there must be something about us, something about me, that tells something about the mystery of God. Of course, not everything I say or do points to God. My sin, fear, laziness, selfishness and such do not tell me or others about God, except the divine love that shows itself in mercy.

But, when I am at my best, then I do show something about God to the world. When I love, when I forgive, when I serve, when I abandon self-centeredness, then I show the world something about the loving Triune God.

Jesus no longer walks among us to show the world what the Trinity is like. Instead, he has founded a community, the Church, to carry on his vocation of showing God to the world. Today, the most real representation of the Trinity is we Christians ourselves. We are the body of Christ. To know ourselves as we are meant to be, we look to Jesus. To know Jesus as he is, we look to one another, especially to those who suffer on the cross in various ways today.

That is our glory and our shame. Our glory as Christians is that God has chosen us to carry on the mission of the Son to be the love of God incarnate in creation. Our shame is that we so often fail as a Church and as individual Christians to live that mission.

On Trinity Sunday, we know what God looks like. God looks like Jesus. And we know what we must look like. We must look like Jesus.

The Body and Blood of Christ (A)

Our Eucharistic celebration preserves actions that once served practical purposes. During the Middle Ages, some of them were misinterpreted as allegories. So, the priest's washing of his hands after the gifts were brought to the altar was seen as a re-enactment of Pilate's washing his hands of responsibility for the crucifixion of Jesus. In fact, the origins of the hand washing are more prosaic. In the ancient liturgy, the priest washed his hands because they were dirty.

If his hands were dirty, why didn't he wash them before the liturgy? The problem was that they were dirtied during the liturgy, during the presentation of gifts.

I once celebrated a Mass in Nigeria where the gifts went far beyond the—to me—usual bits of bread and wine and possibly the money collection. This offering included a goat that looked and acted willing to charge me. Folks more used than I to dealing with goats held it back while with a city boy's nervous scrutiny of its horns and teeth I laid a hand on its head as I had been told to do. I also accepted dirt-covered yams and other vegetables and fruits as well as a few chickens. The hand-washing afterwards was more than a symbolic gesture.

Offerings in the ancient Church were more like that one in Nigeria than many of us are used to. The members of the community offered bread, wine and other foods and gifts. The bishop or priest would accept all of this, and then take only a bit of the bread and wine, barely enough for everyone present, and put the rest aside for distribution later to the poor. Then, he would wash his hands.

So, the bread and wine that became the Body and Blood of Christ was part of the service of the Church to the poor. The Eucharist is a communion with Christ first of all, but, in Christ, also a communion with the community of believers and with those whom the community serves.

St Paul reminds us, 'Because there is one loaf, we who are many are one body, for we all partake of the one bread'. (This was much easier to comprehend in the pre-host days when, in fact, one or more loaves were broken and shared as the Eucharist.)

Each celebration of the Eucharist is a declaration to the world that the People of God are united in Christ. How often do I recall this fact when I am celebrating the liturgy? Desultory singing, half-hearted responses, daydreams, judgements on fellow worshipers, rehashing of old arguments and theological or catechetical mind games—all sorts of things go through my lips, mind and heart during worship. Most of them detract from, rather than building up the Body of Christ we call Church.

I am willing to admit that the Mass is a proclamation of unity among those sharing the action, a sign of union with the whole Church and a re-commitment to serve the world. The problem is that when I look around me at the real men and women who are supposed to be one, I often allow myself to be separate from them. I would rather pick and choose those with whom I am 'loaved'.

Fortunately, Christ is not so choosy. He is willing to be present in the bread and wine that his people share. He is willing to be present in that people and in what they do as individuals and a community to show the love of God to the world. It is his real presence in the sacrament that makes us really a community and really able to serve.

That union with one another in Christ for the service of the world is our foretaste of the eternal life to which we are invited. 'The one who eats this bread will live forever,' says the Lord. By being 'loaved' with one another in Christ, we become heaven on earth.

This is the link between our celebration of the Eucharist and our mission to evangelize the world. Our liturgy is a sign that Christ calls us all to unity. It is an experience of that unity. It is a unity that is meant to be carried beyond the walls of the church to the whole world, since the whole world is the source of the fruits of the earth and the work of human hands from which we make our offering.

Body and Blood of Christ (B)

We Christians have had some two thousand years to practice following the commands and example of the Lord. And we have had some two thousand years of failure. No one who looks honestly at the history of the Church or its members, at its current state or even at such Christians as (pardon me for saying this) you or me could claim that we have done a good job.

There is one good thing that we have consistently done, however, even though not all Christian communities do it, and not all do it regularly. It is one of the central elements of Catholic Christian life. That is to repeat the actions of Jesus at the Last Supper. We take bread, speak words of blessing over it, break it and share it among ourselves. We also repeat the action of Jesus over the cup and share it. We call it by many names: Eucharist, Holy Communion, the Breaking of the Bread, the Holy Sacrifice, Mass, the Divine Liturgy, the Source and Summit of the Christian Life and so on.

One aspect of the prayer that marks the action is known as *anamnesis*. The word is Greek, as is much of the technical language of the liturgy, since the original language of most of the Church outside of its Palestinian birthplace was Greek. Even in Rome, Latin did not become the language of the Church's worship until some time in the second century.

The word anamnesis means remembrance, or more literally, not-forgetting. Not having amnesia. Before we had the New Testament, before we had Church organization or church buildings, we had the simple act of sharing bread and wine to enable us to not forget the Lord and what he had done and said.

Remembering is not simply something that happens in my head. In Scripture, to remember is to place oneself in the original events. For example, at the Passover meal, the Seder, Jews don't talk about what God did for their ancestors more than three thousand years ago. They speak of how those at the table themselves were brought out of Egypt. So, when Jesus told his disciples to 'do this in remembrance of me,' he was not telling them to learn answers for a quiz. He was telling them to over and over again join him at the table, in his ministry, in his glory.

When we gather to break and share the bread and drink from the cup, we are really present with the Lord and he with us. The presence of Christ in the sacrament is a cure for and a protection against amnesia, against forgetting that the Lord is with us at all times. He calls us, challenges us, empowers us, comforts us and forgives us. The Eucharist helps us to not forget. And, remembering, we can repent, reform and carry out our vocation. That vocation is to be the real presence of Christ for the world even after the liturgy is ended.

When the Mass was translated from Latin to Japanese, the words, 'The Body of Christ', used by the minister of the sacrament were translated into a respectful form of the language. After all, the proclamation to which we answer 'Amen' is about the presence of God the Son. But, shortly afterwards, the translation was changed to a form that is used when talking about ourselves.

The reason is illustrated in a sermon preached by St Augustine in 408. 'If you want to understand the body of Christ, listen to the apostle [Paul] telling the faithful, *You, though, are the body of Christ and its members*. So if it's you that are the body of Christ and its members, it's the mystery meaning you that has been placed on the Lord's table; what you receive is the mystery that means you. It is to what you are that you reply *Amen*, and by so replying you express your assent. What you hear, you see, is *The body of Christ*, and you answer, *Amen*. So be a member of the body of Christ, in order to make that *Amen* true.'

So, on this feast of the Body and Blood of Christ, we once again say 'Amen' to being Christ for the world, confident that his real presence with us will help us act as we truly are, his ongoing real presence for the world.

The Body and Blood of Christ (C)

The Eucharist appears to be an 'in-house' affair. We do not share it with those who are not Christians. Except in extraordinary circumstances, Catholics do not share the Eucharist with non-Catholic Christians.

So, the Feast of the Body and Blood of Christ would appear to be a day for a family celebration. But the Mass readings bring gate crashers into our party. The first is Melchizedek, king of Salem and priest of El Shaddai, God Most High. That is all we know about him. He was a pagan foreigner. 'God Most High' was some locally worshiped deity of the people of Salem. Since the god belonged to the kingdom and the kingdom to the god, the king naturally served a priestly function.

Melchizedek is probably in the readings because his blessing is connected with bread and wine and the Eucharist is bread and wine. But, whether he is with us for some deep theological reason or merely because of his menu, it is good to have him.

Why? Because of what he does. Melchizedek blesses Abram, ancestor in faith of all who believe in the one true God. But, look at what is happening. There is only one true believer in the world, and he is being blessed by a non-believer in the name of some non-existent tribal god!

God's love and blessings are not limited by the belief of the men and women through whom God chooses to work. A pagan priest-king not only has a place in the building of the Reign of God, but God uses him to bless believers.

Today there are many more believers than in Abram's time. Jews, Christians and Muslims—all of whom worship the same one God—number about three billion. Even so, the people for whom Melchizedek stands still outnumber us. Perhaps they always will.

Because Melchizedek has joined our celebration, all those other billions are part of what we do. They, like we, can be a means for God to bless the world. So, the whole world is with us as we worship, no matter who, what, how or even if they themselves worship. Do you feel a bit crowded?

Luke's Gospel continues this theme of universalism. Jesus tells the disciples to feed everyone. When the disciples are unable to do so, he provides the wherewithal to feed them. Now, everyone there had made some effort to come to Jesus. Perhaps some of them were true believers. Perhaps others were merely curious. Perhaps some went because a friend was going. Whatever their reason for coming, 'they all ate until they had enough.'

This miracle is about the Eucharist. It is for all who follow Jesus, no matter how mixed their motives. But there is more to it than that. Luke tells us that what they had left 'filled twelve baskets.' The number twelve symbolizes the whole People of God and so the leftovers show that there is enough even for those who were not there. They were somehow remembered in the action of Jesus. Feeling more crowded?

It is St Paul, however, who makes the point most strongly. 'Every time, then, you eat this bread and drink this cup, you proclaim the death of the Lord until he comes!' We share the Eucharist not for our own sakes, but for the sake of showing the world the saving presence of Jesus among us. What began by looking like a family meal now appears to be a meal the family shares not for its own sake at all, but for the rest of the world!

So, Melchizedek and the mob belong in our thoughts and prayers today. When we share the Eucharist, we do so on behalf of Melchizedek and all others who do not know Christ. God works through them to bless the world, and us with it. We should keep them in mind and heart, giving thanks for them and on behalf of them.

Sacred Season:

Ordinary Time

First Sunday of the Year, Baptism of the Lord (A)

Once the Church moved beyond Aramaic-speaking Palestine, the language of Christians was Greek. So, Christians used Greek words to describe themselves and what they believed.

Some of the earliest surviving Christian writings are graffiti, pictures and sayings scratched on ancient walls. Among them are pictures of fish because the Greek letters of *ichthus*, 'fish' begin the five words that make up the Greek statement, 'Jesus Christ, Son of God, Savior.'

But the popularity of this image was not merely due to a word game. There was a message in it as well. Fish are born and live in water. Christians, too, come to new life in the water of Baptism. So, the fish symbolizes those who say 'Jesus Christ, Son of God, Savior' and who live because of the sacrament of Baptism.

Some fish are beautiful. Some are grotesque. When they are in water, they generally move gracefully and even the most grotesque have a certain beauty. Out of water, they flop around, their colors fade, they die. If I separate myself from Jesus Christ, Son of God, Savior, I become a fish out of water. I will lose my true beauty and gracefulness. A Christian's true self is a fish self.

What kind of fish? Perhaps the finny fish that best symbolizes Christian fish is the salmon. A salmon is born in water and then the water carries it out into the vast sea. There, the salmon wanders and grows until the time comes for the big event of its life, the return to the place where its journey began.

When I was baptized, I was born as a new creature. God looked upon me, as upon Jesus, and said, 'This is my beloved child with whom I am well pleased'. That was the beginning of my journey of faith. My baptized life has carried me into the great sea of the world, and I have grown as a member of my species, the Christian fish.

Someday, I will return to the point at which I started, and I hope that God will say, 'Here, once again, is my beloved child, worn with the journey of life, coming now to the fulfilment of the union with me that started in Baptism. I am well pleased'.

I am a fish; I am something else as well. The baptism of Jesus was a declaration of his son-ship. In that baptism, God declared who Jesus was. The same happened less dramatically, but no less really, in my own Baptism. When the water shows us to be fish, the sacrament declares us to be beloved sons and daughters of God.

That has implications for our lives. When God declared Jesus to be 'my beloved son', his ministry and his journey to the Cross began. Baptism is not merely a ritual that happens once for all. It is a beginning and a responsibility.

It is a responsibility because we have it in our power to make God look like a fool. God has declared us to be sons and daughters. The world, then, is right to look for some family resemblance between us and God. We should be loving, serving and forgiving, not because that is the way to earn God's favor, but because that is how we are true to the favor we have already been granted.

If we fail to resemble our Father, then God's hopes are thwarted. The life of Jesus declared at every point that he was the true *ichthus*, Jesus Christ, Son of God, Savior. God says that we can be fishlike, that we can imitate Christ. How like him am I?

In today's reading from the Acts of the Apostles, Peter tells the crowd what they can expect of fish people, followers of Christ who 'went about doing good and healing all who were oppressed by the devil'. We should do likewise.

It isn't hard to find good that needs to be done. It isn't hard to find the oppression of evil. We must be willing to swim into the mess of the world and show that God's life can be lived there.

The sea looks like a forbidding place, yet that is where fish live. The world can look like a forbidding place, yet it is a natural habitat for those who have been made fish in the water of Baptism.

First Sunday of the Year, Baptism of the Lord (B)

'She's more Christian than most Christians.'
Have you ever made a similar comment? The implication is that being Christian means being gentle, generous and gallant. Since gentleness, generosity and gallantry are not monopolies of the baptized, just about anyone can be called 'Christian.'

The feast of the Baptism of the Lord, provides an opportunity to reflect upon what my own baptism means, what it means to say, 'I am a Christian'. Obviously, I could not be claiming to be notably generous, gentle or gallant.

Could it be that there are two kinds of Christianity—the nice kind practiced by the unbaptized and the mediocre kind preached by the baptized?

According to the Acts of the Apostles, followers of Jesus were first called 'Christians' in Antioch. The word means 'partisans of Christ.' It has nothing to do with the way people act, but refers to whom they follow.

In other words, a Christian is not defined as a nice person. To be a Christian is to have a relationship with Christ, to be one of his partisans.

So, we are wrong to say of someone who is not baptized that he or she is very Christian. He or she is very good. Virtue is not a Christian monopoly. It's a form of spiritual imperialism to call them Christian. They are good (by the grace of God that comes through Christ) on their own terms, not ours.

However, the problem is greater than calling Buddhists, Hindus, Jews, Muslims or even atheists Christian. The real problem is a poor understanding of Christianity that allows us to make the mistake in the first place.

Perhaps the greatest internal threat to the Church comes not from theological disputes, nor sectarian divisions. The danger is an attitude called 'moralism', the belief that the Christian life consists in living a special way, acting in a particular way, doing certain things and refraining from others. It puts the focus on me rather than on God.

Basic Christianity is found in this week's Gospel: 'You are my beloved Son. On you my favor rests.' God chooses to make us sons and daughters. In baptism, we are united with Christ, the Son, and enter into a special way of meeting God, a way chosen by God, not us.

Our duty, then, as Christians is to grow in that relationship. Good deeds, a good demeanor and good intentions are not enough. In prayer, reflection, study and action we must deepen our relationship with God.

If we do that, then we will, in fact, act in a particular way toward others. As we grow more aware of and awed by God's parental love, we can only respond by showing that love to others. Might that be the reason that after hearing the Father's voice, Jesus embarks on his mission?

God has said to each of us at our baptism, 'You are my beloved child. On you my favor rests'. What am I going to do about that?

First, of course, I give thanks. Then, I give witness. I try to live a life that proclaims to the world that God loves us. I may be a very pleasant person while doing it. I may be an ogre. My personality may repel certain people, and even myself. That does not matter.

What matters is that God loves me even in my unlikeableness. Life would probably be nicer for my fellows if I were as gentle, generous and gallant as many who are not partisans of Christ. But, it is the partisanship, not the personality, that makes a Christian.

Baptism of the Lord, First Sunday of the Year (C)

People who went to be baptized by John were looking for a Messiah, an anointed one who would fulfill their deepest needs and hopes.

What were those needs and hopes that brought them to the desert? For some, they took a political form, release from the Roman Empire's taxation and oppression. Others wanted to see the unambiguous presence of God among the chosen people.

For still others, it was probably vaguer and, therefore, perhaps deeper. They sought some sort of inner peace. They hoped someone could give them a good reason to risk getting out of bed in the morning and take the bigger risk of closing their eyes at night. They wanted some sign that their lives were noticed by God, important to God, embraced by God and sustained forever by God.

In other words, those folks at the side of the Jordan were like us.

Among those folks was Jesus. He, too, had come to John. He, too, received John's baptism. Perhaps he, too, was looking for something, some assurance of his relationship with God. In other words, Jesus at the side of the Jordan was like us.

'When all the people were baptized, and Jesus was at prayer after likewise being baptized, the skies opened and the Holy Spirit descended on him in visible form like a dove. A voice from heaven was heard to say, "You are my beloved Son. On you my favor rests".'

In that moment, Jesus received the assurance he was waiting for, the answer to his heart's desire. So, too, did everyone else. That is the reason for the Spirit's appearance in visible form. The assurance to Jesus that he had God's favor was also an assurance to the rest of the crowd that in Jesus, God's favor was on them, too. It is our assurance as well.

The difference between us Christians and the rest of the world is the knowledge that there is an answer for our anticipating hearts, and the answer is the Son of God present among us. That was Good

News to the people on the banks of the Jordan River. It is Good News for the whole world.

The celebration of the baptism of Jesus is a proclamation of who he is, the first public proclamation of the identity of Jesus, the Son of God. The Holy Spirit tells those who have been full of anticipation that their hopes are realized.

In fact, their hopes have been exceeded. They were willing to settle for John as their messiah. John, however, told them that the real messiah would be vastly more powerful than himself.

What they—and we—were given is the Son of God. Sometimes we take that for granted. We treat the title as if it were an interesting batch of words. Perhaps the marvel of what the words mean is too great for us to grasp them even slightly, so we shrug them off.

However, the voice at the Baptism of Jesus was telling the truth. God has given us not only the answer to our hearts' anticipation; God has given us the fullness of God-ness to be with us, to stay with us.

So what are we to do? Should we sit back and luxuriate? The answer to our hearts' desires does not entail resting or relaxing. It doesn't even bring much comfort. It brings something else, something that is a theme of the Gospel of Luke that we reflect upon this year. It brings a call to spread the Good News, to share it with the whole world.

The same thing happened with Jesus. After receiving the Baptism of John and the declaration of his identity, he headed off deeper into the wilderness to be tempted, and then began his mission.

We, too, have been baptized—in our case, with the Baptism of Jesus. We, too, face temptations. We, too, are given a mission as a result of our Baptism and the declaration that Jesus is the Son of God. We are sent into the world to be advertisements in our words and deeds for the answer to the heart's anticipation of the world, the Son of God, Jesus Christ.

Second Sunday of the Year (A)

Ordinary Time in the Church calendar has nothing to do with the humdrum, the everyday. It refers to the fact that we use ordinal numbers (first, second, third . . .) to count the weeks.

Though this is right from a historical and linguistic point of view, the fact of the matter is that we really are in a humdrum, everyday period of the year. Christmas is past, Lent and Easter are weeks away. We are in a 'same-old, same-old' time when nothing dramatically different goes on in the worship of the Church.

It is the most important time of the year.

John the Baptizer said, 'I myself did not know him, but I came baptizing with water for this reason, that he might be revealed to Israel'. In other words, John's whole vocation was meant to point to Jesus, but when Jesus was actually standing right in front of him, John did not recognize him. It took a vision of the Spirit descending from heaven like a dove to make John see what was before his eyes. How can he have missed what was most important to him?

The answer might be 'ordinary time'. John was going about his business, doing what he always did. Granted, standing at the Jordan River wearing camel skins, eating locusts, preaching and baptizing might not be our idea of ordinary, but they were the ordinary things of John's life. The day Jesus came to him to be baptized was a day like any other day.

When Jesus showed up, he was just one more of the people who came to John. John might have been tired, distracted or bored. He was not alert. So, John baptized Jesus as he had baptized many others. Nothing special, just the ordinary. Why should it have been otherwise?

We fall into a routine, and even resent anything that might upset the patterns of our lives. We like each day to be pretty much as the day before. We neither want nor need surprises. We like to live in ordinary time. We like it so much that even if something out of the ordinary were to occur, we might not notice it. Jesus came to John to be baptized, and John did not notice.

But, the ordinary times of my life, are not necessarily enemies. It was in his ordinary time, after all, that John met Jesus. It is in ordinary time, in the day-to-day of my life, that I, too, encounter Jesus. That is the reason ordinary time is the most important time of the year.

The Christian life is not about doing good deeds or conducting beautiful ceremonies or saying fervid prayers or preaching the Gospel or thinking profound thoughts. It is about growing in love of God through Jesus Christ. All the rest comes along with that as aids to that end and results of it.

In the Incarnation, God has come among us in order that we might have that relationship. That coming was not in drama or in power. It was in the life of a carpenter who walked the roads with fishermen—an ordinary man with ordinary people in an ordinary time.

That is when and where we, too, can meet him. My day-to-day life is the place where Jesus is.

Spirituality is not so much a matter of prayer as of awareness, about sensitivity in ordinary time to the ordinary events and people around me. Christ is there among them as he was among the events and people of Israel two thousand years ago. Prayer can and should help me become more able to see God at work in my ordinary time, lest like John I miss seeing Christ as he stands in front of me in the people and events of my life.

And so, the ordinary is, in reality, the extraordinary. There are no ordinary times. There are no ordinary places. There are no ordinary events. There are no ordinary people. There are no ordinary lives—not even my own. Christ the Lord is in them all, calling us, encouraging us and enabling us to know, love and serve God.

There is, then, no need to search for God. Rather, as the Jewish theologian Abraham Joshua Heschel said, God is in search of us. God saves me the trouble of the search by coming into my life, into my world. Meeting Christ is the most ordinary thing there is. I can't avoid it, only ignore it.

Second Sunday of the Year (B)

Once upon a time, a young man visited a rabbi.

'Rabbi,' said the youth, 'I do not believe. Convince me.'

The rabbi said, 'Go, and for one year act like a believer.'

The youth left, thinking, 'I came looking for wisdom, and he tells me to play act!'

However, since the rabbi's advice would not be difficult to follow, he decided to give it a try. A year later, he returned and said, 'Rabbi, I believe.'

Today's Gospel passage contains the first words of Jesus in John's Gospel: 'What are you looking for?' He addresses disciples of John who like the young man in the story, are seekers.

However, when Jesus asks what they are looking for, they can't come up with any answer except to ask where he is staying. Are they too shy to ask what this 'Lamb of God' business means? Or, could it be that they do not know what they are looking for?

Jesus answers, 'Come and see'. He does not offer explanations. He merely tells them to join him. If they go with him, they will find what they are looking for. By the end of the day, Andrew proclaims, 'We have found the Messiah!'

I often feel something is missing in my life, that there must be more to it than counting the days and years till I die. Something's missing, but I can't even say for sure what it might be. If the Lord were to ask, 'What are you looking for?' I, too, might answer, 'Uh, where are you staying?'

The 'Come and see' of Jesus was not an invitation to see where he was staying. It was an invitation to come and find what they really were seeking.

The paradox of faith is that we only learn what we seek in life and from life as we find it. I know I want something; I don't know what I want; I'll know it when I get it.

The disciples had no idea what was in store for them. They could not have conceived of the cross, the resurrection, their own mission to the world, martyrdom, eternal life.

Like the young man, the disciples became believers through acting like believers. They followed Christ to where he lived near Bethany and where he lives in glory. Now they know where he stays.

I, too, approach Jesus looking for something. If someone were to ask what I'm after, I could only give partial answers, because I do not yet know the full answer I will receive through a lifetime, an eternity, of following the Lord.

So, Jesus says to me, 'Come and see. Come and see where I am to be found today. Come and see what it is you are really looking for. Come and see the fullness of life to which I will lead you.'

How do I go? It's not a matter of waiting on a street corner for some prophet to point out Jesus walking by.

The Church, the community born when Andrew and his friend decided to follow Jesus, serves the function of the Baptizer, pointing to the presence of Jesus. So, one way to go after him is to be part of this community.

That means more than spending an hour a week at some ritual. This community is one of worship and service. We worship individually and communally. In addition, we serve our neighbor as Jesus did. When the disciples went with Jesus, they entered into a path of healing, forgiveness, and liberation for others. Such lives will lead us to what it is, whom it is, we are seeking.

'What are you looking for?'

'I don't know, Lord; show it to me.'

'Come and see.'

Second Sunday of the Year (C)

John's Gospel tells us that Mary was at a wedding party. Then, it mentions that Jesus and his disciples 'had likewise been invited'. It sounds as if their invitation had been tacked onto Mary's.

Why would someone have asked her to bring them along? I can't imagine any other reason than that Jesus and his disciples were the kind of folks you want at a wedding party. They must have been witty, good singers and dancers and a good audience for other people's jokes. We seldom think of Jesus and his disciples in that way, but there are plenty of reasons why we should.

The story of the wedding feast at Cana actually focuses upon a joke, a pun by Jesus. Unfortunately, like all word plays, the puns of Jesus get lost in translation, so unless we learn Aramaic (with a Galilean drawl besides), we miss the joke. Anyway, Jesus joked with his mother.

Mary said to him, 'They have no wine'. Had she said it in English, Jesus might have responded, 'Of course not, it's a happy day. Why should anyone whine?' Mary then would have made a face, groaned and pretended to ignore the pun.

Well, that is what happened. Of course, Jesus and Mary did not speak English. But, in the Galilean dialect of Aramaic (a dialect ridiculed by the sophisticates in Jerusalem because of its sloppy pronunciation), it was possible to make a pun connecting 'wine' and 'lamb'. Jesus did so, acting as if Mary had said, 'They have no lamb'.

This makes sense, then, of the answer Jesus gave Mary: 'My hour has not yet come.' Just before the account of the wedding feast the evangelist tells us how John the Baptizer had pointed to Jesus and said, 'Look, there is the Lamb of God!' Mary talked of wine, but Jesus affirmed John's declaration, adding that the time had not yet come for him to show himself as the Lamb of God.

Like many mothers who've spent years listening to their children's jokes, Mary made a face and ignored her son's pun. Instead, she in effect told him to get down to business and do what the Lamb should do. And he did it.

He gave wine. Jesus knew the difference between a good and a mediocre wine. According to the waiter in charge, he gave good wine. There were good reasons for his doing that. The most obvious is that he drank wine and knew how enjoyable a really good wine can be. The second reason is linked to who he is.

In Scripture, wine is a symbol of joy and peace. The joy is easy to understand, but how is wine a symbol of peace? There is more to drinking wine than uncorking a bottle. The wine has to be made. That requires vineyards. They require lots of care. Then, the grapes must be harvested. Finally, the wine must be made. If soldiers or marauders destroy the vineyard or drive off the workers, there will be no wine. If we have wine, that means we have peace.

Jesus makes wine. That is, he brings a time of peace to the world. We live in that time.

We do? The world certainly does not look peaceful. Even the Church is not peaceful. And, while we're at it, neither am I. What is this peace that Jesus is giving when he turns mere everyday water into wine?

We must return to his pun. The wine he gives is himself, the Lamb of God who takes away the sin of the world. The real lack of peace in the world and in my life is not something political or psychological. The real lack of peace, and the cause of all other lack of peace, is spiritual. It is enslavement to sin.

Jesus the Lamb presents us with the wine of peace because he overcomes the sin of the world in his death and resurrection.

What remains for us is the task of the head waiter, the one who recognized the good wine and served it to the guests. If, through prayer, refection and service, I imbibe the Good News and, intoxicated by it, go out to the world filled with the Spirit of Christ, I and the world will know peace.

Third Sunday of the Year (A)

If we look at what Matthew says about the ministry of Jesus, we can see many things that would have caused him problems had he tried doing them as a Christian.

First, he does not stay put. Standard wisdom tells us that anyone trying to build a Christian community should stay in one place, working with people, working on people, working through people to build up an effective public presence. Buildings must be erected, programs must be initiated, committees must be appointed, leaders must be chosen and trained. Jesus failed to do any of this.

Then, there is the way in which Jesus invited people to discipleship. He apparently just picked people at random 'as he was walking along the Sea of Galilee'. No catechumenate or RCIA, no novitiate, no testing, no training, no retreats or seminars. Just, 'Come after me'.

The biggest problem, however, would be what he failed to do. Though he did tell some people to follow him, he did not tell most of those he met to follow him or join a new community of faith.

He did not tell them to abandon the religion of their ancestors. He did not tell them to go and do anything. In most cases, he merely told men and women that the kingdom of God, the fulfilment of God's will for creation, was at hand, and then he went on his way with the small group he had invited to come along. Even after performing miracles for people, he simply sent them home.

Matthew's Gospel is, more than the others, concerned with what the Church should look like, what sort of community of faith it should be. Right at the beginning, it challenges what most of our communities of faith are and what we expect them to be.

Looking at our structures, our hierarchies, our parishes, our congregations, our orders and our organizations, and then looking at the billions of people whom we are not reaching with the Good News of God's Reign, we can only feel uncomfortable. Can it be that we are going about it all wrong?

In one sense, Jesus had an easy time of it. He had no Church that needed all these things in order to carry out its activities and vocation. We do not have that luxury he had. There is a Church; we are that Church. We have to learn to live with it and in it and proclaim the Kingdom through it. Without it, neither we nor the rest of the world could know the Good News.

And yet . . .

We will never find an ideal form for our life as Church. So, what are we to do? We cannot abandon the developments that have brought us where we are today. After all, they do in fact sustain the community of believers. At the same time, we cannot honestly claim that they all contribute to the most effective proclamation of the Gospel. Whatever we have or do as a Church either locally or globally must be directed to proclaiming the Good News. Structures and ways of doing things, even venerable ones, are of secondary importance and must serve those ends.

We depend upon our structures and customs, but we must never lose sight of the reason for their existence. We need a sense of perspective. Jesus had such a sense. Rather than worry about other things, he devoted his ministry to proclaiming everywhere and to everyone that God's love was real and really present among them. When that proclamation required disciples, he called disciples. When it did not, he did not. The proclaiming was more important than the follow-up.

The Church that follows Jesus must be as willing to subordinate everything else to the proclamation of God's love. If that means downplaying or even abandoning certain ways of doing things, so be it. If it means not looking for institutional results, no problem.

Even if it means seeing people continue in their old religious traditions, but with a new confidence in God's love, then we must not define our mission as a search for converts. Like Jesus, we must be content to proclaim in deed and word the Good News, and call to fellowship those who are needed to further that proclamation, confident that God's love is bigger than the Church.

Third Sunday of the Year (B)

Long ago, on the way home from school, I saw an elderly woman with two shopping bags stopping to rest every few steps. I offered to help her.

'How far are you going?' I asked.

'Not far—just down the street.'

We walked a few blocks. My arms were tired, but I was too proud to rest. Every so often, I asked if we were getting closer. Each time, she answered, 'Not much farther—just down the street'.

Finally, she turned into a side street.

'Is this the block?'

'Not far—just down the street'.

We plodded a few more blocks. My fingers were aching and numb at the same time. Finally she led me into an apartment building.

'What floor are we going to?'

'Not far—just upstairs.'

At each floor, I asked if this was the one she lived on. By the time we reached her fifth-floor apartment, I had been 'not far'-ed into exhaustion.

Jesus in today's Gospel seems to have something in common with that woman. 'The reign of God is at hand!' Well, he said that 2,000 years ago, and it still seems to be a long way off.

Something else Jesus says complicates matters. 'This is the time of fulfillment.' Is he referring to his own time, or to any time we hear his words? Why say this is the time of fulfillment, and then that it's still on its way?

So, where is it? If it's already here, we should be able to recognize it. Well, the reason we can't recognize it leads to the third thing Jesus says: 'Reform your lives and believe in the good news!' The reason we don't see the reign of God is that our lives need reforming.

The reign of God is the fullness of God's presence with us, resulting in the forgiveness of sins, the establishment of just relationships among peoples, the sanctification of all creation as an offering to our Creator.

Can we see signs of that?

The clearest presence of the reign is Jesus, God's reign made flesh. 'The time of fulfillment has come' is another way of saying, 'Here I am!'

But are we too late? Have we missed the chance to experience the reign of God? Must we wait till the end of time?

No, because God's reign present in Jesus is carried on through the Church, sinful, weak and divided though it be. In the community of men and women struggling to be faithful to Christ, sharing God's love with friend, foe and stranger, there is the reign of God, even if not in its fullness.

And the reign of God is not confined to the Church. There are signs of that reign throughout the world.

The breaking of shackles that bind the bodies, minds and spirits of men and women, the advance of knowledge, the work of artists and the growth of solidarity among nations, cultures and religions of the world are all signs that God's reign is here, that the world is growing toward the vocation God has set for it.

The symbol of all this, our truest experience of God's reign, is the Eucharist. When we share the body of Christ, we are in the reign of God, united with all Christ's people in all times and climes.

I often miss that, which is why Jesus calls me to reform my life, to make it a sign of God's reign. Living a reformed life will clear my eyes, heart and soul to see God's reign in the Eucharist and in all it stands for—Jesus, the Church, the world.

This is the time of fulfillment. The reign of God is at hand. Let us reform our lives so that we may see it present and coming.

Third Sunday of the Year (C)

The Bible is reputedly the best-selling book in history. There is, however, no evidence that it is the best-read book.

In the past century, Biblical scholarship has made great progress in providing tools to gain a deeper understanding of Scripture than has been possible for centuries. That scholarship has borne fruit in translations, courses, books, pamphlets and programs aimed at drawing us to a new encounter with the Word of God. Have they done so?

Unfortunately, they have not succeeded. Too few people nourish their faith at the banquet of the Word. Of those who turn to Scripture, too many do so in a fundamentalist way that ignores the tools of scholarship and the guidance of the Church.

Why should we be more familiar with the Bible? Isn't it enough that on Sunday morning we hear three passages and a psalm read (or, if we are lucky, proclaimed) in church? Why should we spend extra time reading and studying a book written long, long ago in strange times and tongues?

One reason is that it is our book. I was once in an ecumenical group where the leader held up a Bible and asked, 'Whose book is this?' The Protestant members present each answered, 'It's God's.' Then, the leader turned to me and said, 'I hope you get this one right, because I want you to give us the Catholic position. Whose book is this?' I answered, 'The Church's'. The leader was satisfied.

For a Catholic, one who sees the Bible as first and foremost the Church's treasure, that book belongs to us as intimately as anything can. It is we, the Church, who in response to God's action among us wrote it, or, in the case of the Old Testament, made it our own. It is we, the Church, that handed it on from generation to generation. It is we, the Church, that have striven to make it come alive in every age in the lives of Christians.

The Word of God is, or should be, a reminder of God's presence among us. That is the reason we treat a Bible or Lectionary with special respect. It is the reason liturgists cringe when they see the Word being proclaimed from a leaflet or photocopy.

When Ezra read the book of God's Word to the people they also listened to his explanation. Ezra spoke to the community on behalf of the community. He was its own voice, commissioned to explain the community's understanding of the Word of God.

The Church, too, has explained the Scriptures over the centuries. Those explanations take various forms: doctrinal teachings, homilies, classes, scholarship and Scripture sharing in small groups. The important point is that we try to read and hear the Word of God as the Church's word and reflect upon it guided by that community.

In the opening of his Gospel, Luke gives a simple description of what Scripture is, 'a narrative of the events which have been fulfilled in our midst.' God's relationship with us is not a matter of words or a book. God relates through deeds, 'events'. Scripture provides a narrative of those events and of the community's response to them. It also provides a model of how to view God's action in our own lives. Scripture is a 'lens' through which we look for, find and understand God at work in the world.

Jesus in the synagogue shows us how it is done. Isaiah had written about a time when God's promise would be fulfilled, 'a year of favor from the Lord.' It would be a time of liberty and healing. The passage describes that time as one of comfort, joy and justice. Luke does not show Jesus reading the whole passage because people were familiar enough with Scripture that hearing the opening would bring the entire passage to mind, but Jesus is certainly referring to the entire section.

He is using the Word of God to announce to the people of Nazareth that the time had come for the fulfillment of God's promises. The new age has dawned. Folks in the synagogue understood that and its implications because they knew the Scriptures. We live in that new age. If we wish to understand what that means for us and the world, let's start by deepening our knowledge of and love for the Word of God.

Fourth Sunday of the Year (A)

For Matthew, Jesus on the mountain is like Moses who proclaimed God's law from Mount Sinai, and the Beatitudes are the new commandments.

So, what do the Beatitudes tell us about how we should live?

The key to them all is the first. 'Blessed are the poor in spirit, for theirs is the kingdom of heaven.' All the others are ways to live out this one.

To be poor in spirit is to understand my relationship with God, to understand that I have nothing to offer God that is not first of all a gift from God. Poverty of spirit frees me to accept God's greatest gift, the Kingdom, because I am not holding on to any illusions that my talents, my possessions, my time, or my life are my own.

If I am willing to settle for less than the Kingdom, allowing myself to be satisfied with the gifts rather than the Giver, I will not be able to see and accept the greater gift.

On the other hand, if I admit that before God I have nothing, I can live the Beatitudes and receive God's gifts.

'Blessed are those who mourn, for they will be comforted.' When I admit that I cannot find comfort anywhere but in God's grace, God will comfort me. That does not mean that everything will turn out as I wish. It does mean that I will know the love of God that embraced Jesus on his cross.

'Blessed are the meek, for they will inherit the earth.' Knowing my true worth before God makes me better able to know the true worth of other people. They, too, are God's gifts to the world. So, I cannot abuse them or treat them as if they were mine to use as I please. Rather than 'lord it over' others, I stand with them in humility before God.

'Blessed are those who hunger and thirst for righteousness, for they will be filled.' Righteousness, holiness, is not some other-worldly way of life. The Incarnation of God the Son shows us that the place for holiness, the encounter with God, is the real world in which I live from day to day. To be holy is to recognize in every event of my life the grace of God giving me life and love, and the call of God to share that life and love with others.

'Blessed are the merciful, for they will receive mercy.' God's love is limited only by my refusal to share it. That is the reason Jesus taught us to pray that we be forgiven to the extent that we ourselves forgive. The key to being merciful is to be honest with myself about how much I need mercy. If a sinner such as I can be forgiven, then it should be no great task to forgive others.

'Blessed are the pure in heart, for they will see God.' To be pure in heart means to have a heart that is not distracted from God. To be single-hearted means to be open to all that God offers, fully attentive at all times to the work of God in our lives. If we look for God at work, we will see God.

'Blessed are the peacemakers, for they will be called children of God.' Even many Christians make the mistake of thinking that peace is merely the absence of conflict. Scripture, however, shows that peace is not an absence, but a presence. It is justice, joy, generosity, gratitude and fellowship. To be a peacemaker is to work at building those virtues in the world.

'Blessed are those who are persecuted for righteousness' sake, for theirs is the kingdom of heaven. Blessed are you when people revile you and persecute you and utter all kinds of evil against you falsely on my account.' Have I ever suffered because of my Christian commitment? Not much. That is disturbing. Perhaps I do not live my faith in such a way that others even think of me as a Christian. Most of my 'persecution' is self-inflicted, a voice inside me that discourages me from living out my good intentions.

An ancient tradition of the Church calls upon us examine ourselves each night before going to sleep to see what sort of day we have lived. Perhaps the best way to do that is to learn and then each night repeat the Beatitudes, seeing how our day has shown us to be poor heirs of the reign of God.

Fourth Sunday of the Year (B)

Interesting, isn't it, that an unclean spirit recognizes the Lord, but people cannot. In fact, the unclean spirit is the first one in Mark's gospel to proclaim Jesus as 'The Holy One of God'.

The people marveled at Jesus' words, liking what and how he taught. They focused on his message. It's easy to imagine them discussing his teachings for days. In fact, some folks have been discussing them for two thousand years. The unclean spirit, on the other hand, does not talk about the message of Jesus, but about Jesus himself, who he is.

Scientists speak of 'anti-matter,' the absolute opposite to matter. Contact between matter and anti-matter results in the annihilation of both.

The unclean spirit knew that in the presence of Jesus it was faced with its opposite. So, it shrieked, 'Have you come to destroy us?' The spirit knew who Jesus is because in Jesus it saw not teachings, but absolute good. The spirit saw the presence of God.

Eventually, people recognized who Jesus is. Christians know that he is, indeed, what the unclean spirit proclaimed him to be, 'The Holy One of God'. We follow the unclean spirit in proclaiming God's presence among us in Jesus Christ.

It is not hard to think that I have more in common with an unclean spirit than that. There is much in my life that is as anti-matter compared to the reality that is Jesus.

When I look beyond myself to the Church, I nearly despair. Our track record is not good at all. The terrible weapons that plague our lives were developed in the part of the world with the longest, most intense Christian influence.

Some of the world's worst persecutions have been perpetrated by Christians who tortured one another in inquisitions, and went after non-Christians in crusades, forced conversions and the Holocaust.

The destruction of the environment God created as a home for all, the creation of economic, social and political systems that deprive men and women of their dignity as children of God—all these can be laid before followers of Christ with the words, 'Here are your real children'.

Is this cause to give up, to decide that since we have so much of the demon about us we should not presume to proclaim Christ? Should we give up doing what the unclean spirit did?

The rest of the world is no less soiled and sordid than we. In fact, we can stand as a symbol of the world, know Christ on behalf of the world, and proclaim him for the sake of the world precisely because we are tainted with evil.

It is when I recognize how far I am from the goodness of God that I can understand the awesomeness of God's love. When we confess our sinfulness, we can see its opposite, the Holy One of God.

The first step in repentance is to admit our guilt, as when we go to confession. We admit our faults and failures out loud, making them painfully and embarrassingly real to ourselves. Then, we are presented with the sin-overpowering love of God when we most recognize our need of it.

And we come to a key difference between ourselves and the unclean spirit. The demon feared; we rejoice because we know that Christ, the Holy One of God, is only our opposite in terms of evil. In terms of love, we are beloved children of God.

Therefore we proclaim that the Holy One of God is among us, that there is hope for us in our uncleanness. We proclaim, like the spirit in the gospel, that Jesus is the opposite of our sinfulness.

It might even be proper to say a grateful prayer for that spirit, that it, too, might know Christ not as its enemy, but as the love of God offered to all us unclean ones. Perhaps in God's mercy, we and that spirit will one day share the joy of heaven.

Fourth Sunday of the Year (C)

Folks in Nazareth knew Jesus well. He had grown up in their village. They knew his family. Probably some of them were relatives. They were a bit mystified at his wisdom. After all, 'Isn't this Joseph's son?' Perhaps that was the problem.

Folks in Nazareth had their own ideas of a savior, whether or not they talked about them or even brought them to their own minds. What did they get, though? 'Joseph's son'. How prosaic! Could they really be expected to accept as their savior someone they had known since he was a kid?

On top of that, he told them they should not expect him to work wonders for them, even though he knew they wanted them. 'You will doubtless quote me the proverb, "Physician, heal yourself", and say "Do here in your own country the things we have heard you have done in Capernaum".'

All in all, Jesus is a disappointing savior. He certainly does not fulfill the job description the folks in Nazareth would set for him. He does not fulfill mine either. Jesus is an underachiever.

Either there is something wrong with Jesus, or there is something wrong with our expectations. We either have to abandon him as a savior or accept him on his own terms. There seems to be no other possibility.

That is probably why so many do not bother with him. It is also the reason that many of us who claim to be his followers actually do not follow him. We give him lip-service, but in fact do not live as if we really thought of Jesus as our savior. Sometimes we reinvent him, deciding to believe in someone whom we call 'Jesus Christ', but who bears only passing resemblance to Christ himself.

The problem with Jesus is that he is not extraordinary enough for us. He really is 'Joseph's son'. He really is someone from a small town in northern Israel. We want special effects and we get a carpenter's son. Why don't we like that?

If the savior of the world is to be found talking in his hometown synagogue to the people among whom he grew up, then we must face the fact that salvation does not occur in some sort of special state where everything is wonderful. Salvation happens in our own villages, whether they be small towns like Nazareth or the global village.

We don't want that because, as often as not, we think salvation should rescue us from our humdrum or painful lives. We don't want our everyday homes, our everyday work, our everyday lives to be the place where God saves. However, our savior does not save us from our lives, but in our lives. Like it or not, our lives are sacred.

What can we do about that? Well, presuming that we agree to accept Jesus on his terms, we will have to do something about the way we live. That means looking for God's work of salvation in day-to-day prosaic events, the joys and pains of our lives.

How can we do that? The first step is to remind ourselves often throughout the day that the Lord is with us, is loving us. Morning prayers, prayers before meals, a quick prayer before doing something, night prayers—all these are helps. Then, perhaps all we need do is wait and see what happens.

Had the folks in Nazareth waited and paid more attention to Joseph's son instead of expelling him from the town, just think of the surprises that would have been in store for them.

Fifth Sunday of the Year (A)

Once upon a time, a researcher from a far planet visited Earth and joined a group of earthlings to learn by what means we exotic creatures take nourishment. When the group sat at table, the visitor asked about a white chemical compound that was in a vial on the table. 'Oh, that's salt', was the answer. 'We put it on our food to improve the taste.' So, the researcher poured out a sample and swallowed it. Accusing the earthlings of being poisoners, the researcher immediately returned home in a huff and with an enduring mistrust of all things terrestrial.

That night, a fisherman hauled in a fish from the deepest, darkest part of the ocean, a fish that had never seen light. The fish said to the fisherman, 'This place looks no different from my home'. The fisherman replied, 'It's dark, so it's hard to see; you need some light', and shone a light in the fish's eyes. The dazzled denizen of the deep leapt overboard.

Hearing that the followers of Jesus are salt of the earth and light of the world would not predispose either the alienated alien or the frazzled fish to value the role of Christians in the world.

Their problem would be thinking that salt and light are themselves the focus. Salt is not something we use for its own sake; we put it on foods to improve and preserve them. Looking at a source of light is blinding. It is light reflected off of things that makes it possible for us to see them. When it comes to our use of them, salt and light do not exist for their own sakes, but for the sake of other things.

So, when Jesus tells us we are salt of the earth and light of the world, what is he saying about us? Obviously, our call to follow Christ is for the sake of the world, not our own. We are supposed to give the earth its true taste, to enable the world to see its true self.

When we look at the world, it is clear that it needs a little salt, needs some light. No one believes everything is as it should be. If the world were well salted and well lit, what would it be like? Well, certain words—'atrocity', 'injustice', 'poverty', 'violence', 'betrayal', 'unfaithfulness', 'falsehood' and such—would be obsolete.

Most people probably don't think it's possible to get to such a world from the one in which we live. But then, most people are not God. God seems to think it is not only possible, but possible for us.

But how can we make the whole world over? I might make me and a few others happy, but the world is a big place with big problems. Is my little bit enough to really make a difference, enough to change the world?

Look again at salt and light. They are not much in themselves. A grain of salt is pretty small. A photon, the unit of light, has zero mass. Yet, they each make a big difference.

The proverb says that 'one bad apple spoils the whole bunch'. That may be true of a crate of apples, but in today's Gospel, Jesus tells us that it does not apply to people. Good is contagious. 'Let your light shine before others, so that they may see your good works and give glory to your father in heaven.'

My bit of saltiness, my little light, can draw others to know the true taste, the true look of the world and become themselves salt and light, for to give glory to God is to be salt and light. The problem may be that the world is not getting its full ration of salt and light from us Christians. If each of us were living as Christ hopes, then the world would indeed be a different place.

Fifth Sunday of the Year (B)

Jesus had a problem finding time to pray. Whenever he tried to get away for some prayer, folks in need tracked him down. 'Rising early the next morning, he went off to a lonely place in the desert; there he was absorbed in prayer. Simon and his companions managed to track him down; and when they found him, they told him, "Everybody is looking for you!"'

That problem is not limited to Jesus. We all live with the fact that as we grow in love of God, there seems to be no time to pray, to meditate, to contemplate. Studies must be done, jobs must be performed, families must be raised. Whenever a free moment appears, someone or something seems waiting to steal it.

So, we feel guilty that we do not give God the time we think we are supposed to. But perhaps it is a mistake to make too great a separation between prayer and our everyday lives. Over the centuries, we have allowed a special vocation in the Church, monasticism, to become a sort of norm for what our religious life should be. We feel guilty when we do not (even though we cannot) give ourselves over to hours of daily prayer.

But most of us do not live in monasteries where the day is built around our prayer schedule. Most of us live in situations where the day is built around nothing in particular, unless chaos be something in particular. Our days are devoted to reaching the end of them with a modicum of dignity, energy, health, sanity and holiness.

We must look to someplace other than the monastery for a model, and we can find one in Simon Peter's mother-in-law. When we first hear of her, she is in bed with a fever. We all know that experience. Had she been a younger woman with little children running around, she might not have been able to take to her bed. She would still have been taking care of the kids who probably brought the fever home with them in the first place.

Jesus came to her, took her by the hand, and helped her up. Immediately, the fever went away. How did she respond to this healing? Did she glorify God? Did she thank Jesus? Did she tell the neighbors? Did she congratulate her son-in-law on his choice of friends? No, 'she immediately began to wait on them'.

In other words, her immediate response to the healing love of God in Christ was to get back to her everyday activity. She began to look after her guests, setting a table, making a meal, seeing to their comfort. The sorts of things we all, in varying ways, do all the time. Normal stuff.

The mystery of the Incarnation, the presence of God among us as one of us, means that the place to find God, the place to meet the Lord, is not on some special sacred mountain, nor in a desert cave. It is not in the forest nor in a cathedral. The place to meet the Lord is in my daily life, in normal stuff.

Therefore, it is a mistake to think that we must be engaged in prayer if we are to meet the Lord. We can meet him and serve him at every moment of our lives. Peter's mother-in-law knew this. When she encountered the saving power of God in Christ, she did the right thing. She got on with her everyday life.

Does that mean we need not pray? No. Prayer is a special time to experience our relationship with God in a less ambiguous way than we might while sitting at a keyboard, wiping runny noses (our own or others') or waiting for a traffic light to change.

Because it lacks the ambiguity of such times, my prayer time is, indeed, precious, and a hunger for it is natural. We want to spend time with the One who loves us best. However, Jesus' own experience teaches us that we must be willing to sacrifice our prayer time for the sake of others. Like Jesus, we must be ready and willing to leave our prayer for those who seek us out. Like Peter's mother-in-law, our encounter with God must get us back to normal stuff.

Fifth Sunday of the Year (C)

Feeling unworthy of God's call is nothing new. Isaiah had the same problem: 'Woe is me, I am doomed! For I am a man of unclean lips, living among a people of unclean lips.' Peter says, 'Leave me, Lord. I am a sinful man'.

God, however, seems to be less demanding of us than we are ourselves. God will accept or, rather, work with and through our weaknesses.

In Isaiah's case his unclean lips were burned clean by a seraph-borne ember. Peter got words: 'Do not be afraid. From now on you will be catching people.'

Their reactions are important. The first words that pass Isaiah's newly-purified lips are, 'Here I am; send me.' Peter does not say anything; he acts. He and his partners 'brought their boats to land, left everything, and became his followers.'

'Vocation' comes from a word meaning, 'call.' A vocation, though, is not simply a call, as if God were yodeling in the heavens. It is a call to do something. Usually, we use the words 'calling' or 'vocation' about some work that involves one's whole being in service.

What are Isaiah and Peter called to do? Isaiah hears the voice of God saying, 'Whom shall I send? Who will go for us?' Peter is told that he will become a fisher of people.

Apparently, the call is not so much to be something as to do something. A vocation is not to some special state of goodness. Even less is it a call to a special status. It is a call to a special task.

The error of Isaiah and Peter was that they thought they had to be a special kind of person to respond to God's call. They thought that the sort of persons they were, rather than the task to which they were called, should determine God's work in the world.

God's answer is simply, 'Yes, I know you're not perfect. I'm not interested in that. I'm interested in having word of my love shared with the world. In a world where everyone is my specially loved child and everyone is imperfect, I am calling you to do something special for me. I don't need someone who can earn my love by being perfect. I just need you.'

Catholics tend to identify the word 'vocation' with a particular kind of response to God's call: priesthood or Religious life. However, they are not really vocations. They are ways of living the vocation each Christian has. Each of us Christians is called like Isaiah, like Peter, to do something for God. Just like Isaiah and Peter, we are called to proclaim God's message to the world, to be fishers of people, drawing them into deeper communion with God.

Like Isaiah and Peter, we have responded. In our Baptism, we have said, 'Here I am; send me.' In our Baptism, we have left our old life behind to follow Jesus. Baptism is an answer to a call, even though we might not fully realize it at the time.

So, to be Christian is to have a vocation. We are not perfect. Like Peter, I am sinful. Like Isaiah, I live among an unclean people. That is not important.

What is important is that God has called me. I am unworthy. I know that. God knows that. The people to whom God wants me to go either know that already or will know it soon enough.

It's not a matter of worthiness. It's a matter of the call. We should not get the two mixed up. My sinfulness is, in a sense, irrelevant. What counts is the task to which I have been called as an individual and to which we have been called as a Church.

The world is starving to hear of God's love, to see God's love. The world is swimming around in confusion, waiting to be brought into God's net. That is what counts. That is the vocation you and I have as Christians. God is willing to work with sinners like Isaiah, Peter, you and me. Let's give thanks for that and get to work.

Sixth Sunday of the Year (A)

Jesus taught the adults and blessed the children, but the Church has gotten it backwards. We teach the children and bless the adults. That was not the case in the early days of the Church. The section of Matthew's Gospel that we call 'The Sermon on the Mount' was intended by Matthew as a sort of catechism for adults.

What Jesus says about what has been taught in the past is uncomfortably clear: those rules are not enough. His followers are allowed no anger, no abusive language, no lustful thoughts, no divorce, no oaths. It is hard to avoid the demands of these teachings. We try to water them down, claiming they apply only to certain people or are meant as ideals. It doesn't work. Jesus spoke them to the crowd, not to a specially chosen elite.

My first reaction to what Jesus says is to decide that what he wants is impossible. There is no way that I can meet his demands. So, I ignore them. But, is Jesus in fact calling upon me to do the impossible? Is the problem that he asks too much, or is it that I am unwilling to give what he asks?

When I say, 'I cannot,' do I really mean, 'I will not'? I certainly cannot say, 'I've tried to live as Christ has commanded and I know from experience that it is impossible'. As GK Chesterton remarked, 'The Christian ideal has not been tried and found wanting; it has been found difficult and left untried'.

In fact, the life Jesus calls me to has been fully lived by another. Jesus did it. It was no easier for him than for me, if what the Church teaches about his being fully human is true. He spoke from experience when he told us to go beyond the normal rules.

Those 'normal rules' are the commandments of God as taught in the Old Testament. Jesus makes the claim that God's law does not go far enough, that it is inadequate. His willingness to overrule the law of God is a sign of the divine power and authority with which Jesus taught. And that power and authority is the guarantee that somehow or other, I can, indeed, live as he calls me to do.

The reason that I can is my Baptism. In Baptism, I am united with the risen Lord, the One who has overcome death. Nothing, then, is truly impossible in living as he did. I can do it if I be willing to try.

But, how do I start? I do not have enough practice and experience to be able to easily start living according to Matthew's catechism. My fear, my weakness and my laziness are too deeply ingrained. It will take a long time to overcome them, so I must not delay.

Where do I start? Jesus talked about going beyond the usual, so perhaps the place to start is with the usual and then to go beyond it. For instance, I often limit my life of faith to part of Sunday and other spare moments during the week. So, perhaps the place to start is some day this week. Can I take time this week to live a weekday faith, for one day trying to go beyond what I consider normal? Doing so will require attention and courage. I will have to be alert to all the opportunities to live as a child of God. I will have to beware of my tendency to take the easy way.

More than anything, trying to live what Matthew presents will require prayer. I must beg the Lord for his strength, so that I may overcome the habits of a lifetime that keep me afraid or unwilling to live as he calls me to do.

It may seem as impossible as I always thought. But, it will not be impossible. The Lord does not tell us to go out and do the impossible. He does, however, command that we do nothing less than all that is possible.

That is adult faith, a faith that does not rely upon custom and rules, but goes beyond them, to a relationship with God that requires all: all my thoughts, all my talents, all my time, all my attention, all my acts.

Sixth Sunday of the Year (B)

I told a well-educated open-minded couple about a heartwarming encounter I had recently had with a boy whose body was badly deformed. The woman's face showed shock and disgust. Her education and values could not overcome some sort of inborn taboo against contact with someone who seems to be 'unclean' in some way or other.

In our more honest moments, we can each find the same sense of taboo in ourselves. It may be directed toward those who look different, those who 'have something wrong' with them, those of a different nationality, class, religion, sexual orientation or race, or any of a number of other things. Death is a sure case of it; our reluctance to touch corpses is not rational.

I am not immune to feelings that 'something' about another might be somehow contagious or contaminating, and I have never met anyone totally free of such feelings. The particular thing by which we are repelled may vary from person to person and culture to culture, but the repulsion seems to be universal.

So, the restrictions that the Law of Moses put on lepers were not unusual. Even the leper crying out, 'Unclean, unclean!' felt repelled by his or her own self.

Since such feelings are natural, perhaps we should just accept them, live with them, and try to disguise them when expressing them might be impolitic or impolite.

But, we Christians believe in something beyond the natural, the supernatural. Just what does that mean?

Movie makers have one definition of the supernatural. It's usually darkly threatening, especially to attractive women. Some shops have another definition involving crystals, mythological beasts, candles, aromas and angel lapel pins. Religious goods stores sell statues, books, posters and soupy music that purport to show the supernatural—usually as an other-worldly realm notable for its sentimentality and poor taste. What definition best expresses the reality of the supernatural?

None of the above is even close.

If you seek the supernatural, you will waste your time searching in movie theaters, shopping centers and church gift shops. You will even waste your time if you search for it by shutting yourself away from the world in order to pray and meditate.

The supernatural is not some realm apart from the world in which we live. Super-nature happens here, in nature, just as the comic-book character Superman lives in Metropolis with other men. The mystery of the Incarnation is that the realm of the supernatural is this world. If you want to see the supernatural, there is only one certain model— Jesus, and especially Jesus as we see him in today's Gospel.

What does he do that makes this passage such a clear picture of the supernatural? Is it the healing of the leper? No. Is it his telling the man to go to the priest to fulfill the religious code by making a sacrificial offering? No. The lesson in the supernatural comes in the words, 'Jesus stretched out his hand and touched him.'

As a man of his time and place and religion, Jesus would have been repelled by the sight of a leper. It was natural. Yet, Jesus overcame what was natural. He went beyond it to what was super-natural, literally 'above nature' or 'beyond nature'. He touched a leper.

That touching healed the man. When Jesus went beyond what was natural, a miracle happened. The leper could be restored to membership in the community, to self-respect and to cleanness. His restoration was the result of a supernatural action, a touch.

We followers of Jesus are called to be supernatural. In other words, we must be people noteworthy for our willingness to go beyond the natural in us. That means developing the ability to look upon others as the sons and daughters of God, our brothers and sisters.

When we do that, we can transcend the 'given,' the natural, to get more deeply involved in the world— healing, teaching, forgiving, loving— being super-natural.

That is not easy. We must combat some of our deepest instincts in order to overcome our 'taboo reflex'. It is a battle we cannot hope to win without God's assistance, so when we succeed, we are signs of the supernatural power of God.

It is essential to the world that we succeed. In a world torn by our reluctance to see each other as beloved children of God, our only hope is in the supernatural. Continuing to live naturally will destroy any possibility of truly human life, and maybe even of any kind of human life.

Sixth Sunday of the Year (C)

At the surrender ceremony marking the end of the American War of Independence, the British military band played a tune called 'The World Turned Upside Down'. The lyrics talk of cats chasing dogs, cheese eating mice and fish swimming in the air. When it comes to the world being turned upside down, however, the song cannot match what Jesus says.

The poor have everything. The hungry are full. The sad are happy. The insulted are blessed. The rich are losers. The full are hungry. The happy are pitiable. The popular are doomed. That certainly sounds like the world turned upside down.

Or, does it? Does Jesus really turn the world upside down? Perhaps the world is upside down to begin with, and therefore we cannot recognize it when it is set right. Maybe Jesus is calling us to be right-side up.

That's hard to believe. I've known rich people and I've known poor people. The poor do not seem happier than the rich, nor do the rich seem miserable. Hungry people are really hungry, and when I finish a big meal, I don't feel empty. Happy people really do seem happy. Suffering people really are miserable. And, people who are liked really seem happier and healthier than those who are unpopular.

All of that is so obvious that we base our lives on those facts. We live in the real world, and that world has rules for getting along. If we follow them, we may be successful. If we don't follow them, we will almost certainly not be 'healthy, wealthy and wise.'

But, what if what we think of as the 'real world' were not real after all? What if the things we have to do to live effectively were as ridiculous as bouncing around on our heads from place to place? Should we pick ourselves up by the toes and begin to go around looking upside down? On what basis could we make such a radical decision?

The only reason we have for thinking that the world might be upside down is Jesus's say-so. Should we take his word for it? That depends upon who he is. If he be one among many moral or religious teachers, then the risk that instead of merely appearing to be upside down we might really turn ourselves upside down is great. Maybe he had a vision problem that I would buy into without evidence or good reason.

On the other hand, if Jesus be indeed who the Church has proclaimed him to be, then we had better take his word for the way the world is supposed to stand. After all, if anyone knows which end is up, it should be he.

I recite a creed that proclaims Jesus to be 'true God of true God'. But, if I really believed what I say, wouldn't I be turning my world, or letting him turn my world, upside down?

If today two billion Christians were, for the sake of our brothers and sisters, to stop looking for material comfort, what would happen to the world? There might be economic chaos. There might also be an end to hunger and injustice. The world would be turned upside down.

If today two billion Christians were, for the sake of serving others, to stop looking for our own pleasure, what would happen to the world? The 'entertainment' industry might collapse. There might also be a healthy sharing of friendship, fellowship and joy. The world would be turned upside down.

If today two billion Christians were, for the sake of standing upright before God, to give up doing what makes us fit in and be popular in our twisted societies, what would happen to the world? We might be called fools and might even be persecuted or crucified. We might also be the light of the world. The world would be turned upside down.

The Gospel presents us with a decision and a consequence. We must decide who Jesus is, and upon what authority he says some very strange things. If we decide that he knows how the world is meant to function because he made it, then we have to accept the consequence. We have been living upside down.

In that case, we have to get right-side up. It will look upside down. It will, after a lifetime the other way around, feel upside down. But, for the first time, we may see the world the way it looks to God.

Seventh Sunday of the Year (A)

Does God have problems? Can God have problems? It certainly appears so. Look at the evil in the world that goes counter to God's will. Look at the amount of unbelief in the world. Look at the things that believers do that give God a bad name. Look as some of the things you do. Look at what a hard time people have in trying to believe. At the very least, God has a public relations problem.

But if we grant that the Creator of the universe can have problems, what evidence is there that there might be a solution? Might we be that solution? And, even if it is possible that I am the solution or at least a solution, what must I do?

I once asked a political activist what he hoped to achieve in life. His answer was simple. 'I want to be holy'. That is what God needs of us and what God wants of us.

God tells Moses in today's first reading to give a command to the people: 'Be holy, for I, the Lord your God am holy.' That is the basic reason for all the commandments of God. The commands of God, or for that matter, of the Church, have one object, the formation of holy people.

In the gospel, Jesus tells us 'in a word, you must be perfect as your heavenly Father is perfect'. My becoming holy is obviously very important not only to me, but to God. But why?

The first reason, of course, is that God loves me and therefore wants me to grow more and more as God's image that I am meant to be. But there is another reason as well, one that touches upon God's public relations problem.

I must be perfect as God is perfect, for otherwise how will the world know how God loves?

How am I to do this? There is much I can do to show the world that God is real, that God really cares about men and women, that people can know God and become holy like God. I can be God's PR agent, loving and being holy like God and thus becoming a solution to God's problem.

What would this perfect holiness look like? Is it faultlessness? In that case, God is out of luck. I'm not able to be faultless. I'm not even sure what it would look like, since I have never met anyone else who is able to be faultless.

The same gospel passage that tells us to be perfect tells us what perfection looks like, and it is not a matter of being free of sins or defects. Neither is it some unchanging state of being. The perfection that God needs and wants from me is an activity.

It is acting like Christ in the face of his murderers, offering prayer and loving service instead of revenge. It is generosity toward those in need. It is treating all men and women as members of my family, whether they or I like it or not. That is, when you think of it, what families are all about anyway; we cannot choose our families. We can only decide to love them.

What makes other people my sisters and brothers is not a decision on my part or theirs. The choice is God's. God has chosen to be Father not only within the relationship we call Trinity, but has created, loved and redeemed us, making us children of God and therefore brothers and sisters of one another. God's choice does not depend upon whether we are good or bad. The rain falls on us all. God's choice is made out of love and we have no say in the matter.

Therefore for me to be perfect as my heavenly Father is perfect means that I must love as my Father does, without being choosy.

That's not easy. I don't know how God could manage it except that 'God is love'. But I am not love and so many of my sisters and brothers are not lovable. What can I do?

I must remember that for Catholics our highest activity is called 'Eucharist', thanksgiving. That means that my faith is about recalling God's love for me. In return, though I cannot love as God does, in gratitude I can try. That willingness to try is perfection enough to satisfy our doting Father.

Seventh Sunday of the Year (B)

People who have taken St Augustine's words, 'Outside the Church there is no salvation', at face value have done marvelous work to spread the Gospel. They have suffered pain, ridicule and martyrdom in order to save as many as possible who would be damned without the Church.

Sometimes they even forced people into the Church. Many of us are Christians because some ancestor was given the choice between baptism and death. Methods that we cannot approve bore blessings for us.

Were Augustine and so many others right? Is the Church essential to God's saving love for the world?

The story of the paralyzed man is about salvation. Jesus gives him spiritual healing, the forgiveness of sins. Jesus later gives the man physical healing as a sign that the forgiveness was real.

On what condition was the paralyzed man given salvation? Did he express faith in Jesus? Did he join the community of disciples? Did he ask for forgiveness or healing?

No, the man did and said nothing. We don't even know if he said 'Thank you'.

So, why was he forgiven?

The man was forgiven and healed because he had believing friends who carried him to Jesus. When they could not get into the house, they went up on the flat roof and tore part of it away. (Roofs were made of sticks covered with straw and mud, so it was not difficult to break through or to do repairs later.)

Once the four had opened a hole in the roof, they lowered their friend to Jesus. The man was probably terrified that he might fall. He may have tried to stop them from doing something so potentially dangerous. Faith in Jesus was probably the farthest thing from the man's mind.

But it was not the man's faith that moved Jesus. It was the faith of his friends. 'When Jesus saw their faith, he said to the paralytic, "Son, your sins are forgiven".'

The situation is similar to the case of the baptism of an infant who makes no declaration of faith. The child is baptized into the faith of the Church, present in the parents, godparents, the gathered community and the entire communion of believers in all times and climes.

So, the paralyzed man, like the baptized infant, is offered salvation because of the faith of others. Apparently, God's action on our behalf does not depend directly upon our faith—a comforting thought, since I probably most need that forgiving love at times when I am least faithful and least faith-filled.

What does that tell us about the Church? Might our vocation be that of the friends in the Gospel, believing, praying, worshiping and serving on behalf of the world?

The Incarnation teaches us that God acts through creation. We celebrate this every time we take bread and wine and share them as the sacrament of the Lord's presence among us. We speak of the Church as 'the sign and sacrament of salvation,' a community that makes God's saving action really present.

Perhaps God has made the faith and prayers of the Church the necessary instrument of salvation for the whole world. In that case, Augustine was right, but in a way he might not have realized. It may be that there is no salvation without the Church, but one need not be inside the Church to be saved.

If that be so, then what of the Church's vocation to mission? Is it sufficient to say our prayers for the rest of the world and otherwise leave it alone? We must look again at the friends of the paralyzed man.

They did not merely send a message to Jesus asking him to do something about their sick friend. They did what was practically necessary to ease the burden of the sick man.

We must do likewise for our sick world. There are two reasons for this. The first is that God works through our practical actions to bring healing, hope and wisdom. The second is that people have the right to see God's saving power at work. Jesus gave the man physical healing because he and those around him needed to be shown that God's forgiving love is real.

If through our service and witness our brothers and sisters can walk through the world with more hope, even if it means walking away from us, we must give thanks. If some of them decide to join us, then we rejoice, since the world will have yet others to be the Church without which the world is paralyzed, awaiting salvation.

Seventh Sunday of the Year (C)

The problem with having a verb 'to love' is that we can think of loving as a thing that concerns primarily ourselves. If I say, 'I love', then I am the subject of the sentence. It can easily become a matter of me and my feelings. So long as my feelings are 'warm and fuzzy', then I can consider myself a lover.

In Japanese, one does not 'love', one *'does* love'. The verb is 'do'. That means that the focus is not on my emotional state, but my actions.

Today's Gospel passage says much the same thing. Everyone knows that Jesus told us to love. We are to love God and our neighbor. Does that mean that we are to cultivate warm feelings about them?

Apparently not. The only reference Jesus makes to feelings is, 'Do to others what you would have them do to you'—figure out what you like, what makes you feel good, and then do it for someone else.

Unfortunately, that's not all that Jesus says. He doesn't tell me to find people I like and then do nice things for them. The entire list of people he says we should do love toward are the sort of people with whom I'd rather have nothing at all to do: people who hate me, people who abuse me, people who steal from me, strangers who beg from me—all sorts of unsavory folk.

It's not that I hate such people. I just want to live far away from them. But Jesus tells me that though I do not have to work up warm feelings toward their ilk, I have to overcome my cold feelings enough to serve them.

So, must I grit my teeth and inflict my goodness on those people? Saint Paul, who had a good memory for personal injuries, quotes Proverbs approvingly: 'If your enemies are hungry, feed them; if they are thirsty, give them something to drink; for by this you will heap burning coals on their heads.' Be nice to them so as to embarrass them? This is not Paul at his best.

No, the model has to be Jesus on the cross, not only forgiving his murderers, but making excuses for them. 'They don't know what they are doing.'

Can we actually do that? Isn't it impossible to do love for all those people I'd rather avoid? Perhaps I could just have good feelings for them from afar.

But, the Lord will not allow that. I will have to eventually take a deep breath and plunge into actually meeting and serving those very people.

How can I do it? I wish I didn't know, but I do. In fact, I am experienced at it.

There are many people who have harmed me. There are people who have deprived me of what is rightfully mine. There are people who have made a fool of me. In most cases, I avoid them. There is one such person, however, that I cannot avoid.

My worst enemy is myself. The one who keeps me from living the life God calls me to is none other than myself. And yet, in spite of all I've done to myself over the years, I still feed myself, clothe myself, and, in general, look after myself. Like Jesus on the cross making excuses for his enemies, I even make excuses for myself.

So, it is not totally impossible for me to do love toward an enemy. I just have to do for others what I do for myself. I have to be as willing to love the one I cross the street to avoid as I am to love the one I see in the mirror. That still is not easy. But, knowing I can do it for my worst enemy is an encouragement that I can do it for others.

There are other examples available to me. There are people who do love toward me, though I have harmed them either intentionally or unknowingly. Then, of course, there is God.

I am in many ways an enemy of God. Yet, God does not give up on me. God nurtures me, encourages me and challenges me. In a word, God does love toward me.

So, in my own life I can see the love of which Jesus speaks being done. I love myself, others love me, and God loves me. That's a good head start. All I have to do is stretch myself a bit to do likewise for others.

Eighth Sunday of the Year (A)

Birth, growth, work, achievement, disappointment and death—we must all go through them, but God has done so, too. God has even been ignorant with us. Jesus apparently did not know much about birds.

He says birds do not sow or reap, but almost the entire life of a bird is a search for food. The high rate at which birds use energy means that they can starve in a short time if they do not keep searching for food.

Human metabolism is slower than birds', but maintaining our health and growth requires food, water, shelter, clothing and community. We can do without some of them for a while, but the quality of our physical, emotional and even spiritual health will suffer and eventually our lives will be shortened, sometimes quite dramatically and drastically.

So, why does Jesus tell us today to not concern ourselves with such things? Does his ignorance extend to not being able to talk sensibly about human beings? Or, is he talking about an attitude toward the things we need or think we need?

'You cannot serve God and wealth.' Yet, without a certain degree of wealth, we cannot serve God. Keeping alive costs money, money we get through effort. Some people work solely for money. That is, their concern in seeking work, carrying out work, thinking about work or talking about work is money.

Some people become monsters for the sake of money. Organized crime with its drug dealing, prostitution, corruption of society and murder is one example of what some people will do for money. They destroy their own humanity and the lives of others for what they 'can't take with them'.

Others work for what money can provide. Yet, even here there are dangers. Money can be used to satisfy our basest desires, to control others, to mar the image of God in us. The First Epistle to Timothy is not kidding when it warns us that 'we brought nothing into the world, so that we can take nothing out of it; but if we have food and clothing, we will be content with these. But those who want to be rich fall into temptation and are trapped by many senseless and harmful desires that plunge people into ruin and destruction. For the love of money is a root of all kinds of evil.'

Money and the work we do to get it can bring problems, but there is a valid and healthful way to view them. The first thing is to work for the sake of the work. That does not mean living for our job; it means finding the value of our work that is not measured in terms of money. What is there about my work that makes it worth giving it my time, attention and energy? There is little work that does not have some sort of value.

Do I work for money, or in order to use God's gift of time to share in the creative eternity of God? If the latter, then the money that comes is incidental to the real reward, an interior reward. The money will sustain me and those who depend upon me, but it will not dominate me.

Considering taking a job, then, should mean more than merely looking at salary and benefits. I should try to find work that is worthy of my time and talent, work that helps build a world worthy of the sons and daughters of God. This is especially important in the case of young people.

Of course, not every situation allows people freedom to work for the sake of the value of the work. Many men, women and even children are forced into demeaning labor. Working conditions can destroy the health and lives that work should enhance. Bosses and coworkers can degrade and abuse. The pay for a worker's time and energy may not be just, not enough to sustain a dignified life.

We need food, clothing and such to survive, but we do not exist for the sake of those things or the other things money can buy. The value of work must be not solely in what we can acquire, but in our time and talent in doing it. When we work for that value, we are relying upon the gifts God has given us, and we will know that their fruits are the gift of God.

Eighth Sunday of the Year (B)

It was common practice among Jews in the time of Jesus to fast. So, when the followers of Jesus did not follow this normal practice, people came to him to ask about it because a rabbi was responsible for his disciples' actions. If they did something that varied from common religious practice it would only be at the instigation of their master.

So, why didn't the companions of Jesus fast? His followers today do so in Lent and at other times. Why not then?

In his answer, Jesus refers to a wedding celebration, a time for food, drink, music, dance and fun. Fasting would be not only foolish, but bad manners as well. It would be a refusal to accept the gift of joy being offered to all who are present.

Jesus is saying, then, that his presence with the disciples is such a source of joy that fasting is out of the question. They should rather be eating, drinking, singing, dancing and laughing.

So, shouldn't our lives be full of eating, drinking, singing, dancing and laughing with never a practice so unjoyful as fasting? After all, doesn't the Church claim that Christ is still present with us today? Isn't the community of believers called the Body of Christ? Don't we speak of a real presence of Christ in the Eucharist?

Yes, Christ is still with us, but it takes faith to realize that. His presence among those disciples in Galilee was obvious. We have to make an effort to recall Christ's presence among us. It is not always easy. Instead of Jesus in front of me, I see other people, I see my work, I see myself with my weakness and failures. I get distracted.

I need training in order to recognize Christ. I must make an effort to force my meandering mind to turn to him. If I do so, then I am ready for joyful eating, drinking, singing, dancing and laughing.

A friend and I once visited a priest who lived in a remote place. Neither of us had ever met him before, nor had we ever been to his town. Our journey was long, hard and tiring. When we reached our destination hours late, our host opened his door to us and without preliminary words of greeting threw his arms out in a gesture of welcome and said, 'First you wash. Then you eat. Then we talk!' He realized that the joyful visit required preparation. So, we washed away the dust of the journey, took care of our bodily needs and then had a wonderful time.

Perhaps that is the reason we followers of Jesus engage in ascetic activities from time to time. It is a way to withdraw from the distractions of our lives in order to celebrate the presence of Christ. It is a sort of cleansing of our minds and hearts from all that would distract us from recognizing Christ among us.

The objective of our fasting, then, is not to punish ourselves. The objective is to know Christ's presence so fully that we become like his first disciples, like guests at a wedding. We fast in order to feast.

But, do we actually fast? Voluntary asceticism seems to have disappeared from the lives of many Christians. We live in a time when any sort of deprivation, whether voluntary or enforced, is considered evil. We do not like to do without.

However, our refusal to deprive ourselves occasionally for the sake of concentrating on knowing the Lord may deprive us of the opportunity to share the wild joy of the earliest disciples for whom being a follower of Jesus was as joyful as a party.

So, might this be the week that I give fasting a try, giving up a meal or a favorite television program or something else if only out of curiosity to see if that will help me know the Lord better, well enough to then eat, drink, sing, dance and laugh in joy at knowing him?

Eighth Sunday of the Year (C)

Matthew's Gospel uses images of blind guides and planks in the eye to criticize Israel's religious leaders.

Religious leaders, whether shamans, imams, lamas, rabbis, ministers, or priests appear to be an integral part of being human. Thirty-five-thousand-year-old cave paintings show what appear to be shamans and some burials from that time appear to be their graves. While some Christian communities dispense with an official clergy, most recognize certain men and women as having a special role in the community.

People have high expectations of these leaders. They are often held to a different standard of behavior and are treated in special ways. Frequently, people even view religious leaders as having access to God that other people lack. That may be why people ask priests and ministers us to pray for them, yet one seldom hears clergy make requests to the laity for prayers.

Yet, they need those prayers, as Pope Francis recognized by his first public act after his election, asking the crowd in St Peter's Square to pray for him. Clergy are, indeed, guides for others, but even the best of them are sometimes blind guides. Even the best of them can be unaware of the planks in their own eyes. Generally, those weaknesses become a problem when they forget that their actions must be the verification of their teaching.

But, why digress into Matthew's message when today's passage is from Luke's Gospel? Matthew probably puts the words of Jesus in their original context, criticism of the religious leaders of Israel. However, Luke makes a very important change that may be easy to overlook. In Luke, Jesus warns all of his followers, whether we be leaders or not.

Why did Luke feel it necessary to redirect the message of Jesus from the Jewish leaders to the Christian faithful? Luke is very concerned with the mission of the Church. That mission is too important to be left to those who are guides and leaders within the Christian community. Every Christian is responsible. Therefore, each

Christian is a leader and guide for the world. The leadership of some within the Church is primarily aimed at assisting the leadership of all outside the Church.

A Japanese poem says 'Those who speak are noble; those who without knowing it themselves speak with their bodies are nobler. Those who give guidance are noble; those who without knowing it guide by example are nobler.'

Actions do, indeed, speak louder than words. The people of the world are not looking for more words from the Church. People want to see the fruits of belief in action. They will find talk of God's love unbelievable if they do not first see that love.

That is the way we are to fulfill our mission as guides and teachers to the world. Luke rightfully takes what Jesus said of the leaders of his day and applies it to all of us.

We will know we are doing the right thing if we look to the fruits of our actions. As Jesus says today, 'each tree is known by its yield.' If through my life others have come to understand even a bit of the love and forgiveness of God, then I am a good tree.

Becoming a bearer of good fruit means that I must make the kind of self-examination that Jesus calls for. Do I really know where I am going in life or am I blind? Do I keep in view the object of my life journey, God? Do I pay attention to what God has taught through the Church and my own experience? Is my vision plank-blurred by sin, selfishness and laziness? Does my own life bear the fruit of a faithful life? Does my heart have an abundance from which I may speak and act?

Repentance, prayer, reflection and study will remove the obstacles that keep me from being a wise guide and a clear-visioned healer for the wandering children of God looking (unaware, perhaps) for a vision of the love of God made real in their lives.

Ninth Sunday of the Year (A)

Benjamin Franklin said, 'In this world nothing can be certain, except death and taxes.' We usually use the saying only in relation to taxes. However much we may dislike them, we'd rather deal with taxes than with death.

However, the death rate really is one hundred percent. I will not escape. I will one day be extinct.

The philosopher Bertrand Russell told of a man who was asked what he thought would happen at his death. His answer was, 'Oh well, I suppose I shall inherit eternal bliss, but I wish you wouldn't talk about such unpleasant subjects.'

It is unpleasant, isn't it? The thought of not being, of decay, of perhaps winding up as an anonymous bone or two in a museum-display, centuries from now, is no less repulsive to a believer than to an unbeliever.

Yet, my refusal to accept mortality as an integral part of God's gift of life is the underlying cause of my sin. I look for power, for possessions, for temporary satisfactions as a way of hiding from myself the fact of my temporary life. The 'cousins of death,' those failures, pains and inconveniences that remind me that I am not all-powerful, drive me to all sorts of sins and absurdities.

Traditionally, Christians reflect upon what are called the four last things: death, judgement, heaven and hell. I must reflect upon my death and to the extent possible accept its reality (though we can probably never fully accept it).

Nowadays, just about the only one of four last things we think about at all is death. But judgement seems far more important to Jesus than death. Death is not an option. We cannot control it. However, we do determine the nature of judgement. After all, God's judgement is not some abstract work; it is precisely a judgement upon what I have done and left undone in my life. I alone provide the evidence.

God takes my life seriously enough to make a statement, an absolutely honest and accurate statement, about it. That does not mean I must live in perpetual fear of God's judgement. After all, our judge is also our loving Father. However, I must not presume upon that love. I pray that I not get what I deserve, but I must not move from there to thinking that I do not deserve to be told I have betrayed God and myself in many ways throughout a lifetime.

Reflection upon judgement should influence my thoughts and deeds, not in order to bribe the judge, but so that I always recall the stakes of my life. The Lord is serious about eternity, and requires me to be so, too. Reflecting upon what I deserve from God—nothing—and remembering what I am offered—loving forgiveness—should be a daily exercise.

Judgement leads to heaven or hell. What can we say about them? Not much. Images of light, clouds, music and angels for heaven. Darkness, fire, stench, noise and demons for hell. We even present them as places, but it might be better to view afterlife as a condition rather than a place, since place is a limitation. Music, because we can neither see nor touch it yet it moves us, may be the best image we have of heaven. But even it falls short because music is of time. There simply is no way to present eternity from within time and place without using images drawn from those limited realities.

The most we can say and the least we must say about heaven is that, based upon our experience of God's love, we know it is better than we can dream of. It is the reason for our creation. We are made for heaven, and our lives should be directed toward that fulfillment of God's dreams for us.

But, we must admit that we might so totally betray those dreams, so destroy our humanity that we cannot experience heaven. Hell is a possibility. We don't know what it is. Some speak of total separation from God, others of total annihilation, the sort of death atheists believe in. Whatever it is, we must not comfort ourselves with thoughts that God loves us too much to take seriously the kind of people we make of ourselves. Jesus speaks today of the possibility of God's rejection of us. It, too, must be a motive for my life, lest I one day beyond all days hear those terrible words, 'out of my sight.'

Ninth Sunday of the Year (B)

Did Jesus oppose the Sabbath? No, he opposed the fact that some people had made what was intended to be a day of rest into a heavier burden than work itself.

What does it mean to rest from labor? Does it mean to do nothing but go to church, to pray, to read Scripture? That does not sound very restful to me. Or, at least, it is not all that rest should be. Rest means relaxation, a loosening of the restraints of our day-to-day lives. It means, in one word, freedom. The Sabbath is freedom-day.

But, freedom from what, freedom for what? What is my normal day like? It is largely a day controlled by others. Other people tell me the work I must do. Other people set my schedule. Other people determine when I rise, when I move, where I go, when I eat, when I have some time of my own. Those are the days when it seems I have been made for others' plans, programs and policies.

In the center of New York City's Manhattan Island, arguably the most driven city on the planet, is a park named unimaginatively but aptly Central Park. Surrounded by skyscrapers, it is a wildlife refuge as well as a people refuge. People leave the busy skyscrapers to stroll along the lakes, nap on the lawns, read on the benches, sketch the birds and trees and watch people watching people. Children go to climb on the statues or view the zoo. It is a geographic Sabbath. It may also be a model for what the Sabbath is meant to be. No one is forced to go to the park. No one is told what to do there. It is a place apart from the hustle and bustle.

A place apart, a time apart. That is the Sabbath. It is a day when we can cast aside our driven selves to be what we cannot be the rest of the week—creative, playful, relaxed. It is a day to be more a child of God than a child of the world. It is the most important day of the week. In that, the Pharisees were right. It is a day that should be treated as something really special.

The Sabbath is for us, and therefore is a day for us to grow in new ways. It is not a 'do nothing' day, as if God created us to sit in front of a TV to watch other people enjoy themselves at play. It is a day to try new recipes, to write a poem, to paint a picture, to make something with my own hands and skills, to explore a new neighborhood, to spend time with friends and family. It is a day to exercise the talents the Lord has given me that my day-to-day life stifles or hides. For the laborer, it is a day to rest weary muscles; for the desk worker, it is a day to exercise those muscles. So, the laborer reads a book while his neighbor digs a garden. It is a day to do nothing more 'economically productive' than plucking the tops off of plants as we walk by.

Perhaps that is the reason Jesus adds a phrase that at first glance is confusing: 'so the Son of Man is lord even of the Sabbath.' Because the Sabbath is for us, Jesus is lord of it? It is justification for his allowing his disciples to be easy-going on the Sabbath, but it is more.

The Sabbath is the day when I have an opportunity (not always taken) to be a true companion of God. That does mean taking time to pray and celebrate our faith with my fellow disciples. But it also means doing much more. When I do so, when I take the time to be truly my own, truly God's, then the Son of Man is indeed the lord of the Sabbath, the day made for us.

Ninth Sunday of the Year (C)

When the German poet Heine was on his deathbed, a priest told him that God would forgive him. Heine replied: 'Of course God will forgive me; that's His job.'

I may not be so cynical as Heine, but in fact I do act as if I have hired God to take care of my spiritual problems just as I hire a plumber to take care of my piping problems or a dentist to see to my teeth. (Actually, considering that plumbers and dentists work in tight, damp, smelly places to seal up holes, they have a lot in common.) Anyway, I feel that God should put up with my failures, should take away all the unpleasantness in my life and not interfere with what I want to do. In return, I will give lip service—generally, if not exclusively, on Sundays and holy days.

But, God is not my employee. The simplest of all facts, yet the hardest to keep in mind, is that God is God and I am a creature. That gives me as much right to presume upon God as a centurion's soldiers or slaves had to presume upon him. None at all.

I should remember that and be amazed by the fact that after I say 'Lord, I am not worthy' I am allowed to receive the Eucharist anyway. I am a sinner. My faith is weak. My deeds are seldom shaped by a desire to follow the will of God. Yet I receive the Body and Blood of Christ.

Obviously, God's care for me does not depend upon me. God loves me, not because it is the divine job description, but because God chooses to love me. And you. And even *them* (whoever they may be in your opinion). All unworthy. All loved.

That does not mean that we need not try to be pleasing to God. We should be anxious to return God's love by striving to be what we have been created to be, the children of God.

When the centurion admitted he was not worthy to have Jesus do anything for him, yet humbly hoped that Jesus would heal the slave, he showed the kind of relationship we must have with God.

The centurion's admission of unworthiness was acceptance of his humanity; his hope was an acknowledgment of God. He thus affirmed that God is God and that we are creatures, that simplest of facts that is the basis of faith. In response to that faith, a healing miracle occurred.

It was not the slave who asked Jesus for healing. He was incapable of going to Jesus himself, and as a slave he could not order anyone else to go on his behalf. It was the faith, prayer and action of one who loved him that brought about his healing.

There are many people who cannot go to God with their hopes and fears. Perhaps they do not believe. Perhaps they have despaired. Perhaps they don't want to bother God with their concerns. Perhaps they feel that their unworthiness makes them unlovable. Prayer is an unexplainable mystery, but we can and should pray on behalf of others, just as the centurion prayed on behalf of the slave.

This gives encouragement to those who ask the prayers of others. God's love is not limited by our inability to make a direct approach. The humble acknowledgment that we are weak and need the help of God is sufficient. For that reason, we need not use special words or rituals, though they are available and useful if we need them.

That does not mean that my prayers will be answered in the way I desire. There were many sick people in Jesus' day. He did not heal them all, or even many of them. He healed enough to teach us that our concerns are not ignored by God. Apparently that is more important than that we be rescued from our pains, doubts and crises. I may not think so when I am in anguish, but I am not worthy to dispute with God, who has declared love for me. With that word, I shall be healed.

Tenth Sunday of the Year (A)

A tax collector in the Roman Empire was not a toga-wearing version of a tax-office bureaucrat. First and foremost, he was a traitor to his own people, working on behalf of the foreign conquerors.

Not only was Matthew a traitor, he was a gouger as well. A tax collector bought the job. He was expected to get a certain amount for the government, and was entitled to grab as much extra as he could to get his money back and then some. It's little wonder that decent folks avoided tax collectors.

It's also little wonder that when Jesus went to Matthew's home for dinner decent folks took note and commented. Since Jesus was a teacher, his meals were supposed to be symbols of the joyous gathering of the saved in the Kingdom of God. If he was willing to sit and eat with Matthew and 'many tax collectors and those known to be sinners,' Jesus was saying something about the Kingdom, something the good people did not want to hear. He was saying that God accepts such sinners and expects the good people to share heaven with them.

The Pharisees did not like to be told that they might have to share the Kingdom with people with whom they would rather not share the planet. Am I really all that different? Indeed, 'good Christian men and women' are often no better than good Pharisee men and women, even though we are supposed to know better.

We share the Eucharist, the foretaste of the eschatological banquet, with all sorts of men and women all over the world, yet we exclude some of those same people from our care, our concern, our service and our love. Heaven is going to be an embarrassing place for many of us, especially if there is assigned seating.

I wouldn't mind being with some of the people who repel me if they were to change. After all, doesn't the Church preach repentance? Sinners and other unsavory characters should change, and then they are welcome to my world.

However, Jesus seems to have gotten things backwards. He did not tell Matthew to repent and then follow. He did not tell Matthew's friends to repent at the door before coming to the table. He shared the table, a taste of heaven, with them without conditions. Apparently, he felt that repentance is easier for those who know they are already loved than it is for those who have to buy love with repentance.

At a soup kitchen in Japan I overheard one of the guests asking the one next to him, 'Why do these people do this for us?' The answer was gratifying and challenging: 'They're Christians; they care about people like us.'

Do we? Do I? Had those same two men showed up at my house, would they have been welcomed? What if they had approached me on the street? Would I share a meal with them? Had they come to a church, would we welcome them? Share the Eucharist with them?

We usually don't even share the Eucharist with non-Catholic Christians. We say that we ourselves must be 'in a state of grace' to share it. Sinners may be welcome at the table of the Kingdom, but not at the table of the Kingdom's servant, the Church. Does that mean that I should welcome any and all to the Eucharist? Perhaps it does, but since it is not my Eucharist, but the Church's, I probably do not have that right. Sometimes being a member of a community means being part of the community's sin.

Be that as it may, there are many parts of my life where I cannot blame the Church or society for my failure to welcome every man and woman as a brother or sister with whom I will spend eternity. My willingness to befriend and serve them will become for some of them the medicine they need to be healed of the weaknesses and sins that repel me. If I can think of their needs rather than my repulsion (or, more often, my reputation and comfort), the very thing that repels me may find healing.

Self-righteousness is not only an ugly sin, it is a foolish one. After all, who am I to decide that others' sins put them beyond the pale? Perhaps self-righteousness, choosiness about with whom we will sit, is the one sin that will keep us outside the banquet hall.

Tenth Sunday of the Year (B)

I once had a 'discussion' with a parish music minister about the hymn *Amazing Grace*. The choir was singing an 'updated' version that changed the line praising God's grace for saving 'a wretch like me'. They sang, 'Amazing grace! How sweet the sound that saved *and strengthened me!*'

The musician preferred the new version because it let us avoid having to look negatively at ourselves. I maintained that throughout my life I have done some things that have made me feel pretty wretched and find comfort in the thought that, even so, God's grace is available to save me.

The word 'wretch' comes from an Old English word meaning 'outcast' and has two meanings. One meaning describes someone who is despised by others, often with good reason. The second meaning refers to someone who is miserable, as an outcast would be.

The hymn was written by a man who deserved to be despised by others, and who through the amazing grace of God was rescued from his misery. John Newton was a slaver. He made his living transporting kidnaped men, women and children from West Africa in floating hellholes to the Western Hemisphere, where the survivors were doomed to spend their lives as slaves on the sugar plantations of the Caribbean and in the tobacco and cotton fields of America. When he recognized what a wretch he was, God's grace gave him hope and brought about his conversion. *Amazing Grace* is Newton's praise of God's mercy that could love even a slaver.

Newton recognized his sin and did not hide from his responsibility for it. He could seek and accept God's forgiving grace. How different from Adam and Eve!

Adam does not say, 'Oh what a wretch I am! Yes, I have sinned.' Instead, he tries to shift the blame to Eve and even to God. 'The woman whom you put here with me—she gave me fruit from the tree, and so I ate it.' *She* gave it to me, and *you* put her here, so it's not my fault, it's yours.

Eve does no better at accepting responsibility. For her, it's the serpent's fault. 'The serpent tricked me into it, so I ate it.'

From the first time we say, 'It broke' as a child right through to the end of our lives, we do not want to take responsibility for the wrong we have done. Perhaps purgatory is the state in which we find ourselves while God waits for us to call ourselves wretches at last. We don't want to admit that we are at times wretches because the admission might make us wretched.

Of course, if we do not admit our wretchedness, we will not open ourselves to allowing God to embrace us, forgive us and welcome us into what St. Paul calls 'a dwelling provided for us by God, a dwelling in the heavens, not made by hands, but to last forever.'

That's where my problem starts. I want to experience the love of God, but I don't want to admit that I don't deserve it. I want God to love me because I am a good boy. So, I spend my life denying my sinfulness, wrapped up in my wretched self and refusing to accept the offer of God's love.

Is that the blasphemy against the Holy Spirit of which Jesus speaks? By refusing to accept God's love on its own terms, I sin against the Spirit of God who is love. That sin cannot be forgiven because it is a refusal to be forgiven. God won't force forgiveness on us.

There is no doubt about it: I am a wretch. And there is nothing I can do about it except accept that fact and turn to the Lord on his terms. Those terms are easy. All I have to do is admit that I am a wretch and accept God's strengthening forgiveness on the terms in which it is offered, unlimited love. Amazing grace!

Tenth Sunday of the Year (C)

In a world where mothers bury their children, God has a lot of explaining to do. Unfortunately, we have no reason to expect the explanations in this life. We can only look at God the Son on the Cross and know that within the mystery of the Trinity there is a parent's love for a dead child.

So, what good to millions of suffering mothers and fathers throughout history are stories of Elijah and Jesus returning two dead children to their mothers? What of the rest? Or, as a bereaved parent would say, 'What of *mine*?' Bringing children to life thousands of years ago was well and good, but what about today?

In Dostoevsky's novel *The Brothers Karamazov*, the sceptic Ivan speaks to his religious brother Alyosha of the suffering of children and how heavenly peace is not worth the suffering of a single child or its mother. 'And so I hasten to give back my entrance ticket, and if I am an honest man I am bound to give it back as soon as possible. And that I am doing. It's not God that I don't accept, Alyosha, only I most respectfully return him the ticket.'

Ivan is willing to face the problem and act on his conclusions. That is one way to deal with the problem. It is admirable, even if inadequate.

Did Luke include the story of the widow's son in his gospel in order to torture everyone who ever hoped that Jesus would interrupt a funeral to bring back a dead son or daughter, wife or husband, father or mother, sister or brother, friend or relative? Or, did the evangelist have something else in mind?

The key to understanding what Luke is telling us is in verse 13 of the passage: 'When the Lord saw [the mother], he had compassion for her.' Until this point, Luke has used the word 'Lord' either to refer to God or as a form of address like the modern 'sir'. Here, for the first time, Luke uses the word that Greek-speaking believers used of God in order to refer to who Jesus is.

For Luke, what happens at the town gate of Naim is the first full presentation of Jesus the Lord as God with us. Until now, Jesus has healed diseases and infirmities and forgiven sins. Now it is time to see who he really is, not just one more wonder worker, but the One who has power over death.

Why would the situation of the widow at her son's funeral mark this change? Why is it here that Luke tells us that Jesus is God?

The greatest of human pains calls forth the greatest of human declarations, that God has walked among us. That is the essence of the good news. This is a world of suffering and death, but it is also the world where God became one with us.

Jesus shows himself as Lord in the situation that calls for the greatest compassion, in the situation that most typifies humanity, grief in the face of death. He feels it as we feel it. He is not a remote deity who cannot know what we feel from the inside. He knows as we know.

But, if he knows the pain of bereavement, why does he not remove it from our lives? He did it for that widow, why not for me?

Faith does not answer all questions. Pain, suffering, confusion and death are facts of life. Every life. Jesus is the Lord of life, yet he, too, dies. So eventually did that young man from Naim, his mother and everyone else in the crowd. So will I. So will everyone I love.

Christianity does not avoid that difficult fact nor explain it away by talking of reincarnation or the unreality of our lives here. To be a Christian is to accept the terrible and fearsome reality of death. We wish it were otherwise, but it isn't. Jesus was not playacting in the garden when he sweated blood at the thought of his death.

Obviously, God does not allow us to avoid death. Instead, the knowledge of death is one of the chief ways God uses to speak to us of love and true life. The death of the young is extra shocking. Therefore, it is an extra-strong call to faith.

That faith is trust in Jesus, the Crucified Son of God, the Lord of life who does not prevent funerals, but makes them into entry rites to eternal life where death's power will be overcome for all.

Eleventh Sunday of the Year (A)

'When Jesus saw the crowds, he had compassion for them, because they were harassed and helpless, like sheep without a shepherd.' It is easy to imagine such a crowd. We have all seen images of refugees fleeing violence or starvation. Their drooping shoulders, shuffling gait, sunken eyes and ragged clothes define for us what it means to be 'harassed and helpless'.

That 'definition', however, is too narrow. Jesus was moved to pity not by encountering an extraordinary situation of suffering, but as he 'went about all the cities and villages'. The harassed and helpless sheep whom he saw were the people he met on the streets of those cities and villages.

Seen through the eyes and with the heart of Jesus, the world of the harassed and helpless is not some far-off place. It is my home, my community. Sheep without a shepherd are all around me. I am often one myself.

What is life like for a shepherdless sheep? Shepherds provide protection from predators when that is needed, but their major task is simply to provide guidance for the sheep, protecting them from the exhausting futility of aimless wandering.

Are the people around me aimless wanderers? If I were to ask them on a street corner as they wait impatiently for the signal that will allow them to cross the busy street, they would deny being aimless. They would say they know exactly where they want to go or have to go and they know how to get there.

A certain job, the right deal, useful contacts, good health, hard work, a little bit of luck and a bit more time will get them where they want to be. However, if pressed, they have a hard time saying exactly where that is. 'Success', 'happiness', 'wealth', 'a sense of being useful'—all these and more might be their answers. But, what do they mean?

Can I really say forthrightly what my life is heading toward? Am I satisfied that there are no doubts about it? Can I honestly say that I and those around me are not harassed and helpless in the face of life? Of course not.

So, I can place myself and those I know among those whom Jesus looked upon as being like sheep without a shepherd. We are the ones he looks upon with compassion.

So, then what? What does Jesus do for us? In the gospel passage, he calls upon his disciples to pray that workers be sent among the lost wanderers so that they may be drawn to God like a harvest.

However, prayer in the abstract is not enough. It will not do to pray that God take care of the problems of the world without being willing to be the means God uses to do that. So, the next thing Jesus does is to give a new commission those whom he told to pray.

The disciples whom he chose are named, but the names are not important. In fact, we do not know for sure the names of all of the Twelve. The Gospels do not agree on the list. That does not matter. Jesus picked them not because of who they were, but because of the vocation he offered them. Any Tom, Dick or Harry would do. Apparently, even you and I will do. In fact, if we obey Jesus' command to 'ask the Lord of the harvest to send out laborers into his harvest' we should expect to be chosen to be those laborers.

We are chosen to go to the 'lost sheep' and tell them the Good News that 'the kingdom of heaven has drawn near.' The evidence that we give for the truth of our message is our work to heal the sick, to restore the outcast, to relieve physical, mental and spiritual suffering and our offer of this service and Good News to all without seeking return for ourselves.

My life as a Christian is not some sort of fortuitous accident. I have been chosen by God just as the Twelve were chosen. I have been sent as they were sent. Somewhere in this world there is someone for whom I am God's gift.

Eleventh Sunday of the Year (B)

Today, St. Paul says, 'We continue to be confident... We walk by faith, not by sight. I repeat, we are full of confidence.'

What is it of which we are confident? The simple truth is that we are confident that God loves us, that the love of God is stronger than anything else in the universe and beyond it. We can sin, we can turn away, we can hide, we can die. Even so, the life-giving love of God will prevail.

So, there is nothing to be afraid of. Whatever happens to me, I will not be separated from God. Even if I were to lose my faith, God would still hold me near and dear.

Sounds a bit naive and even stupid, doesn't it? After all, there is plenty to be afraid of in this world. One needn't be neurotic or faithless to worry when crossing certain streets, let alone if living in an area prone to violence or natural disaster.

My faith is surrounded by doubts. The 'bad guys' prosper. Children suffer. Thousands die in famines, floods, earthquakes and violence. Friends grow apart and relationships sour. I will die. Where can I find unambiguous proof of God's love for me? I doubt I can.

I cannot deny those doubts without being dishonest. Non-believers have an easier time of it. They can just say, 'That's the way it is' and get on with their lives. We believers have to face the hard questions.

According to today's Gospel passage, Jesus recognizes the problem. He came to proclaim the Kingdom of God, but the evidence for it seemed slight, no greater than a mustard seed. Most of us would agree that it seems no bigger today.

The strange thing about Jesus's talking about the Kingdom as a mustard seed is that he intends that as encouragement. Why should I be encouraged to know that the fulfillment of God's action is barely visible? I want more than that. I want big-as-a-blimp certainty.

One reason for the ambiguity is the fact that God has chosen to make us the builders of the Kingdom. Its final fulfillment will be in

God's hands, but our cooperation and efforts are part of the building. Knowing that, and knowing us, makes it clearer why the signs of the Kingdom are ambiguous. I am ambiguous.

I am a child of God, a baptized Christian. That should make things pretty straightforward in how I live. But in practice, I do not live up to my Christian vocation. Sometimes, I am indistinguishable from anyone else.

Oh, I try. I go to church. I pray when I think of it. I read Scripture from time to time. I snatch a moment every so often for quiet reflection when I can't think of anything else to do. I try to at least avoid being nasty if I can't be nice. Not much more than a mustard seed's worth of Christian life.

At times, mustard seed is about as much as I can manage. That's discouraging. No wonder Jesus felt it necessary to speak of mustard seed as an encouragement.

Jesus says to me today, 'Hey, don't sell yourself short. Your mustard seed is what the Reign of God is about. Your little faith, your little effort is enough. Give your little bit and stand by amazed as you see what God will do with it. Your mustard seed will flourish.'

Eleventh Sunday of the Year (C)

We might say a sinner is someone who does wrong and we might even give a list of sins. Frequently confessions are like that. 'Laundry lists', some priests call them, lists of sins that need cleansing.

But, are those sins the whole story? Is my laundry list about dirty socks, or about dirt? Are sins my disease or are they merely the symptoms of something more basically wrong in my life? Sneezing, coughing and a fever are not the illness, but the signs of a cold; so too my sins are signs of something more deeply wrong.

We speak of original sin, an illness that infects all humanity.

Traditionally we have said there are seven forms this illness takes, seven deadly sins that underlie our sinful actions and contaminate our good deeds. They are lust, wrath, gluttony, covetousness, envy, sloth and pride.

God has gifted us with creativity, a power we use most obviously through our sexuality. Lust leads us to use that gift selfishly. We use people for our own pleasure. Sometimes lust disguises itself as a drive to power that might not appear sexual at all. Artists, politicians and bosses are among those in danger of this sin, because power can be used creatively or selfishly. The sin of the schoolyard bully is lust.

We have dreams. They motivate us to pray and work for the Kingdom of God. However, when our dreams cannot be fulfilled, we can give in to anger and attack other people for the sake of our dream. The social reformer, the pacifist, the judge and the preacher must beware of this sin because the visionaries of what can be, when frustrated by what is, can turn wrathful.

God has given the things of the world as supports for our lives. Gluttony refuses to know limits in using them. We eat too much, we drink too much, we buy too much and we destroy the environment because we will not settle for 'enough'.

Covetousness is greed, the urge to stake an exclusive claim to what God has given for all. Since God has given the whole world, this sin is never satisfied. It wants more and more because it wants all.

Theft and war usually are signs of this sin. So are fraud and cheating. It is the one deadly sin with a holiday of its own, celebrated when Christians commemorate Christ's birth.

People are children of God. Envy is the sin that says they must be mine instead, subservient to me. They must not have, be or do better than I. It is the sin underlying 'sour grapes', possessive relationships and 'cutting people down to size'. Look at the smirk on the face of someone who has made another either cry or explode and you'll see envy's smile.

The sloth is such an inactive animal that algae grows on its fur. We think of the sin of sloth as inactivity, but laziness sometimes appears very active. It is the sin of 'Who cares?' Rather than put effort into thought, prayer, duties, learning or relationships, we act like whirlwinds of activity. Couch potatoes and their busy neighbors may have much in common.

Pride is the titanic sin. The 'unsinkable' steamship was an example of pride at work. 'We can do anything!' It is also the titanic sin in that it is the greatest and the foundation for all sin. Pride is the sin that says humanity really does not need the real God. I can be god. All '-ism's' are prone to the sin of pride, including Catholicism. When we forget that sin marks and mars all our creations, pride, the sin that underlies all others, triumphs.

The good news is that Jesus is with us children of sin to declare us children of God. In him, we 'have redemption, the forgiveness of sins.' Knowing that, we can love and then be truly like God. And the world will know that because we love like the woman in the gospel who bathed Jesus' feet with her tears we have been forgiven.

Twelfth Sunday of the Year (A)

We have probably always have had and probably always will have a fascination with the eerily alien—ghosts, demons, monsters, ogres, wraiths, witches, space invaders and the rest of their ilk. Some people's attitudes toward angels, saints and even God probably also fit into this phenomenon.

Modern science, rather than dispelling such ideas, merely gives them new garb. The great-great grandchildren of those who dwelt at the edge of the forest and heard spooks in the rustling trees now fly airplanes and search the skies for UFOs.

Our ghosts, ghouls and goblins share a common characteristic: they are usually threatening. They are the stuff of nightmares. We do not want to meet them, and merely to hear about them or see them on a TV, movie or computer screen is frightening. Frightening, yet fascinating.

In fact, we seem obsessed with monsters. From children's cartoons to pseudo-scientific seminars on alien abductors, we are drawn again and again to considering the possibility of some non-human, anti-human presences lurking in the shadows, ready to destroy us. Some say they are inventions of our minds to help us come to grips with the reality of death. Since in our stories the hero or heroine (in other words, myself in some guise) always wins, we are winning over death.

'Do not fear those who kill the body but cannot kill the soul; rather fear him who can destroy both body and soul in hell', says Jesus in today's Gospel passage from Matthew.

With this admonition, Jesus gives us the answer to dealing with ghosts, aliens and whatever else comes along, including certain fellow human beings. His advice even applies to accidents and natural events like storms, earthquakes, disease and wild animals as well as any other form of danger to my life: Do not be afraid.

Why not? Even if some of our fears are directed toward fictions like visitors from other planets, some fears are based in reality. Isn't Jesus being unrealistic to tell us not to fear?

The answer comes in the rest of what he says in the Gospel. 'Do not be afraid; you are of more value than many sparrows.' In fact, nowadays in Tokyo grilled sparrows cost somewhat less than a bowl of noodles. So, is our worth, while more than that of the sparrows, lower than, say, that of a meal in a good restaurant?

Of all my boyhood toys, the one I best remember was not really a toy at all. It was a broken radiator exhaust valve. It was worth nothing in the marketplace, but with just a little imagination it could be so many things. I valued it immeasurably. Though it is now probably buried in a landfill somewhere or was long ago melted as scrap, it remains a treasure in my memory. Worth and value are two different measures, and Jesus is dealing with value rather than worth.

Our value of which Jesus speaks is not something that we have in ourselves, our market worth. Our value is given to us by God, and it is an inflated value, far beyond what we are actually worth. In fact, it is infinite, because its measure is the infinite love of God.

That is the reason the Psalm says we need not 'fear the terror of the night, or the arrow that flies by day, or the pestilence that stalks in the darkness, or the destruction that wastes at noonday'.

God is in love with us, and therefore we need not fear the real or imagined threats around us. There are terrors in our lives, but measured against the love and power of God, they are nothing. As the Church's Sunday Night Prayer says, 'Night holds no terror for me sleeping under God's wing.'

And so, we go to the housetops to proclaim that love. In a world full of terrors, we have been commissioned to share the Good News that we need not fear. God's love protects us. God's love embraces us eternally, overcoming fear, overcoming death.

Twelfth Sunday of the Year (B)

A hospitalized woman said to me, 'I'm afraid to sleep at night.'
'Why?'
'The doctors won't tell me, but I know I'm dying.'
She was right. She was dying, and the doctors had not yet told her. But, she knew.

It was her knowledge that she would die soon that made her afraid to sleep. Sleeping required a lack of fear and a willingness to let go that she did not yet have.

Going to sleep is certainly a risk. While I am unconscious, the world continues on its course. All sorts of things happen and I neither know nor control them. I am even personally vulnerable. Closing my eyes for a nap or a night is an almost foolhardy act of daring.

The night prayer of the Church recognizes the connection between sleep and death. Our night prayers are meant to be a preparation both for dropping off to sleep and for death, when we will have to let go of everything. Every night, the prayer ends with the wish, 'May the all-powerful Lord grant us a restful night and a peaceful death'. We're supposed to close our eyes at night as if we were practicing to die.

We need a faith that can sleep. We don't often think of faith as something to sleep about. Prayer, action, study, reflection, proclamation—that's what we think faith means. Doing nothing? Sleeping? Is that faith, too?

In the Gospel, the disciples are all very busy. There is a terrific storm raging. They are awake in a nightmare, doing all the things required to prevent their boat's swamping and their drowning. Meanwhile, Jesus is asleep.

Finally, the disciples can bear it no longer. They wake Jesus and give him one of the few bawlings out he receives from the disciples: 'Teacher, doesn't it matter to you that we are going to drown?' They are literally all in the same boat. If the disciples fail in their efforts to keep it afloat, they and Jesus will drown. No wonder they are upset with him for sleeping while they are busy panicking. They are facing death and he's snoring!

Why was that? An obvious answer is that he must have been exhausted. But, that's not answer enough. Perhaps the disciples were right and he just didn't care. After all, they would all die sooner or later anyway, so what's the fuss? Maybe he was just so fed up with the disciples and frustrated with his own mission that he just wished it would all go away. Maybe he was sleeping as a means of escape.

Or, maybe Jesus had a sleeper's faith. Perhaps his trust in God was such that he was able to let go, to relinquish control over his life and events and leave it all to God. He could take the risk of going to sleep, a sound enough sleep to be undisturbed by a raging storm, because he knew that God was on watch.

Jesus could sleep because he knew that God does not sleep. He could afford to let go, to let the world move along, because he knew it will never move beyond the loving care of God. Even in a storm, even in his sleep of death on the Cross Jesus knew that God's watchful care is present.

The same is true for me. When I am asleep I am no less embraced by God's love than when I am awake.

Does that mean that while I sleep there will be no storms, there will be no monsters hiding under my bed? Of course not. There will be. Faith does not scare away the nightmares. It makes us confident that the worst they can do to us will not overcome God's love. That's true as well for the biggest nightmare of them all, death.

So, each night we prepare to sleep by recalling our day, by reminding ourselves that God will bring our efforts to fruition and by making the big act of faith—we close our eyes.

Twelfth Sunday of the Year (C)

We spend much of our lives answering questions. 'What do you want to be when you grow up?' becomes 'When will you ever grow up?' School examinations give way to the questions on various applications. Questions, questions. Today, even Jesus becomes a questioner. But, his question is the most important question anyone can ever be asked. 'Who do you say that I am?'

We can usually give some sort of answer. 'My catechism told me that you are the Son of God.' 'Some theologian says you are the existential encounter between the divine and the human.' 'A novelist says you are a man struggling to understand himself.'

A priest in Kyoto, Japan, once met a taxi driver who had an interesting idea of the answer to the question. My friend got into the cab and asked to be taken to the church at such-and-such a place. Since Japanese cabbies are no less garrulous than those in any other part of the world, he struck up a conversation.

'You're one of those church people?'

'Yes, I am.'

'Pardon my saying so, but you folks don't seem to be doing very well here in Japan. I mean, in movies and TV, the church is a big thing in other countries, but here you don't get many people to come, do you?'

'No, we don't.'

'I can't understand it', the cabbie continued, 'there must be something good about this Jesus guy that so many people in other places follow him. Maybe you're not getting the message across here the right way.'

'That has crossed my mind.'

'Pardon me for suggesting this, but maybe you should go to New York and meet this Jesus fellow and tell him what you're doing and find out if you've got it right.'

The cab driver had an answer to the question of Jesus—he is someone who runs a religious business out of a big office in New York.

But, neither the taxi driver's answer nor those we learn from others really answers Jesus. The disciples gave answers that came from other people—'You're John the Baptist, Elijah or another of the prophets.'

'But you—who do *you* say that I am?' In the final analysis, Jesus is not interested in opinions the disciples or we may have heard or read. He doesn't want to know what our mothers or teachers or preachers told us. He wants to know what we think. Or, more accurately, what we believe. Or, even more accurately, what *I* believe.

The word 'believe' is not primarily concerned with an intellectual activity. It comes from an ancient phrase that means 'to be in love'. Even in Latin, the word that comes to us as 'creed' originally meant 'I give my heart.'

'Who do you say that I am? How do you love me?'

So, who do I say that Jesus is? How do I love him? Of all the questions I have ever been asked or ever will be asked, this is the most important. It may even be the single question the Lord will ask of me when my life is judged.

What is the answer? I might say with Peter, 'You are the Messiah of God!' But, those are Peter's words and I don't talk that way. I might say, 'You are the one who has loved me more than all others ever could or would. You are my true friend.' 'You are the one who walks with me in pain and confusion.' 'You are the one who will heal my death.' I am not sure how I will answer the question. Finding that answer may be part of my vocation as a Christian.

How do you answer Jesus? Who do *you* say that he is? Jesus is asking you.

Thirteenth Sunday of the Year (A)

The fourth-century patriarch of Constantinople, Saint John Chrysostom, commenting on the wealth he saw on the altar and in the church around him, gave a sermon that makes reference to something Jesus says today.

'Do you wish to honor the Body of Christ? Do not despise him when he is naked. Do not honor him here in the church building with silks, only to neglect him outside, where he is suffering from cold and from nakedness . . . Of what use is it to load the table of Christ? Feed the hungry and then come and decorate the table. You are making a golden chalice and do not give a cup of cold water? The Temple of your afflicted brother's body is more precious than this Temple (the church).'

Jesus said, 'whoever gives even a cup of cold water to one of these little ones in the name of a disciple—truly I tell you, none of these will lose their reward.'

In Matthew's Gospel, 'little ones' are the disciples whom Jesus has sent into the world to share the Good News. So, as we go about our daily lives trying to show others the difference that Christ has made in our lives, their response to us is a response to Jesus and they will be rewarded. We are an opportunity for blessing for those whom we meet.

However, Chrysostom touches on a point that we should consider today because it is one of the great obstacles to our being a source of blessing to the world. If people do not perceive something of Christ in us, we are not being true disciples of Christ. If we have not taken up the cross to follow Christ, how will our brothers and sisters see him today?

When people see us, what do they see? A community of people who love Christ more than anyone or anything else? Men and women who are willing to give their lives for his sake and as he did for the sake of the world? In other words, do they see Christ in his Church, the Body of Christ?

Yes and no.

Perhaps they see the beautiful churches we have erected to the glory of God. Perhaps, too, they see the poor at the doors of those churches, hoping that Christians won't drive them away from sleeping on the steps.

Perhaps they see our institutions of healing and learning. Perhaps they also see men and women who cannot have access to those institutions because they cannot afford their services.

Perhaps they see our organizations that collect vast sums to assist the poor throughout the world. Perhaps they also see that much of that wealth is produced by economic and social systems that glorify possession over generosity, selfishness over sharing. Perhaps they see us calculating how little we need give to salve our consciences, but not factoring in the pained needs of the world.

Perhaps they see our voluntary acts of service to the world. Perhaps they also see our selfishness, our complacency, our cruelty.

Perhaps they read and are moved by our Scriptures that speak of God's love for all of us. Perhaps, too, they see how little we allow that word to shape our lives.

Perhaps they hear our prayers, sermons and hymns and sense in them the voice of God. Perhaps, too, they hear the backbiting, the slander and the viciousness of so much that Christians say even about each other.

Perhaps some of them even see me.

Part of the call of Christ is a call to repentance. It is not something I can reserve to Lent or an occasional confession. Because nearly my whole life is a nay-saying to God, my whole life must be repentance.

I must beg God for the grace and courage to say in deeds the 'Yes' I said in Baptism when Christ called me to take up his cross and follow him.

In fact, the grace and courage are always offered. When I am ready to accept them, perhaps then I will truly become one among the prophets and little ones who will draw the world to Christ.

Thirteenth Sunday of the Year (B)

What kind of person thinks there are destructive drugs in the world? What would you call someone who insists that corpses are dead? 'A realist', right?

Today's first reading denies the existence of destructive drugs and in the Gospel Jesus tells mourners that the dead girl in front of them is asleep.

Are believers not realists? Do we live in a world of make-believe, refusing to accept facts?

That is a question we must not avoid. And the answer is not a once-for-all exercise. Each day, we are faced with facts that should call into question our faith in God.

The philosopher Miguel de Unamuno said, 'Faith that does not doubt is dead faith.' An untested, unchallenged faith is not faith at all, but a willful refusal to inhabit this universe rather than a world of make-believe.

So, what are we to make of our readings today? Are the realists right or is faith right?

Perhaps the real question is: 'What is reality?'

The 'realist' is someone who uses a commonsense approach to life. If science and the evidence of our senses indicate that something is real, then it is real. By the same token, what cannot be verified by those means is unreal. Can't see or measure God? Then, God either does not exist or is irrelevant.

But, is this realism? 'Realists' accuse believers of avoiding reality, but might we not say that it is the 'realist' who avoids reality, who cannot accept what will never fit inside human concepts or understanding? Perhaps the atheist is the one who cannot accept reality because it won't fit into a human head.

So then, what is reality? An easy answer for the believer is to say that what God wills is real and that anything that goes against the divine will, no matter how obvious to us, is basically unreal.

In that case, dangerous drugs and death and sin and injustice and all manner of evil are unreal because they are not the will of God. Today's reading from Wisdom says that. 'Through the devil's envy death entered the world; and those who belong to his company experience it.'

It is an attractive idea. But, is it too easy? If only the things God wills as good are real, then what do we make of the Cross of Christ and his call to take up our own crosses to follow him? No, we cannot deny the reality of pain, suffering, evil and death in the world. We cannot claim that only those who belong to the devil experience them. They are not the whole reality, but they are a real part of it.

So, the world as God wills it and the world as we experience it are both real. To accept only one while ignoring the other is not realistic. The atheist and the other-worldly believer are of the same ilk.

It is by accepting the co-reality of good and evil that the Christian is the true realist.

Our advantage is the Cross. The Cross is the place where the highest reality, God, and the lowest reality, evil, come together. By embracing death, Christ makes all reality a way to God.

Because I am a realist who believes that God loves me, I can accept the other realities of my life. I suffer, I sin and I will die. But because reality involves the love of God, I can be confident that my suffering is united with God's suffering, that my sins are forgiven and that my death is a sleep that through God's love will lead to the fullness of reality.

Thirteenth Sunday of the Year (C)

The followers of Jesus two thousand years ago were not always an attractive group. That should be a great comfort for us today, because we moderns are not an especially attractive group either.

Oh, yes, we have had our saints and will have more. We have done and continue to do much good in the world. We have proclaimed the Good News throughout the world and continue to do so. Presumably, we will do so till the end of time. But, all in all, we must admit that our record as a community is not impressive.

But, let's get back to those original followers of Jesus. How were they unattractive?

For starters, let's look at James and John. Jesus is on his way to Jerusalem, going to the cross that will save the whole world. Samaritans along the way refuse him hospitality because of their prejudice against Jews. When James and John see this, they go beyond the Samaritans' inhospitality and suggest that the divine power that will save the world be used to destroy the whole village—men, women, children and goats. As if the disciples could manage to 'call down fire from heaven' to toast bread, let alone a village!

Then, there are the folks who would follow Jesus once they have finished doing what they think more important, like fulfilling family obligations. Those people miss the fact that absolutely no worldly duty or desire, no matter how important, is more important than an immediate response to the Lord's call.

So, where are we in all this? Well, there is certainly too much of James and John in the world. The renewed nuclear arms race and the foot-dragging by the 'old' nuclear powers when it comes to ridding the world of such weapons shows that we are very willing to entertain thoughts of calling down fire from the heavens.

Though our military powers really can call down fire from above, even those of us who still cannot toast bread without mechanical assistance have not grown beyond James and John. If I look into my heart, I find a sordid mass of resentments, vengeful thoughts, and a library of nasty things I 'could have said' and a museum of nastier things I 'should have done'. How much of my conversation consists of attacks upon people who have offended me or who I think have offended me?

Yes, I am a member of the apostolic Church, a follower of James and John.

But, it does not stop there. I am also a follower of those people who were too busy or who had so many important alternatives to following Christ. I have a job. I have appointments. I have commitments to family and society. I have a reputation to uphold. I have relationships that need to be nurtured and enjoyed. I have to study. I need some rest. I have so many truly important things to do. And yes, I also have a lot of unimportant things to do that I like to think are important.

It is true that I have responsibilities to the world, to others and to myself that I cannot lightly abandon. The point is, though, that there are times in my life when it is clear that the Lord is calling upon me to do something else.

I am presented with a person in need. I read or hear the Word of God and feel a stirring within me that calls for new directions in my life. I spend time in quiet prayer, and my heart knows I am being invited to a new way of following Christ, perhaps by getting rid of the resentments and anger that make me like James and John. Do I abandon or delay my other responsibilities? Or, do I say, 'Thanks, Lord, but I'm terribly busy right now. Perhaps next week'?

When the Lord calls us, it is because he wants a response in action from us *now*, not a minute from now, not an hour from now, not next week or next year. He does not call upon us by appointment. He will not be penciled into our over-full schedules.

The good thing about this is the fact that he will call us at the best time for achieving what he intends with our lives. Answering now means answering at the best opportunity—the best for us, for the world, for the Lord.

Fourteenth Sunday of the Year (A)

What if I were to say, 'learn from me, for I am humble'?

The problem would be that I myself could not believe what I was saying. I would know that anything I said about my own humility would be a form of bragging. I might do it with the most subdued tone and downcast eyes, but my message would still be, 'Hey! Look at me—I'm being humble!'

I know my weakness, my fears, my stupidity, my stubbornness, my ignorance and my laziness are too much a part of me to leave much room for anything about which I can brag. I have plenty of reasons to be humble.

If I tried to brag about anything, least of all humility, those who love me would laugh; others would sneer. Both would be correct.

But, Jesus could get away with it. Why do we let him claim to be humble when we know how hollow our own claims to humility are?

It is important to see the context of Jesus' claim to humility. When I claim to be humble either to others or to myself, I am thinking about myself. When Jesus spoke about being humble, he was talking about others.

'Come to me, all you that are weary and are carrying heavy burdens, and I will give you rest.'

The humility of Jesus is an element in his service to others. He presents his humility as evidence that they can trust him to care for them. They can take his yoke upon themselves, knowing that he will make it an easy load.

We sometimes seem to think of humility as a way of speaking— in subdued, self-deprecating tones— or even as a cringing posture. Jesus shows us today that humility is neither words nor appearances, but a quality that shows itself in deeds.

Humility is the quality in us that enables others to trust that we will help them bear the burdens of life. People will know they can trust me to help them because I actually help them without thought of inconvenience to me.

We sometimes confuse humility and shyness. Shyness makes me want to be invisible. However, humility requires being noticed. How can others know they can trust my service if they never see my service? However, what is done is more important than who does it. It is my service that they should note, not me. I should be humbly noticeable and noticeably humble, drawing attention to the work of God who uses me as an instrument.

So, if I wish to be able to say with Jesus that I am humble, I must shut up and get to work. There is no shortage of people in my world who are heavily burdened. They are lonely, they are sick, they are hopeless and unaware of the love that God has for them.

Why should I worry about their burdens when I have enough of my own? The Nobel Peace Prize-winning organist, theologian and medical missionary Albert Schweitzer once told a group of young people, 'I don't know what your destiny will be, but one thing I know. The only ones among you who will be really happy are those who have sought and found how to serve.'

If I hope to share the kind of joyful closeness to the Father that Jesus shows in the prayer that opens today's reading, there is no other way than the way of humble service. I must put the needs of others before my own. When I do so, another's burden is eased, but I, too, benefit from finding a new peace of heart that eases my own burdens.

When I can be humble in this way, then the words of Jesus apply to me. 'All things have been handed over to me by my Father; and no one knows the Son except the Father, and no one knows the Father except the Son and anyone to whom the Son chooses to reveal him.'

When I imitate the serviceable humility of Jesus, I come to know God in a new way, the way of Jesus. The world around me may be in turmoil, but I will be in peace and calm, not because I am apart from the world, but because I am sharing God's deep love for that world.

Fourteenth Sunday of the Year (B)

When I was a seminarian I decided I no longer wanted to believe in God. I was training in a hospital, and I still went through the motions while making a final decision to quit.

One day, as I walked into a room to visit a Catholic, the other patient in the room cried out, 'Hallelujah, Praise Jesus!'

I was in no mood for evangelical Christianity, so I merely nodded and went to the bed of the Catholic patient, where I spent most of the time trying to figure out how to get out of the room without having to deal with the 'holy roller'. I stood up and tried to quickly leave the room. I failed.

'Reverend, Jesus is wonderful! Come over here and let's talk.' I was too polite or cowardly to say, 'Listen, Lady, I'm just going through the motions until I decide for sure to leave all this God business, so leave me alone'.

The woman talked about Jesus, and how she trusted in him to heal the arthritis that had her totally crippled. She could not stand, walk or use her hands. Whenever she said Jesus was wonderful, I would just say, 'Uh-huh'. Finally, I was able to escape. As I left, she made me promise to come back in the afternoon.

I spent lunch and the class after it dreading facing her again. But, a promise is a promise, so I dragged myself back to the ward. Fortunately, when I arrived, there was an emergency, so I had an excuse to not go back to the 'Bible bouncer'.

The next time I was at the hospital, I steeled myself to make the visit I hadn't made that afternoon. Sure enough, as soon as I walked into the room, I was greeted with, 'Hallelujah, Praise Jesus!'

'The other afternoon, I kept waiting for you to come, but you didn't. I just kept looking at the chair you sat in, and wondered where you were. Then I realized that you were bringing the love of Jesus to someone else. I remembered that when you were here and we talked, the love of Jesus was with us, and that love could heal me and I could walk. So, I got up out of this bed to go to the toilet. I saw a nurse in the hall, and she said, "What are you doing out of bed? You can't walk!" And I said, "The Reverend was here and the love of Jesus was with us, so I can walk". And the nurse said, "Oh, OK, but don't overdo it". (I love that response.)

Four days later, I visited the hospital again, this time looking forward to seeing that woman. I saw her, alright. She walked up to me in the lobby, thanked me for healing her and told me she had come to visit patients.

What is the relationship between faith and miracle? Certainly the only faith in that hospital room was hers, not mine. Because she believed, a miracle could happen. She could walk and I could believe.

God does not force us to accept love. In today's Gospel, we hear that Jesus could not perform miracles because people would not believe in him. They were not willing to accept the love God offered them because it came in a form they did not expect. A carpenter? A home-town boy? No wonder 'they found him too much for them.' They wanted something more dramatic, but they got the local carpenter, just as all I got was an old 'Bible bouncer.'

That woman believed, and so the love of God could work miracles. What is hope-giving is that her faith was sufficient to cure one without faith. God was willing to work through her faith to heal the two of us.

Perhaps that why we live our faith in a community called 'Church.' We need each other's faith in order to believe. We support the weak with our faith, and when we are weak, the community will carry us to the Lord. Even when I doubt, I must hold to that community, even if I think I cannot hold to God. Being with believers puts us at risk of miracles.

I still don't know what happened in that hospital room. I know God did something, but I'm not sure what. All I know is that the faith of one made a miracle happen for two and a woman who could not walk has carried me for many years.

Fourteenth Sunday of the Year (C)

The Lord sent his disciples out 'as lambs in the midst of wolves'. What he commanded his disciples two thousand years ago, he also commands us to do today. We are supposed to be lambs among the wolves.

Of course, Jesus was referring not to the four-legged variety of wolf, but to the more dangerous two-legged kind. He thought wolfishness an apt description of such people. That may be an injustice to the canine wolves, but not, sad to say, to the human ones.

The Renaissance humanist Erasmus coined the epigram, 'Human beings are to each other either gods or wolves'. Divine or lupine—which are we? Which am I? What makes a two-legged wolf?

Wolves travel in packs. They hunt in packs. They prey upon the weak. An old caribou or a young deer has no chance against their attack. Neither has a lamb. Wolves use remorseless cunning and inexorable strength.

Sound familiar? Most of history is about the strong swallowing the weak. Strong nations draw resources, wealth and life from weaker ones. Our social and economic structures favor the strong at the expense of the weak. Even in our homes and personal relationships, we engage in domestic devouring, acting out of strength, forcing our will upon others. From children in a playground to nations at war, the strong form packs, and woe to the weak.

How have we disciples fared? Not the way one would expect. Jesus sent us out as lambs, and we have, for the most part, not been devoured. Why is that?

Could it be that we convert the wolves? All one need do is look around to see that is not the case. Actually, something else has happened. We have learned to live like the wolves. We are sheep in wolves' clothing.

Church history is in part the story of the tensions that have marked and marred our community since the time of Jesus. We have compromised, we have accepted the protection of the world's power, we have blessed and even wielded that power.

I, too, have hidden my lamb-ness. I do what I must to fit in. After all, I know what happened to the Lamb of God—they crucified him. I avoid any danger of that happening to me. I go to church and say my prayers, but outside I keep quiet lest I attract attention from the wolves. So long as I am with the flock, I am fine. But Monday morning puts me back in the woods with the wolves. So, when I'm not with the flock baaing out hymns, I imitate the howls of the wolves.

The result is that the world is short-changed. Christ knows what the world is to be, what humanity should look like—lambs. If the world is not rescued from wolfishness, it is not ready to be part of the Kingdom of God. Jesus sent the seventy-two out to save the wolves, to help them become lambs.

We must teach the world's wolves a new way of living. We must teach respect for the weak and service to them. We must teach the wolves that lambs are not for devouring, but for showing us something about God.

We cannot do this unless we are willing to risk being eaten up. That is what the wolves did to Jesus. He talks to his lambs about the rejection we will face in our mission. It appears we will either be rejected by the wolves (except as a meal), or rejected by the Lord. Not much of a choice. Perhaps it is wiser for the time being to masquerade as wolves.

But, we know deep down that we cannot play wolf. We have been baptized in Christ, the Lamb of God. So, we cannot even be good at wolfishness because in our hearts we know we are really lambs.

Jesus is so impractical. When he sent the disciples, he should have told them to wear armor, to carry weapons, to acquire wisdom in the ways of the world. Instead, he told them to expect to meet wolves.

And then, an interesting thing happened. The disciples brought peace with them where they went. They defeated the powers of hell, casting out demons. Some lambs! That's who we really are, if we be willing to give up our own wolfishness, be willing to walk through the world as servants.

Fifteenth Sunday of the Year (A)

There were three stages in the formation of the Gospels. The first was the life of Jesus himself and what he said and did.

The second stage was the period of proclamation of Jesus after the Resurrection, when the presentation was adapted to the missionary needs of the preachers. They combined sayings, arranging them in an effective order for teaching purposes.

The third was the actual writing of the Gospel accounts, writing influenced by the experience and needs of the particular communities for which the Gospels were written.

The Parable of the Sower shows this sort of development. We have a parable of Jesus, an explanation of parables in general and then an interpretation that is presented as his, but which actually comes out of the experience of the later Church. Both the original intent of the parable and the interpretation bear important messages for us today.

The sower in the parable broadcasts the seeds rather than planting them one by one. The ground was plowed and then the seed was sown. Since the weeds in the field were plowed under rather than removed, weeds sprang up along with the crop.

Since the seed was simply thrown around, it could land just about anywhere, including on the paths that had been packed down by generations of people walking them.

What is Jesus talking about? This parable begins a section of Matthew's Gospel that deals with the growth of the Reign of God. That Reign always looks unpromising, but God works in ways that we cannot see to bring it to fruition.

No matter where some of the seed may land and the odds against it, the growth of the Reign of God is unstoppable.

That's the seed, but what of the sower?

The sower is anyone chosen to spread the Good News of the Reign of God. In other words, the sower is anyone who is a follower of Christ. You or me.

But, am I really a sower? I doubt it. I am willing to speak of my faith and live my faith, but usually in certain limited circumstances. There are probably people with whom I work or among whom I live who have little or no idea that I am a disciple of Christ. Even if they know that I carry a Christian label, they may not know what my faith means to me.

'When the time is right.' 'When they bring up the subject.' 'When it won't matter what they think of me.' Not for me the sower throwing seeds on paths, in weed patches, on stones or on fertile soil—anywhere and everywhere.

In other words, I do not broadcast the seeds of faith, entrusting the harvest to God. There is too little about my deeds and words that would give anyone else any idea, or even remind myself, what it means to be a Christian.

It is here that the interpretation Matthew gave the parable becomes important for my life. God will bring the harvest to fruition, but sowers are needed. In other words, God needs me to be a person in whom the Word has borne fruit.

I am one who hears the Word without understanding it. It is not that the Word is difficult to comprehend. The problem is that I do not pay attention. Even paying attention to the Word as read in the liturgy appears beyond me. I seldom go looking for the Word in Scripture or in the events of my day.

I am one who receives the Word with joy, but I fail to persevere in it because I fail to reflect upon that Word in prayer and meditation. That sort of 'faith' is unready to follow Christ to the cross.

I am one who hears the Word, but I am too busy. I have other priorities and responsibilities. Isn't it enough to say I am a Christian, go to church and leave it at that?

But, I am at times also one who hears the Word and allows it to sink roots into my heart. When I do that, my life bears fruit.

Which kind of hearer will I be today? How will I receive the Word today, right now? Am I willing to commit myself for this week, or at least today, to be one who sows the Word in word and deed? Will I live in such a way that could at least give others the suspicion that I might be a Christian?

Fifteenth Sunday of the Year (B)

Jesus gave his disciples many commands: 'Love one another', 'Go into the whole world', 'Receive the Holy Spirit'. But in today's Gospel passage, he gives a command that doesn't seem to make much sense.

When he sent the disciples out, Jesus told them to wear sandals. Telling them to not carry an extra tunic makes some sense if he wants them to live simply. But why tell them to make sure they have their footwear on? Surely there must be more important things to be said.

Many people go through life without ever wearing shoes. Feet can be tough. Through most of our evolutionary past we were all barefoot. It is only in extreme situations that we really need footwear—ice fields, coal mines, city sidewalks.

The shoe that says what 'shoe-ness' is all about may be the steel-toed boot of the construction worker. 'Protection.' That is what shoes are, protection for our feet as we go about our tasks.

Protection for the sake of a task may be the reason the Lord tells us to make sure we're properly shod when going forth to share the Good News.

Our vocation as Christians is the most vital in the world. Billions of our brothers and sisters live without knowing 'the God and Father of our Lord Jesus Christ who has bestowed on us every spiritual blessing in the heavens!' Those men and women have the right to know that. The way God has chosen to give them that Good News is the Church, you and me and all the disciples of Christ in every land and time.

That is an urgent task, and nothing should interfere with it. On a stroll from Jerusalem to Jericho, a thorn in the foot might be an inconvenience. In the spread of the Gospel, the delay is disastrous.

Our life as Christians is that urgent, that important to the world. I am essential to the world and my life as a Christian is too important to the world for me to be sidetracked by sore feet. So, the Lord says, 'Wear sandals'.

Can that really be the case? Am I really that important to the world?

Appearances, inclinations and desires to the contrary notwithstanding, it is true. I am essential to the life of the world. I am one of the heralds of the Gospel, whether at home or on the road. My mission is too important to let any problems or concerns of my own (the emotional, social, or even spiritual versions of thorns in the foot) sidetrack me.

It is hard to believe that God is relying upon me, when I thought I was supposed to rely upon God. But, that's the case. God needs me, needs us, to bring the Good News to a world waiting unawares for it. So, Jesus tells us to wear our shoes, ready to go forth and ready to be ready.

That means more than just wearing Birkenstocks, Nikes or Pradas. It means I should be aware of possible obstacles to living my mission and make provision for them.

Do I lack the words to put my faith into ways others will understand? Study the Word of God and the message of the Church. Do I lack confidence in myself? Unite with the community of believers in worship and sacrament. Am I a sinner? Repent, confess and receive forgiveness. Am I unsure of the way? Serve. Am I afraid? Pray and keep moving.

Perhaps that is the real message of Jesus in commanding his disciples to wear sandals: keep moving, keep being ready to move. Your message, your life is too important to the world for delay.

Fifteenth Sunday of the Year (C)

Perhaps the biggest hero in the story of the Good Samaritan is not a fictional character in the parable, but the real person who questioned Jesus, the lawyer.

In Jesus' day, there were two groups of Pharisees. The group Jesus had disputes with was rigorous in its interpretation of the Law. If God has given laws to the people, those laws must be observed in their entirety. As they say, 'God did not offer Moses the Ten Suggestions.'

However, there was another school of thought which said, in effect, that God's Law was an outline for life and that people had to use faith, love and common sense in applying the Law. The evidence in the Gospels is that Jesus got along well with that group.

The lawyer's question, 'Teacher, what must I do to inherit everlasting life?' was one that anyone would ask in order to find out what side of the argument a teacher stood for. Jesus turns the question back to the lawyer: 'What is written in the law? How do *you* read it?'

The lawyer gives the non-rigorist answer. There are 613 laws in the Bible, but they boil down to two in accord with which all the others are to be judged and lived. Love God and love your neighbor. Jesus commends the lawyer, showing which side he himself tended to favor, though he later says, in effect, that it, too, is wrong.

The lawyer isn't finished. He wants to know how broad the definition of neighbor should be.

The priest and the Levite who passed the injured man were not bad. They were obeying the Law of God. Their duties at the temple required that they remain ritually pure. Contact with blood or with a non-believer would make them incapable of serving God's people in the liturgy until they had undergone purification. The injured stranger might be a heathen. He might be a leper. He might bleed on them. They owed it to their vocation to avoid him. They may have said a prayer on his behalf as they passed—the way I might when I pass a beggar on the street. They did what the Law seemed to require of them.

The Samaritan was not bound by the same rules as the priest or Levite. He was not even a Jew. Being outside of the Law, he was free to respond to the call of his heart.

Now, imagine the lawyer hearing this. He is not a rigorous follower of the Law, but he is no Samaritan, either. He would obey the Law, but would adapt his obedience to circumstances. It would be natural for him upon hearing Jesus to become a defense lawyer, offering some explanation on behalf of the priest and Levite. He might have complained that the right thing was done by someone totally outside the Law. He might have resented the implication that his own position on the Law took second place to lawlessness.

But, he did not. When Jesus asks him to react to the story, he merely answers the question about neighborliness. Jesus, in effect, told the lawyer that the law does not really matter. It's like telling a baker that bread does not matter. The lawyer did not dispute that; he was a hero. He was ready to be told by Jesus, 'Go and do the same.'

What about me? Do I live by the rules? Do I look at every situation and ask what the law of God or the Church or the laws and customs of my society demand of me? Do I run my life according to the unwritten law of 'What will the neighbors think?' Do I decide that my role as student, worker, spouse, parent, priest, man, woman or child should be the main consideration when I am faced with a situation that demands some response from me?

Jesus ran afoul of the religious authorities in part because in their dispute among themselves about how to live the Law he did not take sides so much as he rejected the whole premise of the argument.

As followers of Jesus, we are commissioned by him to serve any need we see, no matter what reasons we think there may be for passing by. When it comes to our brothers and sisters at the side of the road we travel through life, absolutely nothing should hinder us in being brothers or sisters—neighbors—to them.

Sixteenth Sunday of the Year (A)

Jesus talks of a field where wheat and the weed darnel are growing. Darnel resembles wheat, so it is hard to go into a field of closely growing grass and separate it from wheat. Even if you can tell the difference, the roots are so intertwined that pulling up one plant will destroy several others.

When the evangelist put this parable into his Gospel, he aimed it at an experience the Church faced in the first century and still faces twenty centuries later. Weeds.

We are the crop of Christ, sown in the world to show the love of God. But, something has gone wrong. There are weeds in the field. They look like wheat, like the true harvest of saints, and sometimes it is hard to tell one from the other, but weeds are among us.

One need not be an expert in the Church's history or current events to know that we are a very mixed crop. There is not a single sin from which we Christians are exempt. We've committed them all and might even be responsible for inventing a few new ones.

There are some weeds that fool me into thinking they are healthy fruit bearers. On the other hand, I have no problem pointing out some of the more obvious weeds in the Church.

Christ went to the cross for me, but he is not getting his crucifixion's worth out of me, that's for sure. I am, too often, one of the weeds in his Church.

My problem is that I am a sort of hybrid. The Lord sowed me as good seed for the growth of his Gospel. But, there is some degree of weed in me. Not only does his field, the Church, contain weeds; even the wheat is a bit weedy.

Which way will I go? I can become weedier; that's for sure. Can I become grainier? Am I tending toward one or the other today? Am I a seed for the growth of the Kingdom of God?

Fortunately, God's Reign does not depend totally upon me. It does not even depend totally upon the whole Church. God will make it happen. Even small, hybrid seed like me can somehow bear fruit because God will make us do so. Mustard seed is not actually the smallest seed and the mustard plant is only a moderately large shrub, but the bush it becomes is much greater than one would expect from looking at the seed.

So, I have reason to hope that the good in me will not be totally overwhelmed by the weedy and will be of some use to God in making the Kingdom come. My little bit will serve, like a bit of yeast, to bring the whole world to God.

How can I cooperate in this? How can I nurture the mustard seed of God in me, how can I be leaven for the world, when I know that I am so weedy?

I cannot do it on my own. Just as the Kingdom will be brought about through God's power, so, too, will my part in building that Kingdom be brought about through God's power. I need only prepare myself for that power to work in me.

But how?

St. Paul tells the Christians in Rome that he faces the same problem. Our weakness is too strong for us to overcome it. But, Paul tells us that 'the Spirit helps us in our weakness'.

We gather on Sunday in order, among other things, to pray that the Kingdom come. Prayer is the operation that allows the good in us to overcome the evil. It is the means by which we hybrids can become more and more like good seed.

In our prayer, God makes the seemingly impossible happen. The seed of good flourishes, the world is leavened. All we need do is pray.

But how?

No matter how much God may be satisfied with my prayer, I am not. I want it to be deeper, more fervent, more frequent and more 'effective' than it actually is. That is because I look upon it as something that I do.

But, Paul tells me not to worry, because 'we do not know how to pray as we ought, but that very Spirit intercedes with sighs too deep for words.' If I wish to pray to be better seed, the Spirit of God will do that praying for me. And then, little hybrid though I may be, I will take my place in the field of the Lord, being good grain for the world.

Sixteenth Sunday of the Year (B)

I went to a monastery because though I was very active and talked a good deal about the Christian life, prayer and a sense of God's love were missing in my life. I asked the prior if one of the monks could give me some direction during my week there. His answer was 'No.'

In response to my surprised look, he said, 'You don't need guidance. You're a busy man, working hard for the Gospel. Too hard, perhaps. No, you don't need guidance beyond this: Sleep. Get up for meals and then go back to bed. If you want to come to our community prayers, you are welcome, but don't get out of bed for them. When you find you can no longer sleep or rest because you no longer need them, then you'll know what to do. After all, you're a priest, you tell others how to live a Christian life. Do it yourself.'

So, I slept for three days, after which I told the prior I was relaxed and comfortable. So, he sent me into the orchard to help the novices pick fruit and do other work that would let my mind rest as my body had. I have met many wise men and women; he is one of the wisest.

In today's Gospel passage, Jesus gives the same advice to the apostles. He had sent them out to heal and teach. They have returned to him excited and full of stories about all they had been doing and all that God had been doing through them. So, he commands them, 'Come by yourselves to an out-of-the-way place and rest a little.'

God is not a taskmaster. In the view of eternity, what need has God of time cards to track my every moment and make sure I am giving full value for the divine investment in my creation? Can God who created monkeys and kittens (and ridiculous me) be all that serious? Can the Creator who allowed billions of years for life to evolve really be anxious that I be working all the time, busy all the time?

I suspect part of my problem is a lack of trust in God. Deep down, I fear that if I am not doing something at every waking moment (and staying awake nights to get it done or at least to worry about it), things will not happen as they should. If I were not on duty, the whole universe would be lost.

Certainly, God has expectations of me. There is a vocation I have been given that no other man or woman can fulfill. But, I cannot live that vocation if I am so anxious, so busy, so driven that I forget that ultimately the work is God's. Nor can I live it if I am too busy to take time simply to be quiet and hear what the Lord might be trying to say to me through the din of my activity.

Why not from time to time take the time to stop my efforts, to realize that even when I am not running about doing what I think God and the universe need, God will still be caring for, loving and giving life to the world?

There are, perhaps, people for whom life is such that they never need an honest break. Either their life is so grace-filled that their everyday activities are spirit-renewing, or they never do anything that leaves them in need of rest. I am neither.

The apostles and, more than we suspect, most of us are busy in our own ways. We serve, we pray, we study, we serve some more. We do.

So, the Lord tells the apostles and us to pack up the picnic basket, get in the boat and get away from it all. Our bodies, minds and souls all need an occasional break.

Sometimes, to find prayer and God's love, all I need do is not do.

Sixteenth Sunday of the Year (C)

When I was a boy, an old-fashioned gentleman who was related to our family through marriage would make it a point to politely stand whenever a woman entered the room. He certainly got a lot of exercise as my mother and aunts ran in and out of the room trying to corral a herd of unruly kids. Years later, Mom confessed that sometimes they would even go in and out just as a bit of mischief.

Posture is important. We tell children to stand up straight. Soldiers stand at attention when a superior speaks to them. In civilian society, citizens are expected to stand during their national anthem. At various times in the liturgy, we sit, stand, bow, genuflect or kneel. When a bishop or priest preaches, he can either stand, or sit in the presider's chair as Jesus did in the synagogue.

In the story about Jesus in the home of Martha and Mary, Mary's posture is important. In fact, it is the key to understanding not only the account, but a sign of an important point about those whom Christ calls. According to Luke, Mary 'sat beside the Lord at his feet listening to him speak'.

Over the years, the difference between Martha and Mary has been used to contrast the so-called 'active' life with a life of quiet contemplation, especially for women, and claiming that passive attentiveness, symbolized by Mary, is holier than action, epitomized by Martha.

But, the story is not about that. To see what Jesus was doing in that house we need not concern ourselves with dinner preparations. We must look at Mary's posture.

She was sitting at the feet of Jesus. In the world in which Jesus lived and taught, that posture had a very special meaning, a meaning that those who saw it and those who originally read Luke's Gospel would have understood. And that meaning would have surprised or even shocked them. It clearly bothered Martha.

The ones who sat at the feet of a teacher were that teacher's disciples. We still speak of a disciple sitting at the feet of a master.

Mary was a disciple of Jesus, entitled to sit at his feet as any other disciple would.

But in that time and place, women belonged in the kitchen, doing what Martha was doing, For a woman to be occupying the position of a full disciple was a radical challenge to the society in which Jesus lived. Mary was claiming equality with men! And Jesus not only allowed it; he even said to Martha that Mary had 'chosen the better part'. And, he added, 'it will not be taken from her'.

In fact, though, not much time passed before it was taken from those women who followed Mary as disciples of Christ. In St Paul's authentic letters, as opposed to those written in his name after his death, we even see women in leadership roles in various communities, including Rome. But, Jesus' and the early Church's radical view of women's equality with men did not long survive. The force of customary attitudes toward women, even on the part of women, was just too strong. It remains strong, though throughout the history of the Church exceptional women like St Catherine of Siena in the fourteenth century have managed to play forthrightly leading roles in our community.

Today, as the attitudes toward women that subverted the practice of Jesus are changing in many places, we in the Church are being challenged to once again accept the fact that Jesus still has something to teach us that seems subversive of the so-called 'normal' ordering of society and the Church.

Today, those who want to restore the equality that Jesus taught are attacked as 'radical feminists' without that charge being really defined. But, the first radical feminist in the history of our faith was Jesus himself.

So, the question we all—male and female alike—are forced to ask ourselves is: What do we do as individuals and as a Church that betrays Mary's vocation to full discipleship, and what must we do to recapture this important aspect of what Jesus meant his followers to be?

Seventeenth Sunday of the Year (A)

Jesus describes something that happens all over the world. The ground can be a handy storage place for treasure, especially in times of invasion or unrest. Since those who do the burying often do not return to reclaim their hoard, it remains in the ground to be discovered later by archaeologists, treasure hunters, house builders and farmers.

We are unlikely to find buried treasure in a field and then sell all we have to buy it. We might be more likely to hear a good stock tip or racing tip and invest all we have in that. The circumstances differ, but the response is the same. When we have the chance to acquire a treasure at a bargain rate, we want it.

Is the Reign of God a bargain? Jesus seems to think so. Using all we have to get it is worth the cost.

Yet, most of the world's people do not seem to think the bargain worth the cost. Christians are a minority. For that matter, though I am a Christian, I am not sure that I am willing to make a big investment. Why do people not respond to a great offer that includes knowing the love of God that gives us life beyond death?

If some scruffy-looking character were to walk up to me and say, 'I have a great investment for you. All you have to do is take my word for it and hand over all you have,' what would I do?

That may be part of the reason the world has not taken up the bargain offered by Jesus. Look at his agents—the Church. We have our glories, but they are often obscured by other things.

That is not merely true of the Church as an institution. Look at the Christians you know. Look at yourself. As the saying goes, 'Would you buy a used car from this person?' What if the asking price were all one had?

There is a legitimate 'scruffiness' in the Church. The Cross does not look like victory. However, it is seldom the scandal of the Cross that keeps people from buying into the Kingdom of God. It is usually the scandal of Christians that does so.

I think the problem is that we Christians have not really 'bought' the Good News of the Kingdom ourselves.

I am a Christian by habit, not by single-hearted desire. When I look at the amount of energy and dedication people put into worldly pursuits—most of them quite legitimate—health, prosperity, career, education, family, relaxation etc, and compare the amount of time and energy I put into being a Christian, I am embarrassed.

If I will not deepen my knowledge of and love for Scripture, if prayer is something I do mechanically if at all, if my service to others is grudging, if my worship is wooden formality, how can I be a convincing purveyor of the treasure of God? If I obviously have not made an investment in it, why should anyone else?

The Kingdom of God is like a dragnet. Everyone who comes into contact with it is drawn in, but the fish who are caught are sent not to the chowder pot, but back to the nets, this time as fishers. Since the whole world must be caught, even the fish must help catch. The life of the Kingdom of God in this world is missionary.

Our vocation is to be bait for the Kingdom. Our lives must arouse curiosity, attraction and, finally, commitment on the part of those to whom God sends us. And God sends us to everyone.

However, if we have repelled others, if our hypocrisy makes the Gospel message of the Kingdom repulsive to them, then we will be judged useless and be thrown away.

How can I become like some learned scribe who can speak with confident knowledge of the Reign of God? St. Paul tells me that if I love God, then all that I do and all that happens to me will somehow work toward the building of God's Reign. I may not do everything well, but God's love will bring about its fruition.

My love for God comes from knowing God loves and calls me. I have been 'predestined to be conformed to the image of his Son.' Just as Jesus was sent to be the sign of the coming Reign of God, I am sent. Can there be a greater vocation than that?

We are other Christs for the world. Let's get out today and help the world find and buy that treasure.

Seventeenth Sunday of the Year (B)

The story of Jesus feeding the crowd is the only miracle account that appears in all four Gospels. Early Christians obviously considered this an important story, one that could not be left out of any account of our faith.

The reason is plain to see when we look at what Jesus does. He takes bread, gives thanks and shares it with the people, who then eat it. Those are the four hallmark gestures of the Eucharist: taking, blessing, breaking and sharing. The story teaches us that the Eucharist is real food for those who follow Christ, and that there is no limit to its ability to feed us or to the number of people for whom it is meant.

Jesus is, of course, the center of the story, but I once saw a children's book that gave a big place to the boy who had the loaves and fish. In fact, he never actually appears. Andrew talks about him, and that's all.

There are two other people in today's account whom it would be easy to overlook. Yet I think they provide an opportunity to put myself into the story in a way that Jesus and the boy do not. I am not a miracle worker. I do not often have exactly what is needed like the boy. Granted, I have needs like the crowd, but I can't identify with a crowd. Philip and Andrew, though, fit me.

Philip is in an uncomfortable position. Jesus looks to him and says, in effect, 'We have an impossible situation here. What are you going to do about it?' Philip has been a follower of Jesus from the start. He has come to look to Jesus for leadership and for signs of God's power. It must have been a shock, then, to have the Lord turn to him for a solution, asking, 'Where shall we buy bread for these people to eat?'

Philip gives the answer most of us would give. 'Not even with two hundred day's wages could we buy loaves enough to give each of them a mouthful!' He sees the size of the problem, recognizes his small abilities, does an analysis of the situation and decides that nothing can be done. Very smart. Very prudent.

Philip and I have a lot in common. I, too, try to be smart. I look around at my world and evaluate the problems and situations I see. I hear the Lord saying, 'We have an impossible situation here. What are you going to do about it?' I look at my own abilities and weaknesses, count up the number of hours in a day, think it all over, and answer as Philip: 'No can do!' Very smart. Very prudent.

But there's Andrew to look at as well. Andrew has looked at the same situation. He knows the size of the problem. However, rather than admit defeat, he looks for what can be done. So, he comes to Jesus and says, 'There is a lad here who has five barley loaves and a couple of dried fish, but what good is that for so many?' He knows that nothing much can be done, but he is at least on the lookout, keeping his eyes open for anything that might alleviate the situation.

Andrew does not offer much, but it is enough for the Lord to work a miracle. He did what little he could, and everyone ate.

There are times when I am like Andrew. There is not much I can do, but, I can do something. I can remain sensitive to the world's needs and alert to all that might answer those needs.

The Eucharist is the miracle in which Christ takes 'the work of human hands' and presents it to the Father as himself. Our own little bit, our own willingness to search out what we can do, becomes part of that. God is looking for the Andrew in each of us.

Seventeenth Sunday of the Year (C)

Do you pray as well as you wish? I don't mean, 'When you pray for something, do you get it?' The answer to our prayers is up to God, and though God always answers our prayers, we know that sometimes the answer is, 'No' or 'Not yet'.

I mean, when you pray, do you really feel that, as the old catechism definition put it very inadequately, that you are 'lifting up your mind and heart to God'?

In today's Gospel, one of the disciples sees a chance to find the formula. Jesus has been praying. The disciple realizes there is something about the prayer of Jesus that seems to make it a deeper communion with God than the disciple thought himself or herself capable of.

So, the disciple approaches Jesus and says, 'Lord, teach us to pray as John taught his disciples'. A rabbi usually taught his disciples prayers they could use as a way of bringing his teaching into their prayer. And Jesus does it, teaching a prayer that has become the hallmark of his disciples through all ages in all places and among all the different groups that call him Lord.

Having taught the words, though, Jesus goes on to say that they are not really all that important.

Our problem (and this is where the catechism definition was misleading) is that we think that praying is primarily something that we do. It is, of course, something we do, but what we do is not the most important thing. Prayer is our relationship with God. God is the chief actor.

When I focus upon myself and what I do in prayer, I become so caught up in formulas, postures, breathing exercises and such that I forget that the whole reason I pray is to remember who God is, and within that relationship, who I am.

Jesus gives us two important lessons as a commentary upon the disciple's request.

The first is a story about someone awakened in the night by a neighbor who needs bread. At first, the groggy one is unwilling to help. However, eventually he gets up and helps his neighbor, if only to get back to sleep.

'So I say to you, Ask, and it will be given you; search, and you will find; knock, and the door will be opened for you. For everyone who asks receives, and everyone who searches finds, and for everyone who knocks the door will be opened.'

What Jesus is telling us is that the important thing about our prayer is not so much *how* we do it as *that* we do it. God will hear us.

If sleepyheads like us respond to prayers addressed to us, we can be sure that God will hear us and respond. Therefore, we can and should pray with confidence. The first principle of prayer is that God will always hear us and respond.

Jesus' second point is, perhaps, more important to those of us who worry about praying well or properly. He uses examples to teach us.

The first example is of a child asking a parent for a fish. In such a case, the child will not receive a snake. The second example is of the child asking for an egg. The child need not worry about getting a scorpion.

On one level, Jesus is telling us that when we pray we need not worry that God will do evil to us in response to our needs. God does not tease. But, there is another level to what he says. It involves puns.

In the Aramaic Jesus and his disciples spoke, the words for 'fish' and 'snake' and the words for 'egg' and 'scorpion' sounded similar. Perhaps there were even situations where mixups could occur: for example, when someone, warned that there was a scorpion in a basket, reached in planning to make an omelet.

Jesus is telling us disciples that we need not worry that God will not understand our prayers. We do not have to use proper formulas, the right words. God loves us so much that our inadequate prayers suffice. In other words, the disciple's anxiety to learn the right words to use in prayer was misplaced. There are no right words; there are no wrong words. God will not misunderstand us.

So, what need we do? Pray.

Eighteenth Sunday of the Year (A)

God is a great disappointment, the ultimate underachiever. There are probably more people who think this way than there are actual atheists in the world. Believers who are honest some time or other face the problem that God does not seem to be measuring up to the job.

Look at the evidence. Each year, tens of thousands die because they do not get enough food. Even more are so weakened that they are not able to live with any semblance of the dignity that belongs to those made in the image of God.

Diseases that we once thought defeated are once again becoming epidemic and a new one, AIDS, is destroying whole societies in Africa and Southeast Asia as well as bringing suffering and early death to many in other parts of the world.

Millions of people are refugees, driven by poverty and violence from their homes. Injustice is rampant. Natural disasters occur again and again.

Closer to home, my life is not as I wish. Friendships end, plans fail, selfishness and laziness overwhelm hopes and dreams. I sin, I fail. I die.

Atheists have chosen the easy answer—they do not have to face the difficult facts of life while holding a faith that says there is a God and that God is love. Believers have the harder task of admitting that God does not meet the standards we set.

Yet, many of those who suffer the failures of God continue to believe. We seem more willing to accept lower performance from God than nonbelievers are willing to do. The reason may be that we somehow realize that God's performance is actually better than we give credit for.

In Exodus, God tells Moses to tell the people, 'The Lord, the God of your fathers, the God of Abraham, Isaac and Jacob, has appeared to me and said: 'I am concerned about you.''

Is that it? God is concerned? Is that enough? Even if it were enough to satisfy God, would it satisfy me? No.

'When Jesus went ashore, he saw a great crowd and he had compassion for them and cured their sick.' The compassion of Jesus is proof that God is not insensitive to the pains and needs of the world. God feels for us, but does more. Jesus heals, God uses Moses to lead the Hebrews to freedom.

But, that was long ago and far away. What about today? If God feels compassion today, what does God do about it?

The disciples come to Jesus and tell him the people are hungry. They are not unlike us when we pray, telling God to fill the hungers of the world.

Jesus gives a clear answer to them and to us: '*You* give them something to eat.'

Jesus has given us the task of answering the prayers of the world. Can it be that the problems of the world could actually be solved by us, the disciples of Christ? It certainly looks impossible, as impossible as feeding more than five thousand people with five loaves and two fish.

It has certainly not worked. Of course, perhaps it has not really been tried yet. When Jesus fed the crowd, there were twelve baskets of food left over. In other words, each of the apostles worked, carrying a basket. Could it be that we are hoping that someone else—God, for instance—will do the task that requires every set of Christian hands?

What would happen if we were to take seriously God's willingness to do the impossible through disciples? Am I willing to take the risk today to find out?

The feeding of the crowd is the only miracle of Jesus to appear in all four Gospels. It apparently contains a message for us that no account of the life and teaching of Jesus could be without.

The Gospels present it in terms of the Eucharist. Taking bread, blessing it, breaking it and sharing it are the four elements that describe the action of Jesus and his Church in our most important activity.

However, in all four Gospels, the Eucharist is linked to the responsibility of the disciples to feed the multitude. Can bread be the Body of Christ? We declare that it can be his real presence among us. Can we say that it is any less likely that God will work through you and me?

God is not shirking. The answer to the prayers of the world has been given. We are that answer. Who, then, is the disappointing underachiever, God who has provided the answer, or we, the answer provided?

Eighteenth Sunday of the Year (B)

Jesus says, 'No one who comes to me shall ever be hungry, no one who comes to me shall ever thirst again'.

Well, we gather to share the Eucharist. But, when I leave the celebration, I want a bite to eat. Feasting on Word and Sacrament does not lessen my need for ordinary food and drink. Has Jesus lied to us?

An obvious answer is that the Lord was not talking about physical hunger. He is speaking of spiritual hungers, and he is the answer to them.

But my spiritual hungers remain. I know I am not alone. Many, maybe all, Christians, feel a famine of the spirit.

We are hungry, and probably will remain so throughout life. In fact, it seems that the more we grow as Christians, the more hungry we get. So, the problem remains: was Jesus lying to us when he said that those who come to him would never feel hunger or thirst?

Since the Lord spoke in terms of physical hunger, let's take a look at it. Two kinds of people are hungry. The obvious ones are those who have gone without eating for some time. The time may be only that between breakfast and a morning coffee break, or it may be a prolonged period of starvation.

The second group is those who eat even when they have no physical need: compulsive eaters, food addicts, gluttons. It does not matter to them what they eat, or they prefer non-nourishing foods to healthful ones.

When I was a boy, my aunt took me to a well-known restaurant. I was too young to appreciate the menu, so I asked for a hamburger and french fries. Throughout the rest of her life, Aunt Sally joked that faced with a choice of fine foods, I chose a burger.

I wonder if my unfilled spiritual hunger is the kind I had that day. The Lord offers to feed me, but perhaps I am so full of spiritual junk food and looking for more of the same that I do not and cannot take in the nourishment the Lord actually presents. I don't know what's good for me because I don't recognize real food.

What is spiritual junk food? It's different things to different people. For one, it might be a job. For another, beauty. For yet another, glamor or status. For some, it might even be religiosity.

How can I discover what my junk food might be? What can't I do without? What am I willing to make sacrifices to have? The odds are that those things are not real nourishment for the depths of my being.

If I decide to become hungry, giving up junk, I can be filled by God, who comes to me when I decide to open myself in prayer, reflection and service. When I start to feel real hunger for God's presence, I no longer look at myself. I begin to see my sisters and brothers who are also in need of physical or spiritual nourishment. I serve them, and find myself feeling hunger for the presence and grace of God. Then, as I continue my service, I feel a growing sense that I am indeed being fed by the Lord, cared for by the Lord, loved by the Lord.

The Lord sets a banquet before me, but all too often, I look over, under and around the table for the sort of nourishment I think I need instead of feasting on what I am offered, the only real nourishment I need.

Eighteenth Sunday of the Year (C)

In ancient times, the wealth of Croesus was legendary. Midas had so much money that a legend grew up that all he touched turned to gold. Today, I suppose, we would talk of Bill Gates as a modern legend of wealth. Some day, he will have as much as Croesus and Midas have—nothing. You and I will have the same amount.

That simple fact is what makes greed so foolish. It is the reason that in the parable, God calls the rich man, '"You fool!" Jesus warned us that one's possessions do not guarantee life.'

In the Gospel today, greed is for wealth. The man who approached Jesus wanted his share of an inheritance. The man in the parable wanted 'the good life', a life of physical comfort and ease.

But, there are other things for which we can be greedy. In fact, greed for money and goods may be less destructive of my humanity than some other greedy desires. I want to look good, both physically and socially. That's not wrong in itself, but if I am willing to sacrifice health or common sense to that desire, something is definitely wrong.

I want status; I want to win; I want recognition; I want special treatment. I want it ALL. But Jesus says, 'avoid greed in *all* its forms.'

The eighteenth-century English poet Matthew Green wrote of 'avarice, the sphincter of the heart'. Sphincters are muscles that close off openings in the body. They squeeze shut so that nothing can get out.

That is what greed does to me. It squeezes my heart shut. When I act out of greed, I act for myself. At the very least, I put others second or forget or ignore them. At the very worst, I destroy them on my way to what I want. My heart is so squeezed that no love can get out. Or in.

Jesus is upset by greed because it deprives us of true godliness. There are many ways in which I can be godlike in my own minor way. I can create. I can think. But, most of all, I can love. Greed squeezes shut my ability to love God or others. When I am busy grabbing what I can get or holding on to what I have gotten, my hands are not free to give, nor are they open to receive.

'Avoid greed in all its forms, because one's possessions do not guarantee life.'

The love of God guarantees life. Might it be that I am greedy because deep down I am not yet ready to rely upon the love of God? Do I really believe that this world is the whole story? If this world is all there be, then greed is a way of trying to guarantee my life.

If I have it all, at least I will have something to show for having been born. If there be nothing more for me than what I can get my hands on, then greed is common sense. My fame and fortune may not outlast me, but I won't care. As long as I have them, I know I am still alive. Perhaps I am greedy because I fear death. Greed is another name for fear. If I have things (whether tangible or intangible) I know I am alive.

Greed can never stop. Since in my heart I want to live forever, my desire for things that hide death is endless. I will never have enough.

No matter how much of my greed is satisfied (and it will never be fully satisfied), my life will end. My possessions are like a blindfold, hiding death from me. But they will not hide me from death. It will come and I will have nothing.

What can I do? I know that greed is something that puts barriers between myself and God, myself and others. But, I also need it as proof that my life is real, that it has value, even if measured by transitory standards of gold and glory.

The remedy is, perhaps, a willingness to not hide from death. When I really accept death as truly the entrance to a new, deeper experience of God's life-giving love, then I can live without greed. I can allow death to kill my greed before either greed or death kills me.

Nineteenth Sunday of the Year (A)

One of my favorite childhood books was *The Little Engine That Could*, about a small locomotive that goes up a hill that larger engines have failed to climb. The little engine was able to do so because it said over and over, 'I think I can, I think I can, I think I can'. Because it thought it could, it in fact became the little engine that could.

I loved *The Little Engine That Could* because it gave me confidence. That is probably the reason the story was told in the first place—as a way to encourage children facing the big, confusing, grown-up-dominated world.

That may be part of the reason the story of Peter on the water is in Matthew's Gospel. The evangelist wanted to encourage the Church and individual Christians to trust in the power of the Lord.

Peter's walking on water was not Jesus' idea. It was Peter's: 'Lord, if it is you, command me to come to you across the water.' It is a rather peculiar request—'Tell me to do the impossible.'

So, Jesus tells him to go ahead and do the impossible: 'Come.'

And Peter does. He walks on water. Perhaps as he got out of the boat and stepped onto the water, he was thinking, 'I think I can, I think I can, I think I can'.

So long as he thought so, he could and did walk on the water.

The problem came because 'when he noticed the strong wind, he became frightened'. His 'I think I can' became a sensible 'I can't do this!' So, he started sinking and cried to the Lord to save him.

Jesus did so, but at the same time he scolded Peter. 'You of little faith, why did you doubt?'

But, why should Peter not doubt? After all, people do not walk on water. One should not even try something so unrealistic.

We are like Peter. We ask the Lord to have us do the impossible—to bring peace and justice, to forgive, to show the love of God to the world—and he says, 'Go ahead!'

How realistic is that? History, reason and our hearts tell us it is impossible. What cause have we to think that we can do the impossible?

But, what is impossible? It is impossible for a little engine to climb a big hill. It is impossible for a Galilean fisherman to walk on water.

The writer Arthur C. Clarke said, 'If an elderly but distinguished scientist says that something is possible he is almost certainly right, but if he says that it is impossible, he is very probably wrong'.

Clarke's comment is certainly true of other realms as well as of science. We decide ahead of time what is impossible and then fail to do what is actually possible.

And yet, we have imitated Peter in asking the Lord to give us an 'impossible' task. By accepting the title 'Christian' we say that we are willing, even anxious, to do the impossible.

Of course, Peter did not walk on water through his own power even if it was his own idea. It was Jesus responding to Peter's faith that kept him up. Peter's thought may have actually been, 'I think he can, I think he can, I think he can.'

Committing himself to Jesus enabled Peter not only to suggest and accept the Lord's call to come across the water, but to actually do so. When his faith faltered, he foundered.

The Lord is willing to support us in doing the impossible. What we need is enough faith to enable us to step out of the security of the boat we call everyday 'sensible' life. To love the world as God loves it, we need foolhardy courage.

Peter starts his request by saying, 'Lord, if it is you.' If Jesus is the Lord, the presence of God among us, then we, like Peter, should clamor to do the impossible.

Does the world seethe with resentment and bitterness? 'Command me to forgive.'

Does the world suffer injustice? 'Command me to be a peacemaker.'

Does the world stagger under the weight of hopelessness? 'Command me to preach the Gospel'.

All I need is confidence that Jesus is indeed the Son of God.

Then, my motto becomes, 'I think I can because I know he can,' and the world will see me do the impossible. I will be The Little Christian That Could.

Nineteenth Sunday of the Year (B)

Elijah destroyed the prophets of idolatry, and Queen Jezebel vowed, 'So may the gods do to me, and more also, if I do not make your life like the life of one of them by this time tomorrow'.

So, Elijah high-tails it into the desert. He's had enough. He just wants to lie down and die. But, the Lord has other plans. An angel awakens Elijah and gives him food and drink. Elijah decides to top off the meal with another nap, but the angel tells him to eat and drink some more and get on the road. So, Elijah gets up and travels 40 days and nights to the mountain of God.

There are details in the story that are symbolic. Ever since it took 40 years for the Hebrews to reach the promised land from Egypt, the number came to mean 'a very long time'. Whatever the actual number, Elijah went through the wilderness for a very long time.

Another detail is Elijah's destination, Mount Horeb. By Elijah's day, the Hebrews lived in two kingdoms. For people in Israel, God's revelation to Moses took place on Mount Sinai. In Judah, home of Elijah, the site was called Mount Horeb. So, Elijah headed off to the place of God's revelation.

So, what does it mean to say that Elijah journeyed for 40 days to Horeb after eating the food the angel gave him? It means that he spent a long time on the road to meet God, but was sustained on that journey by the strength of God.

I have a lot in common with Elijah. I have times when it seems that all my efforts are useless, that the world is too much to handle. Even if I don't wish I were dead, I want to crawl into bed and pull the blanket up over my head.

But, that's not all I have in common with Elijah. Like him, I am on a journey for which I need help, the equivalent of the special foods of explorers and adventurers. It is a journey that passes through the wilderness of my own pain and sin as well as the pain and sin of the world. It is a journey that will last my whole lifetime. It is the journey to God.

Elijah had hearth cake and a jug of water to sustain him. What of me on my journey?

Jesus says, 'I am the living bread that came down from heaven. Whoever eats of this bread will live forever; and the bread I will give for the life of the world is my flesh.'

The Eucharist we share is food like that the angel gave Elijah. It is food that enables us to persevere in our long journey to God. It is the strength of God.

In the Eucharist, we have an advantage over Elijah. The food he ate gave him energy for the journey. The 'bread that comes down from heaven, so that one who eats it will not die' is more. It is not only bread for us on the way, it is Jesus, the Way and the Destination of our life's journey. In a sense, we are at our destination before we arrive there.

We share the Eucharist, and go about our daily lives empowered like the prophet who reached the mountain of God. Knowing the end of our journey, we travel confidently through this world, aiding our sisters and brothers who may not yet know the way, may not yet realize that the bread of angels is available to them.

Elijah ate the angel's food cake and reached the mountain of God. The Hebrews ate manna in the desert, and reached the promised land. We eat the bread of life and reach eternal life with God.

Nineteenth Sunday of the Year (C)

At every Mass, following the Lord's Prayer, the priest adds a prayer that says that 'we await the blessed hope'. Day after day, year after year, century after century, millennium after millennium we wait for—for what? for whom? Is there really a Savior, a God, to come after all?

Are we deluding ourselves? Are we like the tramps in Beckett's play *Waiting for Godot*, pathetic characters in an absurd world waiting and waiting for no reason for someone who will never come?

One way we have dealt with the problem of waiting is to forget that we are waiting at all. Like the servant in the parable, we say to ourselves, 'My master is taking his time about coming'. We occupy ourselves with all sorts of distractions of the moment, many of them truly worthwhile, but distractions none the less. We serve the world, we worship, we study. We organize an entire Church.

But, today's Gospel reminds us that regardless of whatever else we may do in the interim, we are waiting. The servants may have a dance party while awaiting the master's return, but they still keep an eye out for that return.

So, where is he? Where is the Savior for whom we wait in joyful hope (as an earlier translation of the prayer put it) or bored resignation or inattentive activity?

We may say that the Lord comes to us in various ways throughout our lives. We say that we encounter him in prayer or that we see him in our neighbor; we hear him speak in Scripture; we share his life in the Eucharist—provided, that is, that we have the faith to either hear or see him at such times. But, are we deluding ourselves, taking refuge from the possibility that he may never come by making believe he comes all the time?

Momentary, faith-dependent comings are not the coming of which Jesus spoke. They are not the coming for which we wait. What we await is a different sort of coming, an absolutely unambiguous coming that means a perpetual presence with us. And that is yet to happen. Or, so it seems.

What is waiting? What do we do when we wait for someone to come to us or contact us? If it be someone we are anxious to meet, we try to kill time, but without much success. We pick up a book or magazine, but keep looking at the door, a window or the telephone. Our eyes move across the page, but our mouths could never tell what we 'read' because our minds were not in the reading. We pace back and forth. We look at our watch over and over again. We turn on the TV and stare blankly at the screen.

In some ways, when we await someone, he or she is already present because the expectation of the coming is shaping our activities, our feelings and our attitudes. Whether we wait in hope or in dread, the thing or person or event we await has become a part of our life. In fact, we often pay more attention to the person whom we await than we may to someone who is actually with us. The absent person we wait for becomes more real than the present person.

When we wait for Christ, he shapes us. If we really wait in expectation, he becomes more real to us than the 'reality' we see around us. Perhaps that is what it means to wait in joyful hope for the coming of the Lord. In some sense, while we wait for him, he is with us. He is part of the waiting.

It is his presence with us as we wait that makes our Christian wait one of joyful hope. In our baptism, in prayer, in the Eucharist, in the community that gathers and waits in his name, he is with us.

Waiting is a key part of the Christian vocation. When we 'wait in joyful hope' there is a real presence of the Lord for us. If we lose the sense of expectation, lose the urge to cry out, 'Come, Lord Jesus!' our faith will become a mere matter of ceremonies, words and gestures. It will become absurd, and Jesus will sooner or later become for us no more real than Godot.

So, we keep expecting the unambiguous coming of the Lord. We may have to wait millennia. No matter. We will wait with and for the Lord.

Twentieth Sunday of the Year (A)

More than the other evangelists, Matthew looks to the Old Testament. That may be why he used the ancient designation, Canaanite, for someone from a place no longer called Canaan.

In the Old Testament, Canaanites are the prime example of godless evil. By calling the woman a Canaanite, Matthew is emphasizing her otherness, her probable sinfulness and her total difference from Jews.

It is a difference that Jesus responded to in a typical way. Typical, that is, for his society. He abused her. She was a foreigner and a pagan. Any Jew would have been curt with her. Jesus did not even bother to answer her.

How can that be? How could he have been so cold-hearted toward a woman seeking help for her tortured daughter? The most likely answer was that he was raised that way.

We are all shaped by the society in which we grow up. Usually, we do not change unless something happens that makes us look at our prejudices in a new way. Travel, learning another language, reading literature, studying history, meeting different people, living in another culture or falling in love can give us opportunities to view ourselves and the world from new perspectives.

The Incarnation means that Jesus really was a man of his time, his place and his people. He spoke their language, he dressed as they dressed, he had the same prejudices they had. But, he was willing to learn. That is what happened when he met the foreign woman.

Apparently Jesus did not see himself as having a mission to those outside Israel. That is one reason that the move toward the Gentiles by the early Church provoked controversy. Some Christians wondered why the Church should do what Jesus had not done. It was probably as a response to that attitude that Matthew included the story of Jesus's meeting with the woman in the gospel.

So, what happens in the story? The conversion of Jesus. When he tells the woman that his ministry is not for dogs like her, she betters him in the repartee.

Failing to find a good retort, Jesus admits defeat not only in the interchange, but the defeat of his prejudice as well. He saw faith where he did not expect to find it and learned from the woman that his mission was not bounded by the limitations of his society and human background.

Was Jesus changed merely because he met a woman who was wittier than he? No, the woman's victory did not come from having a quick tongue. She was willing to approach Jesus, a foreigner whose religion differed from hers. Perhaps she wondered if her gods or her neighbors might be offended by that. She endured his silence and persisted in her request. She used her wits in arguing with him.

Where did she get that desperate courage and strength? Her strength was in her love for her child. For the sake of her daughter, she would endure ridicule and rejection without giving up. Jesus, the love of God, could only respond positively to that.

What about me? When I make decisions, do I listen for 'wisdom,' for 'rationality,' for 'common sense,' for 'what's in it for me?' Do I listen to the prejudices of my time and place?

Or do I listen for love? When I hear politicians and leaders do I try to find love, especially love of the powerless, in what they say and do? When teachers, neighbors, family, friends, strangers or organizations make requests or suggestions to me, do I listen for the voices of love? Do I listen when love speaks in my own heart, or do I deafen myself to that voice?

Sometimes I will not find love in what I hear and see. I may find selfishness or stupidity. Sometimes my own self-interest and prejudice blind me to the real message. When Jesus merely listened to the request of that alien woman, he missed the point. When she made him hear her love, he grew. Seeing her love, he did what his own great love demanded and he healed the girl.

I must listen to all who love, even though they differ from me. They may be the voice of wisdom, calling me to understand and show God's love better. I must be willing to listen and look where I might rather not. The voices of love are calls to conversion to God who is love. When I have been converted, then I will do as Jesus did, being a better sign of the good news of God's love for the whole world.

Twentieth Sunday of the Year (B)

Early Christians were accused of atheism because we did not worship the gods. We were accused of being antisocial because we formed tight-knit communities. We were accused of treason because we did not pay proper respect to the authorities and refused to serve in the army. We were accused of immorality because our major gathering was called a 'love feast.' Perhaps the most interesting charge was cannibalism.

Where did anyone get the idea that Christians are cannibals? They probably got it from us, and we got it from Jesus. He claims to be living bread. When the crowd gets squeamish, he says, 'if you do not eat the flesh of the Son of Man and drink his blood, you have no life in you . . . for my flesh is real food and my blood real drink.'

We are so used to hearing 'The Body of Christ . . . The Blood of Christ' that we forget how shocking they are, though some years ago, a popular hymn had the refrain, 'Eat his body, drink his blood'. followed by a pause before the next phrase long enough for some to insert the word 'Yuck!'

Early Christians did not hesitate to say the Eucharist really is the body and blood of the Lord. What we later came to call the 'Real Presence' was so real to them that they spoke forthrightly about eating and drinking the Lord.

Over the centuries, Christians have tried to explain how bread and wine could be the body and blood of the Lord, but no explanation can be completely satisfying. Since the Middle Ages, Catholics have used a theory called *transubstantiation*. This explanation has waned in popularity because it relies upon physics as taught by Aristotle some 350 years before Christ. People attuned to contemporary science and philosophy find the medieval explanation either inadequate or incomprehensible.

Ultimately, the *how* of the Eucharist is not important. What is important is that the Lord said his body and blood are real food, that the bread and wine of the Eucharist are that body and blood, and that we are to remember him by sharing the Eucharist.

For us, remembering is an intellectual activity, though our senses may be involved as well when, for example, an aroma sparks memories.

In Scripture, however, remembering is something more. To remember something is to make it real once again. At Passover, Jews remember the Exodus by talking not about their ancestors 32 centuries ago, but about themselves as escapees from Egypt. They affirm that in remembering Moses and the Hebrews, they, too, are liberated from bondage.

You may have noticed the same style when I spoke about accusations against Christians in the second century as accusations against us. If you remember an event in salvation history, you enter it. It is really present. And so are you.

Thus, when Jesus tells us to 'do this in remembrance of me', he is not enjoining some intellectual activity or nostalgia for some 'once upon a time'. He is saying, 'enter the reality of being with me, meet the real me, eat the bread and wine that are my presence among you'. The Eucharist we share really is Christ present among us, present for us.

Outsiders might not understand. In a sense, neither do we. We believe. We believe that Christ is with us in our Eucharistic celebration. We believe that his presence is not merely something that happens in our memories. We believe that he shares himself with us so that we may live as he did, proclaiming and being the love of God for the world.

Would someone watching us at the Eucharist be so stirred or disturbed by my conviction that the sacrament is the real presence of Christ for me that he or she might think I was involved in some form of cannibalism?

Twentieth Sunday of the Year (C)

From about January 588 BC till July 587, Jerusalem was surrounded by the Babylonian army of King Nebuchadnezzar II. As the siege continued, starvation and disease began to claim lives. According to the Book of Lamentations, mothers even cooked their own children for food. People knew that the fall of a city always resulted in murder, rape, pillage, arson and slavery. Their only hope was in the troops who manned the walls, fighting off attacks, shooting arrows into the besieging troops.

Before the war, Jeremiah warned that it was a mistake to revolt against Babylon, which had earlier conquered the country and installed Zedekiah as ruler. Even after war began, Jeremiah did not keep quiet. He continued to issue his jeremiads against King Zedekiah, his advisors and his policies. In a country at war, in a city under siege, that is treason. Jeremiah's predictions of defeat were demoralizing the troops. So, he was dumped into a muddy well. This would mean his death, but no one would be directly responsible for spilling his blood.

So far, this is a story that could happen—and has happened—in many countries. Even in times of peace, authorities do not take kindly to attacks upon their policies. When it becomes apparent that their policies are disastrous, they are even more inclined to silence naysayers. Zedekiah and his princes have disciples all over the world.

But, the story takes a strange turn. Ebed–melech goes to the king and says, 'these men have been at fault in all they have done to the prophet Jeremiah. He will die of famine on the spot, for there is no more food in the city.'

King Zedekiah relents and tells Ebed–melech to set Jeremiah free. Did the king figure that since everyone was starving anyway, it made no difference where Jeremiah did his starving? Did he feel that since all was lost and everyone knew it, whatever Jeremiah said or did could not really affect the already–demoralized defenders? We don't know. I think it had something to do with his recognition that Jeremiah was, indeed, a prophet, one who spoke for God.

Perhaps the king realized that those who speak for God will say what we do not wish to hear. God's word will always be treasonous to the ways of the world.

In the Gospel, Jesus declares himself to be like Jeremiah, a bearer of what seems to be bad news. 'Do you think that I have come to bring peace to the earth? No, I tell you, but rather division!'

People in Jerusalem did not relish Jeremiah's pronouncements. Neither do we relish hearing Jesus' saying that our families and society will be torn apart by dissension. The Jerusalemites wanted independence and food. We want peace and harmony. God seems to give what we do not want, and then expects us to call it 'Good News.'

Do you know the answer to the question: How do you train a mule? First, you take a large plank, and hit the animal over the head to get its attention. We are mulish, too self-contented, too dense and too self-absorbed to see that what God offers us goes far beyond anything that we are willing to settle for. Jeremiah and Jesus are saying, 'Never mind what you think important. It will not last. In fact, it must not last so that you can receive what will last, God's eternal love.' Sometimes, we need to feel a plank over the head to get the message.

What we think of as reality— the day-to-day world in which we sin, harm ourselves and others, regret but do little else about pain and injustice, forget God and eternity—this so-called 'reality' is falsehood. True Reality is found in the will of God, a will that calls for love received and shared, love that transcends time. It's a Reality that we will only, it seems, turn to when we've been hit with a plank.

So, Jeremiah in his day and Jesus in his (which is ours) say that our dreams shall be shattered against the Reality of God's love. It will hurt. It will hurt as much as slavery or strife. But, it shall free us from the delusion that this world offers what we really need. God offers what we really need, and shall do whatever is painfully necessary to smash anything that makes us willing to settle for less.

Twenty–First Sunday of the Year (A)

Shakespeare may not have thought much of Jesus' calling his chief disciple 'Rock.' In *Julius Caesar* Marullus berates the people of Rome: 'You blocks, you stones, you worse than senseless things!'

That's one way of looking at Simon's nickname. By calling him Peter (Rock), is Jesus saying that the man is 'as sharp as a bowling ball'? The Gospels do not portray Peter as the brightest of the disciples.

The old 'Rocky' movies give another possibility for understanding Peter's nickname. Is Simon the strong man who will overcome, though all the odds are against him? Swinging his sword at Gethsemane certainly shows that he was ready for a brawl.

Might Simon be rock–like in stubbornness, unwilling or unable to be moved by argument or common sense? That might be, though Saint Paul once 'opposed him to his face' for being wishy–washy.

Or, might Jesus have called him Rock because he was dependable, committed, steady in the face of opposition? But then, there was that shameful business of denying Jesus during his trial.

Another possibility is that Simon was seen by Jesus as strong enough to provide support for others, a rock–solid foundation. That is certainly implied in what Jesus says after the naming: 'on this rock I will build my church.'

The Gospel says that Jesus chose to build his Church on Peter the Rock. Did Jesus decide to do so because of Peter's rock–ness? Might it not be the other way around? Is the Church built on Peter because he is the Rock, or is he the Rock because the Lord chose to build the Church on him?

The answer is important for us, because in a sense the Church is built upon each of us. So, must we be rock–like in order to be good Christians?

If to be a Christian requires that I be a rock, there are, indeed, some ways in which the description fits.

Certainly, we can be capable of gross stupidity—blocks, stones, and worse than senseless things. Yet, like Peter, we are capable also of being the recipients of God's inspiration.

We can be like Simon Peter in being rambunctious, ready to rush off on behalf of the Lord, but disappointed and fearful when the battle against our own sin and the sin of the world gets to be difficult.

On the other hand, we can be stubborn in holding to the customs of faith, but too willing to compromise with the world when it comes to the actual living of that faith.

Am I rocklike in steadiness? Well, sort of. But, I worry too much about 'fitting in.' My friendships, my position in society, even my livelihood depend upon not being too different, especially in the ways that faith calls me to be different.

A rock of support, then? Sometimes. But, I prefer to support others at my convenience rather than at their need. I have commitments of my own that are more important to me.

Perhaps most appropriate would be the image of 'rock bottom,' as low as one can go. All in all, neither I nor my fellow Christians are all that impressive.

If Jesus had nicknamed Simon 'Gelatin,' that might have been more accurate not only of him, but also of us, the Church built upon him as foundation—somewhat firm, but wobbly.

Is it sufficient to be gelatin rather than rock? The Lord seems to think so. In the case of Simon Peter, Christ's decision to build the Church upon him turned him into a rock foundation. Simon who denied the Lord, Simon who ran away at the final test of the Cross, became Peter, the leader of the disciples and martyr for Christ.

The key to Simon's shift from gelatin to rock is his admission that Jesus is 'the Messiah, the Son of the living God.' That admission did not turn him into rock, but it was all Jesus needed to declare that he would suffice as a foundation.

Is my weak faith gelatinous enough for Jesus to declare the same of me? It probably is. I say that Jesus is the Lord, and he makes me a foundation for the building up of the Church.

Does that mean I will never again waver, quaver? Of course not. Peter shook many times even after being renamed Rock.

The important thing about Peter and the important thing about me is that Christ has chosen us to be Church. He has set us up in all our weakness and declared that the gates of death will not prevail against us.

Twenty–First Sunday of the Year (B)

When Jesus said that the Eucharist is really his body, 'from this time on, many of his disciples broke away and would not remain in his company any longer'.

So long as Jesus gave inspiring talks and good moral advice, made trenchant comments about the religious establishment and worked wonders, people were happy to follow him.

There is no shortage of such people. Some admire Jesus as a moral teacher. Some paint him as a political challenger of the 'system' of his time. Some make him into a sort of mystical figure who taught esoteric knowledge to an enlightened elite. Some make him out to be a wonder worker who relieves us of responsibility for our world because he will one day fix it. Still others consider him a powerful god who play–acted at being human.

They share something with the disciples who left Jesus. They find him too big. He doesn't fit their categories and understanding, but goes beyond them. Rather than face a reality that transcends their ideas of who he should be, they leave.

They and we are faced with the fact that Jesus is more than we can feel comfortable with. If he were merely a moral teacher, that would be fine. We would have him under our control because we can understand him.

If on the other hand Jesus were some remote divinity we would still be able to contain him. 'Totally Other' is something I can understand, it fits into my head. It means 'Not me'. No connection, and therefore no need to take him into account beyond, perhaps, going through an occasional ritual to make sure a volcano doesn't erupt in my living room. I could box him, and put the box far away.

Our problem, and the problem of those disciples who left him, is that Jesus refuses to be either totally one of us or totally a remote divinity. He talks about ascending 'to where he was before'. He claims divinity. But, he also claims to be with us in a piece of bread and a cup of wine, a claim that the Church makes the center of its life and worship.

Divinity that fits our preconceptions is nice, but beyond them it becomes scary, especially if it gets as close as the Eucharist. We are not in control. We want either a domesticated or a distant god. Jesus is undomesticated, and in my hand! It's like being in a cage with a tiger.

When Jesus turned to Peter and the rest of the Twelve, he in effect asked them if they were willing to live with such knowledge. Could they endure the thought that God, the all-powerful, was with them, asking them questions, offering himself as food?

Peter's answer is an acceptance of the facts. 'Where else could we go? If you are who you say, then there is no place else we could go and still live in the real world.'

If Jesus is indeed who he and the Church say he is, then there really is no place else to go. If he is real, then any alternative is unreal. We have no choice. If we accept the truth of Jesus' divinity, we must accept the reality of the Eucharist we share.

Many that day could be disciples until Jesus started talking about being as intimate with us and familiar to us as a bite of bread and a sip of wine. Our gathering each week is a proclamation to the world and to one another that what he said then is true today. He was, is and always will be God with us.

Twenty–First Sunday of the Year (C)

The person who asked Jesus, 'Lord, will only a few be saved?' may have been concerned for the salvation of others, or just worrying whether or not there would be room for one more. As so often happens, Jesus does not give a clear, direct answer.

That has not stopped others from doing so. Jehovah's Witnesses teach that those who will go to heaven are limited to 144,000. There are approximately two billion Christians in the world today (among whom Jehovah's Witnesses are usually not counted). So if that figure were true it would lead to the Lord hearing a lot of us saying, 'We ate and drank with you'.

Though most Christians have been open to larger numbers of saved, they have not avoided speculating. Occasionally, one may be accosted on the street by someone who asks, 'Are you saved?' It is a not uncommon concern, and the question is probably asked of mirrors more than of strangers.

Many people give a confident 'Yes!' as their answer. Others despairingly answer, 'No'. Some of the world's least attractive—and even repulsive—Christians are those who are so convinced of their own salvation that they feel justified in belittling, persecuting and belaboring their 'unsaved' neighbors. Some of the most heartbreaking Christians are those who are so convinced of their damnation that they forget the whole premise of salvation—God's forgiving love. The correct answer to 'Are you saved?' is probably some variation of 'I don't know, but, God willing, I am'.

But, the answer is not important because the question is not important. Speculation is a waste of time. If my salvation is related to how I spend my short time on earth, I have more important things to do than to speculate on how God's love will ultimately deal with me.

So, Jesus shifts the question. He does not say who is saved, but tells his listeners to act. Rather than speculation, God wants action. Instead of wondering who is saved, and whether or not I am among them, I should be living a particular kind of life.

Those who 'stand outside and knock at the door, saying, "Lord, open to us" are rejected as "evildoers"'. They feel they deserve a place in the Kingdom of God because they have eaten and drunk with the Lord. He says he does not even know them.

More important than our membership in the community of those who know the Lord is that we not be evildoers. We must be 'good-doers'.

The good-doers who will have a place among the saved need not be members of the community of faith at all. 'People will come from east and west, from north and south, and will eat in the kingdom of God.' How one lives, rather than how one believes, will be the important factor.

So, how do I become a good-doer? A burning interest in my own salvation will not suffice. It may even interfere because good-doers must be focused upon others, not themselves. Paradoxically, the best assurance of my salvation is a lack of concern with my salvation.

Instead, what I need is to spend my time and energy for the salvation of others. Does that mean I should accost folks on the street to ask about their salvational status? No. Salvation is the state of being fully what God intends one to be. What God intends is loving communion with each of us and for us to live in communion with one another.

So, whatever I do that helps my brothers and sisters know God's love and share it is an aid to their salvation. And my brothers and sisters are all people. The best way for them to know the love of God is, of course, to see it in the people who can turn to Christ and say, 'We ate and we drank with you and heard your teaching.' I must show practical, here-and-now love to my neighbor, responding to what he or she (not I) thinks are the areas of life that need help, need love.

If we live that way, the Lord's word to us will be, 'Of course I know you. You have been with me all along, but were too busy loving others to notice. You were more concerned with helping others become the image of my Father than you were with your own salvation. Welcome!'

Twenty–Second Sunday of the Year (A)

There is no Christian life without the cross. Yet, we do not want it. As a decoration, it looks nice. As the searing torture of body, mind and spirit that it really is, we want no part of it.

Peter was not the last follower of Jesus who has felt, 'God forbid it, Lord! This must never happen to you—or me'.

In Matthew's Gospel, today's passage follows Peter's declaration that Jesus is 'the Messiah, the son of the living God'. Peter liked the thought of Jesus as the Christ, the anointed one of God, sent to bring about the fulfilment of God's plan for the world. We like that, too.

What Peter could not handle was the fact that 'from that time on' Jesus started talking about suffering and death as his way of messiahship. Peter and we like our gods to be powerful, not suffering. More to the point, we like ourselves to be powerful, not suffering. God, however, sees things differently.

The pains, the crosses of our life, bring us to complain to God. In my own life, some of my most honest prayers have been at such times. No fancy words, no set phrases, just raw pain, confusion and anger. In other words, my true self.

Apparently, God prefers the complaints of Jeremiah to the solicitude of Peter. When Peter tries to head off talk of suffering, Jesus calls him 'Satan'.

Jesus says yet another shocking thing about Peter: 'You are a stumbling block to me.' How can Peter's hope that Jesus not suffer be a stumbling block?

Peter is renewing the temptation that Satan presented to Jesus at the start of his ministry, the temptation to avoid the painful way and take the easy way. Jesus is upset because it is a real temptation that Peter presents to him. The cross was Jesus' vocation, but that does not mean he liked it or did not hope for some other way. He prayed for as much in Gethsemane.

The temptation to avoid the cross is not one that Jesus alone faced. We, too, face it. That is the reason Jesus tells us that we must be willing to take up the cross. We, too, must face and overcome the temptation Jesus faced and overcame.

'If any want to become my followers, let them deny themselves and take up their cross and follow me.' He wants us to follow him to the cross and through the temptation to avoid it.

What is the cross? It is not merely the instrument of torture on which Jesus was killed. It is certainly more than a decoration or a piece of jewelry. The cross is the way in which God relates with the world.

We say that God is love, and that our lives are meant to be signs of that love for the world, but what is love?

Love is not merely the emotion that is a real part of every healthy human life. The kind of love that characterizes God is not an emotion, but an activity. It is a giving of one's all for the sake of the beloved. This is symbolized in Christian marriage, where the couple commit themselves to sharing not an emotion, but a life.

The ultimate self-emptying, the ultimate offering we can make in love, is the offering of our whole life. God did that in Jesus on the cross. If we want to know what God is like, we must look at the cross. If we want to show what God is like, we must take up our cross.

But, that has implications for us who call ourselves Christians. We must be willing to face the cross, willing to sacrifice even life itself for the sake of God and others. We do it knowing that in becoming like Christ on his cross we also become like him in his resurrection. As St. Paul says, 'If we have been united with him in a death like his, we will certainly be united with him in a resurrection like his.'

Does that mean we must go in search of opportunities to suffer? No. We need not search. They will come. What we must do is spend our lives facing the minor crosses that come our way, learning patience, humility and service. Then, when the big demands come, we will already have learned to deny ourselves and follow the Lord.

Then, we will be able to face the Lord in his glory and receive the reward of those who show the unlimited love of God to the world, unlimited life.

Twenty–Second Sunday of the Year (B)

One result of the Church's move into the Roman Empire and beyond was that the Biblical background of Christians was replaced with a pagan one.

Jewish Christians came to the Church a with view of God and traditions connected to the history of God's relationship with the Chosen People.

Christians with a pagan background carried their own customs and ways of thinking into the Church. Many of them, like Greek philosophy and most of our Christmas customs, enriched the Church. Many, like certain attitudes towards saints and relics, presented problems. Most were probably both blessings and curses.

As the Church continues to spread throughout the world, attitudes that differ from Biblical thought continue to enter our way of viewing God and the world. Some enrich us. Some present problems. Some do both.

The difficulty is that we tend to take those attitudes for granted, and fail to measure them against the Scripture and the teaching of the Church. They are so much a part of us that we don't even notice it. I wonder if some of my own attitudes about God can be traced to my horse–sacrificing ancestors in Europe long ago.

In this week's passage from Mark, the Pharisees point out that Jesus' disciples don't follow the customs of their ancestors, and as their master, Jesus is responsible for what they do or fail to do.

Because of their negative portrayal in the gospels, we may forget that the Pharisees were very devout believers who tried to shape every aspect of their lives with reference to their faith. They did not consider following various practices as a replacement for faith. Bringing those practices into their everyday life protected their faith, made it a part of everything they did, even washing their hands before meals.

So, what was the problem? What's wrong with having practices that allow faith to be part of everything we do? After all, we have the custom of praying before meals to remind ourselves that all that we have comes from God, and that the meals we share with others are related to the Eucharistic banquet we share with the whole Church.

There is nothing wrong with those customs. The problem appears when we make particular customs a measure of someone else's faith, or even our own. Because his disciples did not follow certain customs, the Pharisees assumed that Jesus was not a man of true faith.

This brings us back to the practices we have inherited from the cultures and religions our community has met and welcomed through the centuries. Those practices can help make our faith more than an intellectual exercise. They can help us understand God's works and help us actually do something on a regular basis about that understanding.

However, there are two reasons we must always be ready to examine our devotional practices.

The first is that how we show our faith eventually shapes our faith. So, we must always match the practices of our faith with the content of our faith. Do my devotions, practices and thoughts deepen my understanding of real Christianity, or am I in danger of wandering from the truth? Have the customs I learned from my family, from my community and from the teachers of my faith begun to warp or replace that faith?

The second reason I must examine my practices is that I might otherwise inflate their value and decide that all Christians must pray and practice as I do. I will then be like the Pharisees who presumed to know the quality of Jesus' faith by what he and his disciples did or didn't do.

The Church has been, when all is said and done, enriched by a careful openness to many ways to express our faith. As individuals, we must be as open, but as careful.

Twenty–Second Sunday of the Year (C)

A symposium, for me, is a dull affair where opinionated people peddle their opinions. There is a lot of talking *at*, but little listening *to* or talking *with*. Perhaps I have never had the good fortune to attend a good symposium. There should be such things, because the word *symposium* means a good time.

Its ancestry is Greek, a combination of the prefix *sun-*, meaning 'together' and the word meaning 'drink'. Originally, a symposium was a gathering of people who discussed intellectual matters while drinking wine. More than their professors at dull conferences, students who attempt to solve the world's problems while seated around a pizza and a pitcher of beer (or their local equivalents) are carrying on a venerable tradition, the roots of the university.

In today's Gospel, Jesus is at a symposium. Scholars say that Luke took various sayings and deeds of Jesus that he thought belonged together and presented them as happening during a meal. Perhaps it was Luke's Greek background that gave him the idea of presenting Jesus at a symposium.

It is a Friday night or Saturday daytime. People are sprawled around the floor, leaning on cushions. (Chairs were not common, and people ate around a low table.) There is wine, food and lots of talk. As Luke says, all eyes were on Jesus. What he said or did would form the basis of the symposium.

Today, we hear two topics. In the first, Jesus comments upon those jockeying for good places at the table. At first, he merely gives the kind of advice that any teacher might give. 'When you are invited, go and sit at the lowest place, so that when your host comes, he may say to you, "Friend, move up higher"; then you will be honored in the presence of all who sit at the table with you.'

This is not very profound advice. In fact, it seems calculating. I have seen people follow it literally, and their reasons have nothing to do with humility. But, Jesus adds something that puts his advice in a new light. He is not teaching manners or social advancement, but the

Kingdom of God. The host parallels God, who invites all people to a banquet.

My place at that banquet is not one I have earned. It is for God to decide where I belong. It is in humility that I know my littleness. It is in humility that I can listen to the voice of God. It is in humility that I know that all I have comes from God. 'For all who exalt themselves will be humbled, and those who humble themselves will be exalted.'

As the eating and drinking continue, so does the symposium.

Sometime later in the meal (and just because Luke puts one saying of Jesus after another does not mean we cannot imagine more conversation and joking in between), Jesus turns to his host and makes an observation about invitations. 'When you give a banquet, invite the poor, the crippled, the lame, and the blind.'

In a time and place without social welfare schemes, the disabled were almost invariably poor. They were frequently outcasts because some people thought their disabilities were a divine punishment. So, Jesus is not talking so much about physical disabilities as he is about the poor and the outcast. He tells the host to invite them.

On one level, Jesus is recommending charity to those most in need. But, he is also issuing an invitation to the host and to us. He is inviting us to be like God who invites all people to the banquet of eternal life-giving love. In so doing, we show God's love to our neighbor. Through us, our neighbors will know God. We also show ourselves ready to understand and receive God's gift. 'You will be blessed, because they cannot repay you, for you will be repaid at the resurrection of the righteous.'

In Luke's Gospel, the symposium continues. It should continue in our lives. We tend to think that reflection upon the Word of God, upon the Work of God, is something solemn, serious, and private.

But, sometimes, we should be ready to hear the Word in the hustle and bustle of our lives, in the symposium of eating, drinking and gabbing that is our daily life.

Twenty–Third Sunday of the Year (A)

The field of Biblical studies called Textual Criticism compares ancient manuscripts of the Bible to see where spelling mistakes, dropped words and added words may have changed texts. The differences are usually minor.

Today's Gospel passage from Matthew may include such a phrase. Some ancient manuscripts contain it, some do not. Was it dropped by some scribes (remember that until the 1450's all copies of Matthew were hand–written) or was it added? The scholars think it more likely in this case that the phrase was added.

That phrase is 'against you' in 'If another member of the church sins against you, go and point out the fault when the two of you are alone.' So, it is more likely that the original version is 'If another member of the church sins, go and point out the fault . . .'

The difference is not significant, since any sin against my brothers and sisters is a sin against me as well. However, when I expand my view to see sins against others as well as myself, I face questions of social justice. There is more to sin than ill–mannered interpersonal behavior. Anything that deprives people of their dignity as God's children or deprives them of realizing and exercising that dignity is sinful.

So, throughout history, believers have confronted those who sin against their brothers and sisters, sometimes with only a dim awareness of it. The prophets spoke strongly and often against the powerful. Someone today who heard or read the sermons and writings of the fathers of the Church without knowing they were more than a thousand years old might attack them as 'new–fangled mixing of the Church where it doesn't belong'. Medieval sermons, especially those preached to kings and nobles, frequently dealt with the abuses of power that enabled the powerful to oppress the weak.

In the abstract and in the past, it might be easy to accept the idea that the Church should be concerned with such issues. In fact, it seems to have been generally recognized that Christians should confront one another and their societies with the effects of sin in the community. However, nowadays when Christians or Churches try to follow the Lord's admonition to not let sin pass without our speaking up, the reaction can be very peculiar.

'The Church should be concerned with religion, not with society, economics or politics.' That phrase is often used by those who feel threatened by a call to repentance. For many Christians, 'morality' is merely concerned with sex; the justice or injustice of our society, our economy or our politics is not a religious issue.

Something new has happened to make relatively large numbers of Christians feel that concerns of faith are limited to prayer, good works and 'churchy' things. Ironically, considering the tradition of two thousand years, many of those people who have such a new attitude call themselves conservative.

This strange development is probably linked to something that is good, the improvement in the lives of millions of people. More people have more comfort, more security, more power and more of a vested interest in maintaining things pretty much as they are than has ever been the case before.

When calls for repentance, for social justice, for a really adequate provision for the poor were aimed at a king, the peasants could cheer, at least in their hearts. Now, many of the peasants' descendants are more comfortable than any king ever was. And we are as reluctant as kings to give up privileges and the means of acquiring them.

The Lord's command to confront sin in ourselves and others is never easy to fulfill. It is even harder, perhaps, to be the object of that confrontation, whether as individuals or as societies.

So, what are we to do?

For starters, we should learn to listen carefully to those who say we must change. They may be wrong; they may be right. We must listen to them to learn which.

On the other hand, we may be wrong. We must look honestly at ourselves and our society and see where we might betray many of God's children and the world in which they and we live for the sake of a comparative few.

Then, we must take what steps we can (and they might not be big ones) to bring our world a bit closer to what we pray, that God's will be done on earth as in heaven.

The one thing we must not do is refuse to listen to the voices of those who accuse us and our world of sin.

Twenty–Third Sunday of the Year (B)

Jesus went through several actions in curing the deaf man in today's gospel. He touched the man's ears, spit, and touched his tongue. 'Then he looked up to heaven and groaned.'

We tend to look upon the Cross as something that happened at the end of Jesus' ministry. The gospels, however, were written under the shadow of the Cross. Every event in the life of Jesus portrayed in the gospels is connected to the Cross.

Was the groan of Jesus when he cured that man a groan from the Cross?

One of the amazing things about us human beings is that we think that there is something wrong with the world. We think it is supposed to be a different place. Why do we do that?

Why do we feel that something is wrong when children get ill? After all, disease and death are natural.

Why do we think there should be fairness, and even some special breaks for the weaker among us? What about the survival of the fittest?

Why do we feel that accidents are evil, or that volcanoes, earthquakes and typhoons should not occur? This is the planet we live on, and there is no other available.

Something within us rebels against the facts. We may not be able to say what we think the world should be, but we know we don't want what we've got.

In other words, we have a hunger for salvation. We desire to be freed for something better. Christians know the source of our desire is the fact that God has created us to share in the life of the Trinity. We also know that the frustration of that desire has its foundation in sin. We may not be sure of the how, but we know it to be the case, and we know that we are not capable of freeing ourselves from the power and effects of sin.

Whatever healing there is of our separation from God and from each other, whatever answer there will be to our desire for a different world, comes only through Christ and what he did on the Cross. The important point is that there is no other way to bring about salvation. It's the Cross or nothing.

That means that all healing of the world's ills must share in the cross in some way. Therefore, when Jesus healed the deaf man who could not speak, he was in some sense doing the work of the Cross. That is the reason for his groan. That healing was part and parcel of the healing, the salvation, that Jesus achieved on the Cross.

What implications does that have for me? Does it mean that if I decide to do more than wish this were a better world I had better expect to groan? Is the only way to fix the broken world to allow myself to be broken?

Have you ever wondered why the Cross is the symbol of Christianity? The empty tomb could have been. The Ascension could have been. So many comforting and glorious things could have been. But, we use the Cross. It is on our churches, it is in our homes, it is marked on our bodies when we are baptized and we renew the mark each time we pray.

The answer, then, is one we knew all along. The way to make God's love present in this creation is to groan with Christ. Anyone who has tried to share God's love with the world comes to know that. Our willingness to groan, to offer real healing to the world, will be the salvation of the world. Our groans will lead to a Resurrection.

Twenty–Third Sunday of the Year (C)

Luke says that 'large crowds were traveling' with Jesus. But, he turns to them and says things that seem calculated to drive them away.

'Whoever comes to me and does not hate father and mother, wife and children, brothers and sisters, yes, and even life itself, cannot be my disciple.' In the idiom of those days, 'hate' could mean 'not prefer'. So, the crowd would have understood Jesus to mean, 'Whoever prefers father and mother . . .'.

Even if his listeners could put Jesus ahead of parents, spouses, children and relations, putting him ahead of 'life itself' is a big order. It is easy to imagine folks answering, 'Uh, Okay. Well, so long'.

Jesus continues, almost as if he wanted to drive off those who had not yet left. 'Whoever does not carry the cross and follow me cannot be my disciple.' Those folks knew about crosses. A cross was one of the most cruel tortures ever devised, and some of the people with Jesus may have seen it. So, more may have said, 'Gotta go!'

Apparently, there were still some brave souls left, because Jesus continues his discouraging words. Before deciding to follow him, one should weigh up the consequences. What, exactly, will it cost to follow Jesus?

He finishes up by saying, 'So therefore, none of you can become my disciple if you do not give up all your possessions'. That includes such 'possessions' as wealth, family and even life. That is a steep price to pay.

Some people do choose to prefer Jesus over father, mother, spouse and all the rest. Some of them choose Jesus over life itself. Even in Christian families and communities, a decision to follow Christ more whole-heartedly can provoke opposition, tears and ostracism.

What about me? Have I done anything lately because of my faith that at least raised eyebrows? Has being a disciple of Jesus cost me anything beyond what I might put into the collection basket at church? Probably not, and there are two possible reasons for that.

The first may be that I have been lukewarm in my faith. Perhaps I have not made any choices lately that would put my faith in conflict with the world. Perhaps I even continue to call myself a Christian simply in order to avoid problems with fathers, mothers and others.

But, there may be another reason I have not made any hard choices. Perhaps I have not yet been presented with a situation in which I have had to make a really difficult choice to live as a Christian. I think that is what Jesus' examples today remind us. Obviously, every moment of the Christian life is not a call to martyrdom or heroic virtue. Usually, the Christian life consists of getting from wake-up in the morning to bed-down in the evening while trying to live the unheroic virtues.

Jesus tells of a builder estimating costs and a king weighing his resources for war. A builder does not put up a skyscraper or even a pig sty every day. Even the most warlike rulers have days of armistice, if not peace. They plan for the special situations. Jesus is telling us to do the same.

If we embark upon the Christian life, there will be many times of calm. There will be times when our faith seems no big challenge to us or the world. But, if we 'sign on' for the life of a disciple, we must know that we may be called upon at any moment to make big decisions, to take radical actions that may turn our lives upside down.

I once spoke with a man who was the only Christian in the Tokyo fire department. He said his work was like his Christian vocation, because at any moment he might be called upon to give his life for the sake of others.

We are like firefighters. They may be sitting around watching TV together or cooking a meal. But, they know that at any moment they may be called to face unknown dangers, to risk their lives. A training program for firefighters that did not mention anything about fires would be a very strange one. Today, Jesus is telling us to be ready for fire so that when it comes, we will not be surprised, but resolute, knowing that the crisis today is one we took into account from the start.

Twenty–Fourth Sunday of the Year (A)

Genesis contains a fragment of a warrior's song attributed to Lamech, great-great-grandson of Cain. It is included to show the increase of violence due to the growth of the power of sin. 'I have killed a man for wounding me, a young man for striking me. If Cain is avenged sevenfold, truly Lamech seventy-sevenfold.' The desire for revenge is nothing new.

Jesus refutes Lamech's arithmetic. Rather than 490 measures of vengeance, the Lord calls for the same amount of forgiveness. It is not sufficient merely to refrain from vengeful words or deeds. Forgiveness, not seething resentment, is the opposite of vengeance.

Peter seems to have understood this, if only partly. That is why he asked Jesus how many times he should forgive. How much insult and injury must we endure before we are justified in taking revenge? But, Peter is not really asking, then, about forgiveness. He is asking how long we must postpone vengeance. If Peter were to truly forgive each time, he would always be starting his count at 'One'.

I have been hurt in various ways by others throughout my life. Family, friends, enemies and strangers have all done things that annoy, disappoint, damage or enrage me. I have forgotten most of those hurts and forgiven many. But, there remain not a few of the not-yet-forgiven or the seemingly unforgivable. Some offenses seem too great to let me forgive and forget them.

In the parable Jesus tells of an official who owes his master a huge sum of money. In fact, it is an impossible sum of money, ten thousand talents. Since there is also no way anyone could run up such a fantastic debt, it is clear that Jesus is using hyperbole, exaggeration, to make a point.

The point of this debtor's story is not the punishments the king would impose on him, since not even selling the official and his family as slaves would repay the debt. The point is the generosity of his forgiveness. An immeasurable offense is matched by immeasurably generous forgiveness.

The king is, of course, God who forgives our sins. The official? The official is everyone, including me. Does that mean that I have sinned against God to a fantastic degree? I hope not, though I know that some of the sins against me that I cannot or will not forgive in others were not great or even wrong in the mind of the sinner. It is also certain that I have hurt others without realizing it, or without intending the hurt I have caused.

Perhaps my sins against God are equivalent to ten thousand talents though I do not realize it. The point of the parable, though, is not the enormity of the offense, but the magnitude of the forgiving love. No matter how much of it I need, there is an infinite loving forgiveness available to me.

But, the parable does not end with the king's forgiveness. When the official sees someone who owes a few months' wages, he does not forgive. Though he has been forgiven an infinite amount, the official will not forgive a measurable sum.

That is my story. God's infinite love for me means infinite forgiveness of my sins. My too-finite love means limited forgiveness or no forgiveness at all for my fellows.

This is where my problem arises. The final message of the parable is that the infinitely forgiving love of God can be limited by only one thing: my unwillingness to imitate it. I even ask for that limitation each time I pray the Lord's Prayer, asking that we be forgiven as we have forgiven.

At first glance, this seems to result in a Catch-22 situation. I am commanded to forgive others because I have been forgiven, but I cannot be forgiven unless I forgive others first.

The way out of the paradox is to realize that forgiving and being forgiven is not a parade of activities that happen in order—God forgives, then I forgive, then God forgives. God's forgiving me and my forgiving others go on together. There is no progression, but a constant interactive experience. God's forgiveness and my own must become like a dance, with God's forgiving and mine moving together in a mirrored harmony.

Twenty-Fourth Sunday of the Year (B)

Once upon a time, there was a woman who had lived a long life. It wasn't a bad life. She had her share of joys and achievements, of love, friendship and family.

But, as life continued, she also had pains and sorrows. In other words, the woman had a cross to bear. She admitted that it was not a big one, but she still felt that it might not be the right one for her. It seemed to be getting too heavy.

So, one day she went to heaven and demanded a different cross. Saint Peter was surprised, but since she reminded him of his mother-in-law he asked an angel to escort her inside so she could find a cross she felt fit her better.

The angel led her to a warehouse.

'What's this?' the woman asked.

'This is the cross warehouse', said the angel. 'Everyone who comes here lays his or her cross down before going farther in. You should be able to find one here that suits you.'

So, the woman began shopping around. One time, she thought she'd try on an attractive little thing, not too small, but compact enough to not be a strain. However, when she tried lifting it, she realized that it was made of lead. She realized that looking at someone else's cross does not tell us how heavy it might be.

For the fun of it, she then tried a big cross that would certainly attract attention. But, though it looked big, it was so light that she would have been embarrassed to bear it.

In the meantime, the angel was getting impatient. It was after hours, and there's no overtime pay for angels.

Just when the angel was about to lose all patience, the woman finally picked up one cross near the door and said, 'Ah, this is the one. Good fit, heavy enough to be an honest-to-God cross, but not too much for me to handle'.

The angel exploded, 'Lady, that's the cross you came here with!'

Cross-bearing seems an inescapable part of human life. Jesus tells us to welcome our cross, confident that no matter how painful it might be, God's love will not be overwhelmed.

But, the question remains. Why must we carry a cross at all? After all, a cross is not pleasant. It really is a torture to face the big crosses of our lives. Couldn't God just get rid of them for us? Wasn't it enough that Jesus bore his cross? If he's our savior, why wasn't his crucifixion enough to cover for all of us? What good does a cross do me?

There must be something about the cross in itself that has value. After all, the Church has always said that it is the cross, not the empty tomb, that saves.

One of the key messages of the prophets is that God suffers. God is heartbroken over what people do to one another and to themselves when they abandon love. When God came among us, the suffering of God and the suffering of humanity were united in Jesus. The crosses we bear do not merely bring us close to God, they make us like God, God who suffers.

Does this mean that suffering is good and we should seek it out for ourselves and not strive to ease it for others? No, suffering is not God's will for the world. The suffering of the world breaks God's heart.

Christ's call for us to take up the cross is an invitation to learn that though suffering is always with us and may make us think God is far from us, it is actually a share in the life of God who also takes up the cross.

Twenty–Fourth Sunday of the Year (C)

A lost sheep drops to the ground and refuses to move. The shepherd who finds it must pick the beast up. There is no other way to get it back to the flock. It must be carried.

Sheep are too big to carry under one's arm, so a fireman's carry (across the shoulders) is the only way to do it. Since in Jesus' world a lost sheep was probably in a rocky desert, a shepherd staggering along with one on his shoulders would have risked sprained ankles or worse.

If I were a shepherd and one of my sheep wandered off, I would say, 'Tough luck', and leave it at that.

Of course, the sheep would have some right to complain: 'You say *I* don't understand when I'm being helped, but you're no better. God does all sorts of things in your life, sends you all sorts of people, teachings and opportunities, and you complain or ignore them! You would rather sit down in your stupidity, your sin and your laziness than get up and follow the Lord, even though he is leading you to safety.'

Let's leave the sheep (they are getting embarrassing) and turn to money. That's something we all appreciate.

The lost coin to which Jesus refers is not merely loose change dropped by the woman while unpacking the groceries. A woman wore her wealth as a headdress, the coins strung around her brow. The woman in the story has only ten coins, each worth about one day's wage. With only that much of an emergency fund, she is poor. To lose even a single coin is a disaster.

So, she gets to work. In a house without windows, she has to rely on the light that comes through the door and a small flickering oil lamp. Her broom would be her major help. By sweeping the whole place, she might hear a welcome 'clink' as the broom hit the coin and knocked it against something.

In both stories, of course, the searcher is God. God is the shepherd who will not leave the sheep to die in its stupidity. He searches us out and then does the real work of saving us from ourselves, saving us for our real home with the flock of God.

God is the woman who looks for the lost coin. (Jesus had no trouble speaking of God as a woman and the early Church had no trouble passing on the tradition that he did so, something that might shock many today.)

God will do all in her power to bring us back to her. We can lose ourselves in all the dark places of the world and of our hearts, but she will be persistent.

And finally, God is the loving father who embraces his wayward son and welcomes him home to a feast.

Why? Why should God take such trouble with me? I am not worth the effort. I am stupid, wandering away from the way I know leads to full life. I am lost more often than not. Or, rather, I lose myself. Yet, God keeps coming after me, offering forgiveness and wisdom. The reason could not be in myself. Someone so perverse as I cannot deserve God's searching love, but I receive it all the same. It can only be because God loves me regardless of how I act.

I tend to view the Christian life as a project, something to be achieved. We draw up lists of things to do—work for justice, say our prayers, share the Eucharist, contribute to charity (and the collection basket).

All of that is nonsense compared to what Christianity is really all about—God the shepherd who will never abandon me when I stray. God the housewife who will search me out wherever I may get lost. God the father who will always forgive and welcome me.

I am the lost sheep, but God will lift me up on his shoulders and bring me home. I am the lost coin, but God will hunt me down till she holds me once again. I am the wandering son, but God welcomes me home.

This is the Gospel. One scholar describes today's passage as 'the distilled essence of the good news, the gospel within the Gospel.' God is merciful not to 'humankind,' but to lost, bewildered, stupid, unlovable me!

Twenty–Fifth Sunday of the Year (A)

The parable of the workmen was probably included in Matthew's Gospel as a rebuke to Jewish Christians who resented the influx of Gentiles into the community. The Jews had generations of experience at believing in God. Jesus himself was one of them.

Then, from out of nowhere, all sorts of strange people started coming into the Church. Not only did they not come from a tradition of believing in God, many of them were in fact pagans who had recently elbowed their way into the community, claiming the right to be part of the chosen people of God. They spoke different languages, wore different clothes, ate different foods and had different customs.

Matthew's message is a reprimand to those who were uncomfortable with the newcomers.

In the parable, those hired early in the morning and those brought on near quitting time all receive the same welcome from the landowner and the same wage, a denarius. A denarius was the amount one needed to live for a day. So, the landowner gave each of the workers all they needed. Of course, the landowner represents God, who will give us all we need. In the Kingdom of God, we will not be given more than all we really need. Neither will we be given less.

So, the parable is not a story about labor relations or wage policies. It is about how God deals with the world. And yet, it is not totally unrelated to the concerns of the modern world.

All over the world, societies are facing their own version of what the early Church experienced. Migrant workers, refugees and immigrants are 'invading' areas where their races, cultures, religions, speech and customs are alien. They often face ridicule, exploitation, discrimination and even violence.

Another way in which 'outsiders' are becoming a strong presence in many societies is the refusal of women and minorities to remain outside the mainstream of their societies. People who have traditionally been in charge see their power eroded and are challenged to either cooperate or be ignored.

On a global level, nations and societies that in the past were merely objects of colonialism, tourism or exploitation for resources or cheap labor are demanding recognition and a just share of the gifts of the world.

In the Church, too, this phenomenon is arising, and not a few Christians appear threatened by the change, just as the Jewish Christians were long ago. If one wishes to survey Christianity today, the journey must begin in places like São Paulo, Nairobi and Manila rather than Rome or Canterbury.

The response to this on the part of many Christians is like that of the landowner in the parable. They work to ensure that all people have a fair share of the opportunities and goods of this world. They join the struggle for justice within societies, among nations and in the Churches.

Such activity is not always welcomed, even by fellow Christians. The imitators of the landowner are accused of abandoning the Church's spiritual mission for material aims, of being dupes of various enemies of society or religion and even traitors.

However, involvement in social criticism and activism by Christians is none of these. Christian calls for equal justice are not based upon ideology or a commitment to solely material values. We must be involved in order to show what God and God's Kingdom are like. The generosity of the landowner shows that God offers the same love to all. The generosity of Christians aims at doing the same. It is a spiritual mission, even when it looks similar to what others may do from a different motivation.

The Incarnation of Christ is God's declaration that if we wish to learn about God, we must look for signs of God's love in the world in which we live. This world is the place where the spiritual is meant to be visible. Just as the parables of Jesus show the love of God in stories about lost coins, vineyards and generous landowners, the followers of Jesus must make the events of everyday life point to God's loving presence among us.

Therefore, we must root out discrimination and an unwelcoming attitude in our own lives. In addition, as citizens, as members of society, we must use the structures and opportunities available to us to make the world more like the Kingdom of God, more like the field of the generous landowner.

Twenty–Fifth Sunday of the Year (B)

Even though the Gospel of John ends with the declaration 'there are many other things that Jesus did,' we tend to think we have the whole story just as it occurred with nothing left out, no pieces moved around. We haven't.

The gospel writers took reminiscences about Jesus and stories about what he had done and said. Then, they picked and chose among them and put them together to make their narratives suit the needs of the communities for which they wrote.

It's like a quilter who takes different pieces of cloth and puts them together to make a single quilt. In some sections, the seams are barely visible because the pieces look similar. In other sections, the fact that adjoining pieces are very different makes the match–up obvious.

In this week's passage from Mark, the seam is easy to see. In the first section, Jesus and the disciples are going through Galilee, and he talks about his death and resurrection. Then, presumably at some other time, though in the text it appears to follow immediately upon the Galilee walk, the disciples are in the Capernaum area, talking about who is most important. Considering the unlikelihood of the disciples wanting first place after being told that the way of Christ is a way to death, as well as the differences in time and place, the seam becomes obvious.

Why would Mark (or whoever he got the story from) put these two particular pieces together? Why did he think that they were an appropriate match, even that they must be together? What is the connection between the death and resurrection of Jesus, arguments about importance and the welcoming of a child?

We can all understand the argument the disciples had. We spend much of our lives seeking status, protecting our status, or mourning the loss of status.

It is as if my value as a human being depends upon outdoing others. The child's cry, 'Me first!' is the simplest declaration of what it is about. I am self–centered. I worship a false god, one that has my name and face. So long as I serve that god, I am handicapped in meeting the one true God.

That, perhaps, is the reason Jesus says that welcoming a child is welcoming 'the One who sent me'. There is something that happens in that sort of meeting that moves my focus off of myself and allows me to meet God.

At the time of Jesus, children had no legal rights, and were not generally taken into account in the lives of adults or society. They were powerless, lower in status than any adult. For an adult to greet a child, to welcome one's company, would be demeaning.

Yet, that is what Jesus says his disciples must do. They must step down from the pedestals they build for themselves and welcome the unimportant, the overlooked, the powerless. If they do that, they will meet God.

Who might the overlooked be today? There is no shortage: refugees, the poor, abused children, the uneducated, minorities, persons with AIDS, youth, the elderly, prisoners, the disabled, the unbelievers—we need only stop looking at ourselves to find them.

What has this to do, however, with the first piece of patchwork, Jesus' comments about his death and resurrection?

Mark apparently wants us to see that being willing to shift our focus from ourselves to meet the overlooked, to welcome them into our lives, is one of the ways we imitate Christ. It is as if after writing the passage about Jesus talking of his death, Mark asked himself, 'What does this mean for our lives as Christians today?'

Twenty–Fifth Sunday of the Year (C)

St Jerome wrote: 'Our walls glitter with gold and gold gleams upon our ceilings and the capitals of our pillars; yet Christ is dying at our doors in the person of his poor, naked and hungry.' About 1600 years have passed, but though tastes have changed, Christ remains at our doors.

Whether our churches be decorated by Michelangelo or from mail–order catalogues, whether our homes be estates or hovels, whether our clothing be designer jeans or hand–me–downs, we have never given worldly goods the treatment they deserve. Or, rather, the use they deserve.

Jesus speaks of 'dishonest wealth.' His presupposition is that wealth is something that stands against the justice of God. But, Jesus recognizes that possessions are a normal part of life, and that some, whether by fair means or foul, will have more than others. As he so often does, Jesus shifts the focus. Here, he shifts it from possession to use.

'Make friends for yourselves with dishonest wealth, so that when it fails, you will be welcomed into eternal dwellings.'

Wealth will go. Economies collapse, buildings crumble, clothes go out of fashion, we die. 'A fool and his money are soon parted,' says the proverb. In fact, whether we be foolish or wise, sooner or later we and our wealth will be parted. We have no choice in that matter.

We do, however, have some choice in the way we and our possessions are separated. We can wait until they are taken, or we can share them with others, with 'Christ at our doors.'

Who are the 'friends' who will give us an everlasting reception? In the parable of the dishonest manager, it is debtors, those who need relief. In other words, it is the poor. If I wish to 'buy' a place in 'the eternal dwellings', I must, in a sense, bribe the reception committee, the poor.

I have possessions, but they are 'mine' only for the sake of aiding those in need. As Francis Bacon said more than 300 years ago,

'Money is like muck, no good except it be spread'. Jesus put it less picturesquely: 'If you are not trustworthy with dishonest wealth, who will trust you with true wealth?'

Trustworthiness with riches means using them for those who need them and for what they can do. If I so use them, then the poor will stand at the gates of heaven and say as I approach, 'Oh, it's you! Come on in—and thanks again.'

Does that mean that I should give up everything? It may, indeed, mean so. The Church has always presented that as an ideal, though we have never lived it successfully. It's embarrassing to think of how much we spend on crucifixes or Christmas stables while Christ remains at the doors of our cathedrals, churches and homes. Some of us take vows to live in poverty for the sake of others. Seldom, however, does 'religious poverty' involve the rigor, suffering and lack of security of the truly poor.

Such problems do not belong only to the Church at large or to certain people in it. It is a problem for a very specific Christian, myself. I am afraid to let go. I want security for my future. I want a bit of comfort in the present. I want to enjoy what my possessions—wealth, time, talents, health, life—enable me to do. What can I do about that?

Perhaps the dishonest manager in the parable gives a hint. He makes an 'investment' in hopes of reaping later benefits. Investing is a way to wealth in much of the world today. Ideally, an investment grows, leading to yet further investment. Can I do that with my possessions, putting at least some of them forward for the needy?

But, how big an investment is enough? I'm not likely to invest all that I have for the poor. The opposite is the danger; I might not invest enough to profit. There is a simple rule of thumb: it should be at least inconvenient. There should be something I would like to do with my treasure, time or talent that I will not be able to do because I have offered them to the poor.

If I can do that, I may find that the return on my investment enables me, or even impels me, to do more and one day buys my way past the gate-keeping poor of heaven. That may be getting in by hook or by crook, but remember that the Master ultimately commends the devious manager.

Twenty–Sixth Sunday of the Year (A)

What sort of man do you imagine Jesus to be? Kind? Gentle? Good-humored? Intelligent? Powerful? Obnoxiously insulting?

Obnoxiously insulting? Jesus in today's Gospel passage is certainly so. Good manners and proper deference were in order when talking to the religious leaders of the people.

What does Jesus say that is so obnoxious? He certainly cannot and does not condemn the leaders because they violate the rules of their religion. They were scrupulous in fulfilling their duties. So, why compare them unfavorably with thieving, traitorous tax collectors and prostitutes?

The answer comes in the response of the sons in the parable to the task their father asks them to perform: 'Go work in the vineyard today.' One says that he will go; the other refuses. One son says the right thing, the other says the wrong.

The son who said the right thing is like the chief priests and elders of the people. They say all the right things. They teach. They fulfill all their public religious duties (for actions do, indeed 'say' something).

But, there is a problem. The son who says, 'I go, sir', talks a good game, but is useless.

The other son, the one who refuses to go, changes his mind and eventually heads out to the vineyard. Jesus asks the priests and elders which son is actually the obedient one—the one who says the right thing or the one who does the right thing. The answer is plain. Deeds are more important than words.

Then, Jesus springs his insult. The son who says the right things, who looks right, stands for the good people listening to him. The son who looks and sounds disobedient at first glance represents the tax collectors and prostitutes. They, not the nice religious folks, are the ones who really do the will of God.

Does this mean that Jesus is in favor of sin? No. Remember that the right thing they did was to repent when John the Baptist came teaching the way of holiness. What, then, could this passage mean for us today?

In more ways than we might like to admit, we are like the son who said, 'Sure, Dad, anything you say'. In our Baptism, we have been given a call by God, a vocation to go out into the vineyard. In that same Baptism, we have said our 'Yes'.

Throughout our lives, we repeat that 'Yes' in various ways. We traipse off to church on Sunday. We take part in the prayers and hymns, recite the Creed and share the Sacrament. This yes-saying is probably sincere. But, is it enough? What about Tuesday or Thursday?

The test of Christian faith is not merely whether or not we are in church on Sunday. Going to church is the renewing of our 'yes' to the call of God. But, do we follow through on the promise?

What would it mean to actually go out into the vineyard and do the Father's will? Some of the things I should do are similar to what I do in church—prayer, reflection on the Word of God. Other things are, in fact, what I do in church, but they take more ambiguous forms outside. Sharing peace, for example. In the liturgy, it is a gesture. Outside in the vineyard, it may be a kind word, a helpful deed, a principled position.

The main focus of my yes-saying in church is the Eucharist, communion with God and the People of God. Taking that communion out to the vineyard means treating every person I meet as a brother or sister.

On the other hand, many people who do not say 'yes' with me on Sunday spend the week doing the will of God. The world would be a much worse place, a place even less a sign of the Kingdom of God than it is, were it not for the men and women who do not say yes to the Creed, to the Church or to the Sacraments but who live for others. They become workers in the vineyard, making it worthy of the Lord's ownership even though they do not know it and might object if told so.

Jesus presents tax collectors and prostitutes to the chief priests and elders of the people as a challenge to conversion. The same is true today. The men and women who without saying 'yes' to the Lord obey his will and bring the care and love of God to this love-starved world are a challenge to us.

Twenty–Sixth Sunday of the Year (B)

Most people who have ever lived have not been followers of Jesus. Most never even heard of him.

So, are most of our ancestors separated from Christ in death as they seemed to be in life? Are most people alive today separated in the same way? Must one be a Christian to be embraced by the life-giving Spirit of God? There are Christians, some of them Catholics, who say that is so.

In Mark's Gospel, John has a problem because God's saving work is apparently not confined to 'insiders': 'Teacher, we saw a man using your name to expel demons and we tried to stop him because he is not of our company.' John felt that the work of Christ in healing, forgiving and sharing the love of God was a possession of those who called themselves his followers, 'our company'.

Jesus answers that, 'Anyone who is not against us is for us.' Those who do the will of God, whether they know Christ explicitly or not, or whether or not they are part of his 'company'—the Church—or not, are cooperating with Christ in making the Reign of God present in our world.

Even atheists can serve in building the Kingdom. It does not depend solely upon us Christians. God will bring it about through many people, cultures and events.

That is good news for us as we look at a world in which most people will never know of Jesus Christ, let alone become his followers. It is a comfort to think that they and the thousands of men and women who are our ancestors all have a place in God's plan.

In fact, 'outsiders' may be important to us in our vocation.

The original company of believers betrayed Christ. They deserted him when he was arrested and killed.

We are capable of similar betrayal. The history of the Church includes horrifying events and actions that can receive no justification, only forgiveness. My own life, too, contains no shortage of betrayal of my vocation as a Christian. At times, we Christians must be confronted with our sin and be challenged to fidelity. Frequently, it is outsiders who render that service to God and us.

So, men and women who are 'not of our company' have several roles to play in building the Kingdom of God. God's love draws them to a sort of faithfulness of which they themselves may be unaware. Their service to their neighbors is service to God. The good they do helps build the Kingdom no less than the good done by Christians builds that same Kingdom. And, they challenge us Christians to deeper fidelity to the Gospel.

Does this mean, then, that there is no reason for 'our company', the Church, to exist? Is it wrong for us to continue to invite others to join the community of those who proclaim Christ, who worship the Father through Christ in the Holy Spirit?

No. Jesus himself called men and women into that 'company'. We companions of Jesus have an essential vocation. All men and women are called to live in the dignity of children of God. All men and women have a right to know that dignity and a right to rejoice in it and give thanks for it. They are entitled to the support and guidance that the 'company' can give in fulfilling the will of God for the world.

Our 'company' lives in the world as a sign of the Reign of God. That Reign is bigger than our company. It includes men and women of all times and climes. Most of those people have not been, and will not be, part of the 'company'. We rejoice that even so, they are part of that Kingdom.

Twenty–Sixth Sunday of the Year (C)

Am I the rich man or Lazarus? I do not consider myself rich, but compared to most of the world's people, I have incredible wealth.

That wealth is not merely monetary. It is also psychological (I live among friends and with a high degree of personal security), intellectual (I can read and write), physical (my health is protected by preventive and healing care), social (I live in a peaceful place and can exercise a high level of freedom) and spiritual (I have been called to know God's love in Jesus Christ). There is no doubt about it—I am the rich man.

In that case, it is important that I know where he went wrong—unless, of course, I am willing to risk baking in 'the abode of the dead.'

We should not take that risk lightly. Jesus talks on several occasions about those who will be cast off from God. In that light, today's parable is especially frightening, because the hell-bound rich man and I have so much in common.

So, what was the rich man's problem? Was it wealth? No, he is never criticized for that, nor is there any reason to think that he is condemned because of how he acquired it. Was the rich man cruel? Did he oppress Lazarus? Did he call upon the authorities to have the beggar removed from his gate? No, he did none of these things. In fact, he did nothing at all regarding Lazarus.

That was the problem. The rich man at his table may not have even been aware of the beggar at his gate. The rich man would have been busy with his day-to-day concerns, just as I am. He may not have even had time to go outside. Even if he did, he might not have noticed one more beggar in a world full of beggars. The rich man did not know Lazarus.

Mother Teresa offered an excuse in such circumstances. 'The trouble is that rich people, well-to-do people, very often don't really know who the poor are; and that is why we can forgive them, for knowledge can only lead to love, and love to service. And so, if they are not touched by them, it's because they do not know them.'

Mother Teresa was more generous than Abraham—or Jesus. When the rich man begs Abraham to send Lazarus to end his brothers' ignorance, he is refused. Ignorance is no excuse because there is no excuse for ignorance.

This brings us to the core of the rich man's (and my) problem. There is simply no excuse for not seeing Lazarus.

The rich man was indifferent to the world outside his gate. The walls of his house were the walls of his world. Such walls need not be a house, either. We build walls of family, race, nationality, class, religion, education, neighborhood and the devil-knows-what else that shut out some part of the world, some Lazarus.

There is no excuse. God gives us a whole world, and if we close our eyes to any part of it, we are refusing God. We make our private world so small that we cannot see either the good God does or the evil we must combat.

What can I do? I am, without doubt, the rich man of the parable. Am I doomed to hell?

There are signs of hope. The first is that since living in communion with all the world's people in Christ is what I was created for, it may be easier to know and care about my brothers and sisters than it is to close them out of my world.

Another is my discomfort. The rich man came to his senses and saw Lazarus too late for it to do him any good. This parable is a wake-up call to see that each and every man and woman is a child of God, and therefore my brother, my sister. Awareness can be the first step in conversion.

And what will conversion look like? It may be as simple as exercising good manners to strangers I meet, including shop clerks and others who serve me. It may be paying closer attention to news reports of what is happening to my brothers and sisters around the world. It may be learning about other cultures, customs and religions. It may be sacrificing some of my psychological, intellectual, physical, social, material and spiritual wealth for the sake of others.

It will be living in the real world, the whole real world.

Twenty–Seventh Sunday of the Year (A)

Today's gospel parable is clearly about Jesus, the Son who followed the prophets to the Master's vineyard Israel, and was killed. It is unusual in that it talks about Jesus himself, rather than focusing on the Kingdom of God.

The parable is obviously a critique of those to whom the Lord's vineyard, the People of God, has been entrusted, the religious leaders of Israel. They use and abuse the vineyard for their own purposes and not those of God. No matter how often God's prophets call them to repentance, they fail to respond. Even God's sending the Son does not move them.

So, responsibility for the People of God will be turned over to a new laborer, the Church.

The evangelist included this parable in order to give Gentile Christians confidence that their membership in the community of disciples was in accord with God's will. Gentiles were not always welcome because they were frequently unable or unwilling to follow all of the Law of Moses. This parable tells them they are in the Church because God has handed that vocation to them.

Millennia have passed, and a parable that gave Gentile Christians a sense of vocation and legitimacy vis-a-vis the Jews does not have the same emotional force for us. So, what are we to make of the parable? Is it of merely historic interest?

Let's look at the comment of the chief priests and elders. Jesus asks them, 'When the owner of the vineyard comes, what will he do to those tenants?'

They answer: 'He will put those wicked ones to a miserable death, and lease the vineyard to other tenants who will give him the produce at the harvest time.' It is easy for them to recognize that the tenants are wicked. What they fail to recognize is that they themselves are the wicked tenants.

Could it be that we fail to see the same failure in ourselves?

The Church has its own chief priests and elders of the people. Are those called to the ministry of leadership in the Church always and everywhere good stewards of the trust they have been given? No.

That was easy to say. It is not untrue, but yet, might we not repeat the error of those who heard Jesus and recognized others' failings? There always have been, are and always will be bad leaders in the Church.

But who are the tenants of the vineyard of the Lord? Are they solely the clergy? We must think about where that vineyard is today. In Jesus' time, it was the People of God called Israel. Does that mean that today the vineyard is the People of God called the Church?

But, the whole world is called to the Kingdom of God. In that case, the laborers in the vineyard are not merely the leaders of the Church, but the Church itself.

That means that every Christian has the duty that once belonged to the chief priests and elders of the people. We are, each of us, members of the priestly people of God. Our vocation is to give guidance, correction and encouragement to all people that they may yield the harvest God longs for.

How can we do that? Preaching and teaching, explicitly declaring the loving will of God, is certainly one way, an essential one. But, the chief priests and elders of the people did that. It is more important that we practice what we preach. Our daily lives must be examples of living freely as sons or daughters of God.

The Eucharist is the supreme example of that. We (not a lonely I) share full communion with God in Jesus Christ. Carrying that communion into everyday life will draw others to that same communion. They will be a rich harvest.

There is one other thing we must do. We must hear and heed the messengers God sends to us workers in the vineyard. For we, too, need to be converted throughout our lives. We must be alert to the Lord's call to move beyond what we've always done to a deeper understanding, a more effective service. The first messenger is, of course, Christ in his Word and Church. But there will be others. We will recognize them if when they speak we see the sins of others. That will be a sign that we must look to our own.

Twenty–Seventh Sunday of the Year (B)

Evidence for the basic accuracy of the Gospel accounts of the resurrection is the fact that the testimony is given by women. That is not because women are more trustworthy than men. It is simply that unless it were absolutely true, the men who wrote the Gospels would never have said so. Saying so damaged their case.

In the society in which Jesus and his disciples lived, women were not allowed to give testimony as equals of men. So, legally speaking, the Church had no basis for believing in the resurrection. The witnesses were not qualified to give testimony.

The example of divorce in Mark's Gospel is another case of women being treated differently from men. A husband could abuse his wife, deprive her and use her but she had no means of escape. A woman did not have the ability to divorce her husband. (Mark's mention of a woman divorcing is something he added to the words of Jesus out of his own Gentile background; Jewish women could not divorce their husbands.) The right of divorce belonged to the man, and no legal proceedings were required. A woman could be made homeless and deprived of her children and all support on the whim of her husband. One rabbi taught that a burnt meal was sufficient grounds for divorce.

There was another group in the time of Jesus that lacked basic rights: children. Children were possessions. In Roman law, a father who killed his child faced no legal penalty.

Children are still abused by adults throughout the world. They labor in dangerous conditions. They are forced into sexual slavery. They are provided with 'entertainment' that poisons their minds and spirits. They are aborted, deprived of education, forced to live in inhuman conditions, victimized by war and poverty, and physically and emotionally abused.

Jesus defended two groups in his society that had no defense. He forbade discarding wives or denying children their right to a place among his followers.

There is no toleration in the Reign of God for the bias that infected his society and infects our own.

People who differ from some social or personal norm in race, nationality, social class, religion, age, physical abilities, education, sexual orientation, language, tastes, employment (or lack of it) or just about anything else are frequently ignored, deprived and even abused.

Women and children still experience this. Others include refugees and migrants, persons with AIDS, the disabled and racial, ethnic and religious minorities.

The Reign of God is as big as eternity, but it has no room for discrimination.

Discrimination is a terrible sin because it denies creation. The truth that God made the world in love is not threatened by science. It is denied by those who treat others as if they were not children of God's loving creation. Jesus was angry when he saw his disciples discriminate. Dare we assume that his anger is any less when we do it?

What are we to do? The first step in conversion is to recognize our sinfulness. I must examine my life and attitudes. I must pay attention when I meet, see or hear about someone different from myself. Do I judge others by criteria other than their being sons and daughters of God?

Following the admission of sin, there is contrition. I must pray for a heart that is pained by my sin. Then, there is confession. This is true in the sacrament (have I ever thought to confess my bias?) and in my day-to-day life. I must confess to others and myself that I am capable of discrimination, that I fall into the sin. Confession to myself is important because it is the source of amendment.

I must pray for courage to turn from sin, to cooperate with God's call to change my life. That is not easy when the sin is one I may have inherited from my community, family or society. Finally, there is penance, action to heal the damage caused by sin. I must act to bring an end to anything that denies the children of God their full dignity.

To do less is to decide that God's Reign should exclude certain people. Perhaps it can. But, in that case, we may find that the ones who are excluded are we.

Twenty–Seventh Sunday of the Year (C)

When they wanted to make a point, Palestinian Jews two thousand years ago tended to exaggerate when they spoke, so it was natural that Jesus would, too. Therefore, despite what Jesus says, anyone who wants to move a sycamore to the sea should use a chain saw, a crane and a heavy–duty truck instead of prayer.

If flying sycamores are an example of Palestinian exaggeration, can we write off Jesus' words and look for more 'truthful' passages? No, if Jesus exaggerated, it was because he wanted to make an impression, wanted folks to pay attention to what he said. So, what about using a mustard seed to move a sycamore? What can it possibly mean?

The disciples ask Jesus to do something we, too, ask: 'Increase our faith'. We see the horrors of the world around us and wonder if there really could be a God who cares. Our cultures are increasingly becoming 'post–religious', with decisions in the political, social and economic realms made without reference to any beliefs at all. Some say that the rise of fundamentalism among Christians, Muslims, Hindus and others is a last gasp by panicked believers who see impending doom for their beliefs.

But, is the situation really all that new? Habakkuk faced the same problems some 2500 years ago. It never has been easy to believe. It never will be.

So we pray, 'Increase my faith!'

Jesus' answer is not comforting. 'If you had faith the size of a mustard seed . . .' Well, it seems that my faith is not even so big as such a small seed, because it doesn't suffice. I don't even want to shake, let alone move sycamores, I only want my heart to be moved. That shouldn't be harder than flinging trees into the ocean.

Perhaps Jesus is telling us that it is not a problem of amount. Perhaps we already have enough faith. A mustard seed's worth suffices, so perhaps we need not ask for an increased faith. There is something else needed to make us feel that our faith is alive.

That may be the reason Luke linked Jesus' words about faith with an admonition about service. Faith is not something we hold on to like a pocketful of seeds, something that can be increased by the mere asking. Faith is a form of service to God. The amount of faith is not important—a mustard seed's worth suffices. What matters is what we do with that faith, whether it be as small as a mustard seed or as big as a coconut.

Worrying about my faith is self-centered. It's as if faith existed for me and an increase in it increased my spiritual capital. My faith, however, is supposed to be other-centered. That is, it should be directed toward God and my only concern should be whether God is indeed getting a mustard seed's worth of service from me.

That is the reason we are told, 'When you have done all you have been commanded to do, say, "We are useless servants. We have done no more than our duty"'.

Ironically, concern with the depth or breadth of my faith can interfere with my being a slave of duty. I can spend so much time waiting, praying, meditating and contemplating to increase my faith that my mustard seed dries up and dies without bearing any fruit.

Or, I can be ready all the time to respond to the call of God, my master. Even when I think I may have done all, I should be ready and willing to do more.

And, more will come. People and situations will always appear that will need a response from this servant of God. The more I respond, the more opportunities for service will open up to me.

An interesting thing will happen as I am busy with this loving service. My mustard seed will sprout and grow without my even noticing it, bearing more mustard seeds that will spread around. So long as I concentrate upon service instead of my mustard seed faith, it will grow bigger than a sycamore.

Twenty–Eighth Sunday of the Year (A)

Ask someone who is not a Christian to describe the Church and its members. What words will you hear? Dedicated? Misled? Helpful? Fanatic? Generous? Strict? Honest? Rule–bound? Dependable? Superstitious? Mysterious? Judgmental? Hypocritical?—Many words, some more accurate than others.

Will you hear joyful? Good–humored? Fun to be with? Singing, dancing and playing?

Most Christians are probably marked by those things. But, they are not what come to the lips of outsiders when asked to describe us. In fact, would they come to the lips of most Christians?

If Jesus had not described the Kingdom of God as a wedding reception, then joy, good humor and fun need not be marks of the Christian. But, Jesus did describe the Kingdom that way.

If we are signs of the Kingdom, then perhaps we should look more like revelers than anything else. Sure, the world is a place of sin and suffering. But, it is also the gateway to the Kingdom that Jesus describes as a banquet to which everyone, bad as well as good, is invited.

So, must I become grimly determined to be happy, since it is my 'duty' as sign of the Kingdom? Actually, if I could recognize myself as grimly determined to be happy, the irony might help me develop a spark of humor that could make me a more cheerful believer in God who made monkeys, kittens, children and such a ridiculous creature as I.

Perhaps the reason I am not a reveling Christian is that I do not allow the Lord to show me not only what is in store for me, but what I have already.

Jesus has taught us to pray, 'Our Father'. If I paid more heed to those words, at the very least I would start giggling in embarrassment. 'Me—able to call God my daddy?!'

Then, there is the Eucharist. All it takes is a piece of bread and a sip of wine to put me in union with Christ's real presence in the world!

Is solemnity the appropriate response to that, or is a child opening presents on Christmas morning the better model of Eucharistic spirituality?

In the Eucharist, in the worship and service of the community of good and bad folks that Jesus invites to the banquet of God's Kingdom, I am offered a foretaste of heaven. How could I do other than rejoice?

And what of the joyous gifts God has given me— friends, family, children on the street, good art, good music, good books, good food? When I really look at all this, really give thanks for them, I rejoice in God's unbelievable generosity. What did I do to deserve all this?

Nothing. It's all a free gift. All this, and heaven too! Even my pains and confusion, my doubt and my death are embraced by God.

Is it any wonder that 'the source and summit of the Christian life' is called Eucharist, Thanksgiving?

So, how can I increase my wonder, my grateful joy in God's love? The first step is probably to open my eyes to the wonders around me and realize that they are all gifts for me from a Father who is madly in love with me.

The next step is probably to take it easy. The world and the Church will probably survive if for the next week I refrain from being either a dutiful Christian or feeling guilty because I am a shirker. As time allows (and there is usually time to do what we really want to do), let's take pleasant walks, listen to good music, read a good book, enjoy good food and drink, waste time with a friend.

And the best friend to waste time with is Jesus himself. Each day, set aside some quiet time (10 minutes or more) to just sit comfortably still. Don't worry if your thoughts wander. The Asian spiritual masters call that our monkey mind and disparage it, but what's wrong with monkeys, 'the craziest people'?

At the end of the time, tell a joke or funny story to Jesus. It need not be 'appropriate,' just funny. Tell it out loud. That may make you feel foolish, and that can be the beginning of merriment with the Lord.

We may as well get used to being merry with him, since he's inviting us to spend eternity at a joyous banquet with him.

Twenty–Eighth Sunday of the Year (B)

There is a guru in almost every area of human interest, offering enlightenment to those who want it. Even the life of the spirit is not exempt from the pursuit of self–improvement. Books purporting to give easy enlightenment for only the cost of a volume fill the shelves. Most of them are simple–minded; some are downright harmful.

There is a paradox in our age's pursuit of self–improvement. We are looking for easy success. If I read the right book, find the right physical or psychic trainer, attend the right seminar, watch the right video or meet the right person, I will be enlightened.

I need not make too much effort myself—the reading or the encounter should suffice. Lots of people watch exercise videos instead of taking a walk.

And yet, I am not totally irresponsible. I really do want to improve myself. I really want to be perfectly fit physically, emotionally, spiritually, socially and financially. I just want it to happen instantly, with a minimum of effort. I want to improve my life, but preferably without changing it.

The man who ran up to Jesus may have jogged out of our own time. He wanted to improve himself. 'Good teacher, what must I do to share in everlasting life?'

Perhaps Jesus had been recommended by whatever was the first–century equivalent of daytime television. So, possibly to reassure himself that he had really found the right guru, he called Jesus 'good'. Jesus told him not to overdo it, to keep a sense of perspective. 'Why do you call me good? No one is good but God alone.'

Then, Jesus told the man the way to live perfectly, the commandments of God. Now, the man was very earnest, so he could honestly say, 'Teacher, I have observed all these since my childhood'.

So, the Lord gave him a bit more advice, the absolutely foolproof way the man thought he was looking for. 'There is one thing more you must do.'

The man's eyes went wide, his head moved forward so that he would not miss a word of wisdom. 'Go and sell what you have and give to the poor; you will then have treasure in heaven. After that, come and follow me.'

'At these words, the man's face fell.'

The man earnestly sought the answer. So, Jesus gave it to him, inviting him to live without assurance, without guarantees. He told the man to give up all that he depended upon and start wandering the road to who-knows-where.

That was more than the man was willing to do.

The difficulty was that he wanted assurances. He called Jesus 'good' in order to assure himself he had made the right choice. However, the world offers no guarantees. Jesus challenged him to live in the real world, to give up all that might allow him to avoid the truth that there is no easy way to share in everlasting life. (And everlasting life is what we all really want; all our other searches are symptoms of that desire.)

So, the man went off, probably in search of someone who would give him more palatable advice.

I, too, earnestly desire everlasting life. I, too, fear living the kind of life that leads to it. I am like the disciples who 'were completely overwhelmed at this and exclaimed to one another, 'Then who can be saved?"

No matter how earnestly I desire it, I cannot bring myself to do what is necessary to achieve salvation. 'For mortals it is impossible, but not for God; for God all things are possible.' God will provide what I need. I must be willing to accept what I am offered. The man in today's Gospel could not. Can I?

Twenty–Eighth Sunday of the Year (C)

No matter what the modern diagnosis of the people called lepers in the Gospel might be, their ailment was at least uncomfortable, possibly painful and almost certainly disfiguring (which is how people knew them to be lepers).

As if that were not enough, lepers were considered a source of defilement as well as contagion and therefore were cast off from society, from the religious community and from their families. Many people (and maybe even themselves) thought their affliction was punishment for some evil they had done. They were miserable.

Misery loves company, and it is not choosey about the company it keeps. The ten, being outcasts for the same reason, formed a group. The more interesting thing is that they were able to overcome a different sort of prejudice. They were closed off from the world, but they were open minded. At least one of the group was a Samaritan.

Jews and Samaritans avoided each other. But in this group, Jew and Samaritan came together, stayed together and called on Jesus together. People who normally would have had nothing to do with each other shared life because the rest of the world had rejected them. They were a community.

There are other communities that are formed around a common affliction, a common experience of being different and outcast. Those communities often transcend the prejudices of the society around them, bringing together different races, cultures, social groups and genders. The Church is one example.

The Church is a group of lepers? Yes, in its essence it is a community of lepers, and to the extent that it is not, it is probably not true to its vocation. That does not mean that we all suffer from skin diseases. What it does mean is that we are disfigured by the sin of the world and by our own participation in that sinfulness.

Since we live in a world of people marred by sin, perhaps we don't notice the extent of our own marring. If we did, our parishes might be more like communities. If I realized how outcast I am from real life in Christ, I might be more open to others and more forgiving of them. My life would have room for the 'Samaritans'.

And those people whom I would ignore unless I accept how alike we are might teach me something. The Samaritan in the Gospel realized something the rest of his community did not. He realized that when all is said and done, the community's focus must not be upon itself and its needs, but upon Christ.

Jesus sent the lepers to the priests to be verified as clean and offer a sacrifice. On the way, they were healed. That undoubtedly made them joyful and grateful. So, they continued on their way to the temple, following Jesus' instructions.

The Samaritan would not have been with the others. The temple of the Jews was in Jerusalem; that of the Samaritans was at Mt Gerizim. So, they were going in different directions. The Samaritan was not with the crowd, and there was no reason to go along with what the crowd did. Someone who is 'different' can see things the rest of us miss. (Incidentally, that is why the men who run the Church must listen to women, the rich must listen to the poor, governments must listen to minorities, adults must listen to children etc.)

So, the Samaritan disobeyed and headed back to say 'Thank you'. He or she realized that the healing symbolized a relationship with Jesus that was more important than the cure. Verifying the cure was less important than doing what was right in that relationship, saying thanks.

We receive many gifts from God, but it is not the gifts nor even the recipient, but the Giver, upon whom we should focus. For Catholic Christians, the Eucharist is the 'source and summit of the Christian life,' and *Eucharist* literally means 'thanksgiving.'

We should be thankful to the ten lepers who teach us to be Church. Individually and as a body, we are not true to the image of God. If we can admit that, we can rely upon each other and serve each other in humility. We will exclude no one. We will be a community. That is what the group teaches us. One among that group goes further, and teaches us that our community must be alert to the gifts of God and grateful for them, a gratitude expressed in, above all, the chief prayer of thanksgiving, the Eucharist.

Twenty-Ninth Sunday of the Year (A)

The Pharisees and Herodians put a touchy political question to Jesus. The Pharisees desired an end to Roman rule in their homeland. The Herodians, on the other hand, were whole-hearted supporters of cooperation with Rome. Cooperation brought benefits; opposition would bring destruction.

By going to Jesus together, they are trying to catch him in a political web. If he were to answer with the Herodian position that the Romans were a legitimate authority, Jesus could be branded a traitor to his people. On the other hand, if he were to say that the Romans had no authority to collect taxes, he would be liable to arrest by them.

Jesus sidesteps the question by merely saying that since the money belongs to Caesar in the first place, they should give it back to him. Jesus does not answer the question of political legitimacy. He seems unconcerned with who's on top.

Yet, his question to the questioners contains an important message. 'Whose image is this and whose inscription?' Coins were decorated with the image of the ruler and an inscription giving his name and title.

The Pharisees and Herodians answer that the image is that of the Roman emperor Tiberius. So, Jesus tells them to 'give therefore to the emperor the things that are the emperor's and to God the things that are God's'.

The image of Tiberius determines what belongs to Tiberius. What, then, determines what belongs to God? Again, an image. Whatever bears the image of God belongs to God and should be given to God.

Humans have been described in various ways. But for God humankind is the image of God.

The image of God— that's you and me. But, not only that, it's also *them*.

You know who they are. The different people. Different races. Different religions. Different nations. Different gender. Different sexual orientation. Different political views. Different physical abilities. Different economic systems. Different moral (or immoral) behavior.

The past century has been one of unparalleled horror. And most of that horror has been caused by what may be the greatest of all sins against God the Creator. The sin has many names —racism, chauvinism, sexism, ageism, exploitation—but it is basically one sin, the denial of God's claim to have 'created humankind in his own image.'

Having denied that certain people are the image of God, we have sacrificed them to a variety of Caesars—individuals like Stalin, Hitler or Mao; ideologies like communism, manifest destiny or racial purity; nations in chauvinistic 'patriotism'; gender images as in abuse of women or 'gay bashing'; economic power as in exploitive capitalism and so many more.

Even my own little versions of such sin are horrible, because they deny the will of God in creation. Too often, my refusal to see others as the image of God prevents their own realization of their dignity.

We too often refuse to see that our differences—no matter how great they appear— are minor variations of an image, the image of God.

Is the image of God about looks? Of course not. Our variety tells us it cannot be about looks. It is about a vocation, a vocation to resemble God in loving others.

Perhaps the reason I forget that all women and men are the image of God is that I forget that I am made in that image, too. I am too self-centered to give much thought to being a creature, someone made by Another according to a particular model.

That model is Christ, the absolutely perfect image of God.

The more I become like Christ, the more I can see the image of God in myself and all other people and rejoice that our many differences still do not completely exhaust the possibilities of that image. We may mar it, but we cannot erase it. We may make it as glorious as an angel, yet we cannot express it fully.

We Christians have been shown Christ, the image of God, so that we can proclaim that image to all the world. In order to do so, we must clear away whatever mars that image in us. That includes all those sins that deny the creation of humanity—all men and women— in the image of God. It includes giving Caesar in all his manifestations no more than his little due.

Twenty–Ninth Sunday of the Year (B)

The Gospel challenges the world's values and its sinfulness. Few of us have any problem believing that. Our problem comes when we are reminded that the Gospel also challenges the Church's values and sinfulness.

The values of the Church are not solely the values of the Reign of God. They cannot be. After all, the Church is people like you and me. Much of my life is conducted without reference to Jesus. I look for the easy way out. I avoid situations where I might have to make my faith clear to others. I postpone the prayer, study and action I know I should do.

Add to me all the other Christians who have ever lived, and the sinfulness and weakness of the Church should not surprise us. The wonder is that the Holy Spirit is able to work through such a weak community.

James and John were fishermen who left their father, their boat and their nets to follow Jesus. In spite of the fact that they had seen his deeds and heard his teaching, they ask for special treatment. The other apostles are indignant at this. Their indignation, however, is not because James and John have asked for high places, but because they want those places for themselves.

In Mark's Gospel, those with a special role in the community, the Twelve, are the prime example of people seeking a special place. We can see the same situation today. Have you ever been to a Church function at which special places had not been set aside for clergy and Religious? Usually, it is others who have to search for places on their own.

When it comes to titles and forms of address, we do no better. We set all sorts of distinctions, primarily among those publicly committed to being servants. Our bishops wear headgear probably derived from that of Roman emperors. HL Mencken defined an archbishop as 'a Christian ecclesiastic of a rank superior to that attained by Christ'.

Some of our clergy are addressed as 'My Lord', 'Your Excellency', 'Your Eminence' and such. The 'servant of the servants of God' is addressed by his supposed masters as 'Your Holiness'. Even 'Brother,' 'Father' and 'Sister' become titles of rank and entitlement rather than of service.

This does not mean that popes are incapable of holiness, or that priests cannot be true fathers in faith or that Brothers and Sisters never walk with us on our journey. It does mean, however, that over time we have come to invest a lot—perhaps too much—in titles and status.

The temptation to status is not limited to one group in the Church, and no one is exempt. Each of us is tempted to want recognition for what we do, say, or think. It is natural.

Sometimes, being a Christian means going against doing what comes naturally. The whole world does what comes naturally, and that is why it needs salvation. Jesus requires that his followers live the reverse of what the world deems natural, that we be signs of that salvation. We must be super-natural, above nature.

Therefore, he tells the disciples that we must be slaves. We should be concerned with service rather than an egotistical pursuit of status, position or recognition.

Jesus himself is, of course, the prime example of this. The hymn that St. Paul quotes in his letter to the Philippians proclaims that Jesus, who 'though he was in the form of God, did not regard equality with God as something to be exploited, but emptied himself, taking the form of a slave.' He experienced our weakness and temptation. The difference is that he did not yield to them. He remained a servant to all.

Today, he warns us against a real danger to the fulfilment of our mission, the temptation to status, prestige and recognition. He reminds us that his way is the way of the Cross. His followers can expect only that as reward for their faithfulness to him.

Twenty–Ninth Sunday of the Year (C)

The story of the unjust judge is supposed to teach 'the necessity of praying always and not losing heart'. It does not achieve that very well for me, because of the image it presents of God, an unjust judge. So, let's ignore Jesus' purpose for a while and look at the parable from another perspective.

The judge's decision is forced by something the woman does that seems natural but is very precious, speaking out. She was able to go to the judge again and again to call upon him for her rights. It is easy to imagine her accosting him on the street and telling him off in front of his friends. She may have stood outside his home, shouting at him to decide her case. The judge was not worn down simply by whispered conversations or politely worded notes. The widow made his life miserable. He even feared that 'she will end by doing me violence.'

The widow's persistence earned the recognition of her rights. But, what if, like so many people in her day and ours, she had not been able to speak out? What if saying anything against a judge would have cost her liberty or life? It was her freedom to speak that made her able to force the judge to act. Her freedom of speech freed the judge.

Freed the judge? Until the judge acted, he was unjust. The woman was right to expect him to do his job and as long as he failed to do it, he was betraying his position and depriving society of the benefits of his work. The widow forced him to perform his duty. She did not turn him into a good man; he remained one who cared 'little for God or man', but at least he had done his job.

Those in power who fear what people—especially those who have been deprived—have to say deprive themselves of the opportunity to change their lives for the better—in other words, of the chance to repent.

This is not true merely in the political realm. The Church contains not a few leaders who prefer to not hear voices that call for greater faithfulness to the Gospel. Ultimately, they deprive themselves and the Church of the chance to improve.

The widow's persistence is the only answer. Speaking out for the right to those who do not want to hear, whether in society, the Church, our homes or wherever else, is the only cure.

Doing that takes courage and commitment. The widow had to be willing to face the judge, to shout in the streets, to become a pest. Her willingness brought what she was after, action by the judge.

Where can we find that sort of courage and commitment? Perhaps it is time to bring these reflections back to the issue that Jesus was talking about when he taught this parable, prayer.

There are many things that go on when we pray. We petition, we thank, we repent, we adore. More memorably put, the four kinds of prayer are 'Please', 'Thanks', 'Oops!' and 'Wow!' It is in regard to our prayers of petition, our requests to God, that Jesus tells us of 'the necessity of praying always and not losing heart.'

Prayers of petition make little sense intellectually. After all, God knows what we need without our asking. Yet, prayers of petition are the kind Jesus recommends most, and the Lord's Prayer itself is one of them. So, we should continue to offer them, regardless of our intellectual doubts.

Whatever else may be a result of prayers that tell God what to do (even if phrased so as to let us think we are making humble requests), we get experience in turning to the powerful and making our desires heard. We all have total freedom of speech when speaking to God. We can turn to God and demand, 'Give me justice!'

Perhaps our prayers of petition are, among other things, practice in finding the courage to speak. If we can do it with God, perhaps we can become more able to speak out with people, including the person we see in the mirror, saying, 'Give me justice!'

The model in today's Gospel is not God as the judge but the widow as us. We should pray, but our prayer should be practice for speaking out in the world to the unjust judges, the powerful who need to hear the call to justice.

Thirtieth Sunday of the Year (A)

The Sadducees were fundamentalists. They only believed what their Bible told them. Since that Bible did not mention resurrection, the Sadducees denied it. The Pharisees, on the other hand, were open to the development of hitherto unthought-of implications of their faith. So, they believed in resurrection.

When Jesus showed that he opposed the Sadducee position regarding resurrection, the Pharisees may have thought they had an ally. So, they gave him the dignity of asking him a typical rabbinical question about the Law.

There were 613 laws, and obviously some were more important than others. Some were keys to interpreting the others. But, which were the most important? Opinions varied. One could learn a lot about a rabbi by knowing which ones he considered 'heavy' or serious, and which 'light'.

The lawyer asked Jesus his opinion on what constituted the heaviest of the laws. Jesus answered as most Jews then and now would, with words from the *Shema*, the Jewish profession of faith. 'Hear, O Israel: the Lord is our God, the Lord alone. You shall love the Lord your God with all your heart, and with all your soul and with all your might.'

The second law that Jesus cites is another that would not have struck his hearers as unusual. Others had linked the two. 'You shall love your neighbor as yourself.'

However, there are two things that Jesus says that are new, things that tell us the basis of his faith, teaching and activity.

The first is that the two commandments are equivalent. Love of God is shown in love of neighbor and love of neighbor shows itself in love of God. When it comes to the most basic love, you can't have love of God without love of neighbor and you can't have love of neighbor without love of God.

How can this be? God is God, and people are people. How can loving one be loving the other? The answer is in the Incarnation of

Christ. When the Father sent the Son to be one of us, this world, every part of it and everyone in it, became the place where God is to be known and loved. God is not loved in the abstract, but in the concrete details of our daily lives.

But, if we grant that the way to love God is to love our neighbor, that still leaves a question. How is it possible to say that we can only love our neighbor by loving God? After all, there are atheists who love their neighbor without ever mentioning God.

Unbelievers may not know or accept a relationship with God, but they have one nonetheless, and their faithfulness to that relationship constitutes love of God and is, unbeknownst to themselves, the basis for their love of neighbor.

The second striking thing that Jesus says is that 'On these two commandments the whole law is based, and the prophets as well'. The only way to understand Scripture, the only way to understand any revelation of God, is by means of these two commandments.

This brings us back to the Sadducees. Their way to understand revelation was to look at words. They failed to look with love at God who is behind those words. Had they done so, they would have known that God's life-giving love cannot be overcome by death. Love is the way to heaven.

I cannot be absolutely sure that I am loving God. That is why Jesus' making love of God and love of neighbor equivalent is so wonderful. If I am loving my neighbor, I am loving God. And, if I fail to love my neighbor, whatever I may say, think or feel to the contrary, I am not loving God.

Love of neighbor (and therefore, love of God) is not mainly a matter of feelings. Feelings are part of it all, especially gratitude—that is the reason our celebration of love is called Eucharist, Thanksgiving. But love is first and foremost a decision to put oneself at the practical service of another.

The First Epistle of John asks us, 'How does God's love abide in anyone who has the world's goods and sees a brother or sister in need and yet refuses to help?'

The law of Christ is simple. Love. Love God by loving your neighbor. And your neighbor is anyone close enough to be loved, anyone in the world.

Thirtieth Sunday of the Year (B)

Until Bartimaeus cries, 'Jesus, Son of David, have pity on me!' the only others in Mark's Gospel who have called Jesus by any title that recognizes him as Messiah have been demons. Even the men and women who have journeyed with Jesus have not seen clearly enough to realize who he is.

The Gospels do not hesitate to put us followers of Jesus in a bad light. We, represented by the disciples, can be so dense that we miss something that evil demons know and that even a blind man can see. That is, that Jesus is the presence of the Reign of God among us.

Bartimaeus cries out without fear, unlike the demons. Instead, he cries out in hope and faith. Perhaps until the time comes that we really need him, we will never see him as he really is.

Sitting on the side of the road, hoping for some charity that would help him stay alive, Bartimaeus knew he needed help. Real help. His concerns were worth bringing to the Lord.

When Bartimaeus throws off his cloak and jumps up to meet Jesus, the Lord asks him a simple question: 'What do you want me to do for you?' It's the same question we heard him ask James and John last week. They gave the wrong answer. They asked for prestige, something no one really needs.

Bartimaeus gives the right answer: 'I want to see.' That's something we all need, to really see. But, what is it that we must see?

Strangely enough, I am blind about my needs. I think there are many things I need, but do I really need them? Or, do I need them as much as I think I do?

Jesus offers something that cannot be seen with eyes blinded by the offerings and enticements of this world. He offers the Reign of God.

There are times in my life when I realize my true need. Usually, such times come when I am fearful or in pain. Death is an obvious eye opener. So are the 'cousins of death,' the events that threaten what we think we need in this life. When we must face their loss, we realize how much we need the power of God. Then, we can cry out to Jesus, 'Son of David, Savior, have pity on me!' We finally see as well as Bartimaeus.

Then, an interesting thing happens. When Bartimaeus, after having declared who Jesus really is, asks to be given his sight, Jesus does nothing. He merely declares that Bartimaeus's faith has healed him already. The blind man's saying he wanted to see was all it took for him to really see. When he called Jesus 'Son of David', he was already seeing. The healing of his eyes was a symbol of the true sight, the true insight, that Bartimaeus already possessed.

That is very comforting to me, truly Good News. It is enough for me to turn to the Lord and call out in my pain, confusion and doubt. I do not need great understanding or even a faith that is alive and lively at all times. I can spend my life at the side of the road, wondering and hoping. As soon as I call, the Lord is there with me.

Bartimaeus has an interesting response to his healing. He appears to disobey the Lord. Jesus tells him, 'Be on your way!' Instead, Mark tells us, 'Immediately he received his sight and started to follow him up the road'. From now on, the way of Jesus is also the way of Bartimaeus.

Once he has recognized Jesus, once we have recognized Jesus, the only way is his way. We follow him to the cross and beyond to everlasting life.

Thirtieth Sunday of the Year (C)

We are living in the very early days of a phenomenon that will reshape Christianity. It has been called 'the coming of the Third Church', a phrase based upon the history of Christianity. The First Church, that of the early followers of Christ in the Eastern Mediterranean area, became the Second Church, one centered in Europe.

The Third Church has no center, because it is worldwide. For many in the Catholic Church, the first sign of the coming of this Church was the Second Vatican Council, when photos of the world's bishops showed, for the first time ever, large numbers of African, Asian, Latin American and Oceanian faces. In the half century since, the phenomenon has grown.

What is distinctive about this Church? Just as Christianity in the West has been deeply influenced by the religious traditions and cultures that pre-dated the preaching of the Gospel in Europe, so, too, are the Churches of Africa, Asia, Latin America and the Pacific shaped by the religions and cultures that preachers of the Gospel encountered there.

That means that ideas of God, of holiness, of worship, of community, of ministry—of everything that makes a Church—are gradually becoming different from what has been 'normal' for more than a millennium and a half. Cherished and time-honored traditions and formulations of faith are being called into question.

This is where the parable of the Pharisee and the tax collector has something to teach us. The Pharisee says, 'I give you thanks, O God, that I am not like the rest of men'. He goes on to say how he obeys all the rules that have been handed on to him. His boast is that he does what everyone everywhere has always felt should be done.

And he is right. Jesus does not accuse him of lying. He is a good man—he is, after all, trying to pray, and pray with gratitude to God. His problem is that he thinks his own way of appearing before God is the only way. He cannot conceive of someone like the tax collector having a valid relationship with God, even though the tax collector is in the same temple, engaged in the same activity, prayer.

The tax collector, on the other hand, seems barely a member of the People of God. His way of life makes him an outsider. He knows he is different, yet feels that he, too, has some right to be in the temple, praying as best he can.

The tax collector is an apt symbol of those Churches that are not only trying to find ways to believe within their own contexts, but will over time change the way all Christians believe.

Since Christians of the Third Church, especially in Asia, are often a powerless minority in their societies, they tend to view the role of the Church and its institutional forms from a different perspective from that of the West, where the Church is only now beginning to face the loss of political, moral, social and intellectual power.

As a religious minority, these Christians are faced with questions that Western Christians have not faced in centuries, if ever. As they struggle to find answers to new questions, some of those answers will appear inadequate to those who faced and answered different questions. Some will actually be inadequate, as inadequate as Western theological formulas and practices. Our theology of the Trinity, for example, may take now-unforeseen directions as Christians in largely Hindu India try to explain what we believe about God.

On various levels, the Churches of the West (which are still in charge) have had mixed reactions to the coming of the Third Church. Sometimes, there is rejoicing that the Holy Spirit is working in new ways in new places. Sometimes, there is fear of the unknown and a refusal to allow others to make their own mistakes as the West made and makes its own. Many times, the phenomenon is ignored.

Love it or fear it, a new Church is being born. It will take several lifetimes, but eventually the Church throughout the world will be different because of what is happening at the back of the temple. The future is there. It would be a shame to miss one of the biggest events in the history of Christianity because like the Pharisee we thought the way we are is the way to be.

Thirty–First Sunday of the Year (A)

The Church seems self–contradictory at times. For two millennia, we have proclaimed the words of Jesus that say that there should be no titles among his followers. Usually, the proclaimers are addressed as 'Reverend', 'Pastor', 'Father', 'My Lord', 'Your Excellency', 'Your Eminence', or 'Your Holiness'.

The problem for Jesus is a style of piety that attempts to substitute appearances for real faith and faithfulness. Jesus criticizes the scribes and Pharisees not because of what they teach, but because they are unwilling to practice what they preach. They like being teachers and being called 'Rabbi', but their religion is more show than substance.

We all know people who make it easy to know their religion. A Christian may wear a cross. A Jew might dress a certain way. A Muslim may have a calloused forehead from rubbing it against a prayer rug. These people are not necessarily hypocrites. They may be giving witness to their faith. They may not even be concerned with whether or not others notice, bearing the external marks of their religion as a way of reminding themselves of who they are and how they should behave.

'How they should behave' is the key. Behavior is what gives validity to the external signs of religious faith. When Jesus tells us to let our light shine, it is not supposed to be a spotlight on ourselves, but one that allows others to see our good works.

It is more important that God be praised than that I be praised. It is more important that men and women hear and see the Kingdom of Heaven proclaimed than it is that they notice who does the proclaiming.

Most of us know this and struggle against the sin of pride in our Christian life. However, even though we may recognize the danger in ourselves of ostentatious religiosity that draws attention to ourselves rather than God, we frequently fail to realize that we sometimes encourage and abet it in others.

The scribes and the Pharisees loved 'to have the place of honor at banquets and the best seats in the synagogues, and to be greeted with respect in the marketplaces, and to have people call them rabbi'. But, someone gave them those seats, someone greeted them, someone called them rabbi.

The practice continues. Clergy (and religious) receive special treatment more often than not, the sort of treatment one might give an imbecile demigod, one who is semi-divine, but incapable of handling the normal demands of life—like picking up a restaurant check.

And, like the scribes and Pharisees of old, many of the objects of special treatment rather like life on a pedestal. Some even expect such treatment. They themselves become the 'heavy burdens, hard to bear'.

There are others who try to climb down from the pedestal upon which people put them. But people try to shove them back. Why is that? Why do so many people want their clergy to be specially treated and insulated from life? Is it a bribe?

If so, what do people gain by their deference, their greetings, their special treatment toward religious leaders? In the case of the scribes and Pharisees, they sat 'on Moses' seat.' That is, they spoke with authority about the Law of God. Might people think similarly of Christian clergy?

In bribing the preachers, do we unconsciously hope to bribe God? Are we looking for some sort of payback from God? Or, perhaps we are hoping that by putting preachers outside the responsibilities of everyday life, we can keep them from applying the Word of God to those situations of our everyday lives where we'd rather not have to hear what God expects of us.

What shall we do? Most of us can do little about clergy who imitate the scribes and Pharisees. Settling for the material and emotional 'perks' of ministry and missing the spiritual excitement and rewards of real service is their self-inflicted punishment.

We can, however, see what we do to perpetuate the semi-deification of the clergy. For starters, imagine asking a bishop, priest or minister to help wash the dishes. If the thought startles you, ask why it does and if it should.

An aside: Many people wonder why some Churches address their clergy as 'Father' even though it is apparently forbidden in the Gospel.

The rationale is that the clergy are not being put on a par with God the Father, and so there is no violation of the Lord's mandate. The title is used by analogy with physical fatherhood, and even the most stringent fundamentalists call their male parent 'father.'

Baptism is a new birth, and in recognition of the fact that we are born anew, the one who is the usual instrument of this birth is addressed as a parent. So, the title declares something about all Christians rather than merely the one addressed.

Thirty–First Sunday of the Year (B)

The Jewish day begins at sundown, a custom the Church follows to some extent. For example, Sunday and major feasts start the evening before. That is the reason Catholics celebrate Sunday Mass on Saturday evening. In fact, there is no Saturday evening prayer or night prayer. Instead, we pray the first of two sets of Sunday evening and night prayers.

The reading in the first of those night prayers begins: 'Hear, O Israel! The Lord is our God, the Lord alone. You shall love the Lord your God with all your heart, and with all your soul, and with all your might.'

So, the first day of our week begins with 'the first of all the commandments'. It is not only that, however, it is the basic Jewish declaration of faith. Just as Christians can sum up their faith in the phrase 'Jesus Christ is Lord', Jews use these words to declare what they believe. So, it was natural that Jesus would cite them as the prime commandment. From childhood he had recited them daily. After all, he was a Jew.

That should be obvious to his followers. And yet, at many times throughout history followers of a Jew named Jesus have attacked his people. And our failures are not limited to the way we have treated Jews. We haven't treated each other any better. In fact, looking at the way I treat people around me would not be a good advertisement for Christianity. What has gone wrong in our lives?

The way to find out where I have gone wrong is to look at the commandments. And if I want to find the most basic wrong in my life, I should look to the most basic commandment.

The problem with the first commandment is that little word 'all'. I'm willing to love God in a half–hearted way. Church on Sunday and occasional prayers are fine. But, loving God with all my heart, all my soul, all my mind and all my strength? That doesn't leave much for me.

When I carry a grudge, it is with me all the time. Someone in love carries thoughts of the beloved around all the time. But what about my thoughts of God? The commandment says 'Keep these words that I am commanding you today in your heart'.

The fact is, I can go for days without giving God a single thought. Oh, I might think from time to time about religious duties and such. But of God? Even when I am in church, I seldom think of God.

Since I seldom think of God, I don't keep the first commandment. Because I don't keep the first commandment, I fall short in keeping the second, to love my neighbor as myself. Being a Christian is not about behaving toward others in a certain way. It is about having a special kind of relationship with God. All else follows from that.

How can I grow in that relationship? One way is to do what I do to build any relationship. Spend time together, something that is actually easy, since God is always with me. Talk. Carry on a conversation with God. I shouldn't bother calling it 'prayer'. That makes it seem too like a task or too exalted. Just talk. I should do it all day long, or at least when I remember to. I should say anything, even if it's just, 'God, I'm going to feed the goldfish now.'

Such an on-going conversation with God could gradually lead me to keeping love of God in my heart, soul, mind and strength. Then, I would be able to love my neighbor as God does.

Thirty–First Sunday of the Year (C)

Catholics do penance after confession. Penances usually take the form of prayer, but sometimes almsgiving, fasting, restitution or some activity to 'let the punishment fit the crime' are recommended by the confessor.

Originally, what we know as the sacrament of penance was performed publicly, and in some places only once in a lifetime. It was only used in the case of major sins that harmed the life of the community—adultery, apostasy and murder.

However, in Ireland and Wales in the fifth and sixth centuries, the practice arose of people meeting with someone to discuss their life as Christians. Manuals called 'penitentials' were compiled for these guides. The penitentials list sins and the appropriate penances for each. This practice spread and eventually evolved into the way we celebrate penance today.

Why do penance in the first place? Since penance follows absolution, it cannot be that we are buying God's forgiveness. Christ has already won our salvation. It is not for sale.

Zacchaeus was not looking for salvation. He was 'trying to see what Jesus was like.' Eventually he climbed a tree to get a glimpse. He got more than he expected.

Jesus answered Zacchaeus' curiosity by inviting himself to dinner. To eat with someone means to accept that person. Zacchaeus was a traitor, collecting taxes for the conquerors, and tax collectors became wealthy through grabbing all they could get over and above the actual high taxes. Yet Jesus says that Zacchaeus is accepted by God. No wonder the crowd started grumbling.

Zacchaeus was not the type to back down, however. He hadn't let the crowd keep him from seeing Jesus. His career was built on not caring about what others thought. So, he 'stood his ground' and spoke out.

He announced the penance he was willing to undergo in response to Jesus' forgiveness. It would mark the beginning of a new way of living. He would give half his possessions to the poor and repay fourfold anyone he had defrauded.

Jesus' response was, 'today salvation has come to this house'. Every member of Zacchaeus' household — his family, his servants and probably even his dog—had suffered because of his sinful life. Now, they would all be beneficiaries of his being forgiven. God's love was wide enough to include them all.

Like Zacchaeus, I am a sinner. Like Zacchaeus, I am loved by God. Like Zacchaeus, I am forgiven, a forgiveness I celebrate most explicitly in the sacrament of Penance.

Like Zacchaeus, I have caused damage that cannot be revoked. The world is marred by my sin. God will use that marring in building the Kingdom, but it is a marring nonetheless.

Healing is needed, just as repaying the defrauded taxpayers was. Penance is an attempt to aid that healing.

Conversion is needed. I must live freed from the power of sin. Penance is a first step in that new life.

Apology is needed. My sins have hurt others in ways I or even they might not realize. Penance is a way of apologizing.

Awe is needed. I should realize the weight of my sins and the even greater weight of God's forgiveness. Penance, which is usually somehow proportional to my sin, is a measure of the great love of God.

Thanksgiving is needed. Forgiveness is a gift. The Lord looks at me as he did at Zacchaeus and says, 'I want to be with you.' Penance is thanks for that gift.

We usually think of penances as something we do in connection with confession. However, in addition to priest-given penances, I should sometimes impose penances upon myself. I know my sins better than a priest does, and I probably know the appropriate ways to do penance for them.

It is important, though, to remember that penance is neither punishment nor the purchase price for forgiveness. So it should not be extreme. When in doubt, don't do it or consult with someone first.

And what forms should penance take? I can volunteer to help at a soup kitchen, or tutor a child or visit a shut-in. I can make contributions to individuals or organizations that need help. I can work at being a cheerful, cheering presence at home and in society. I can pray for those who have been touched by my sin. I can fix what I have broken. I can fast. With the forthright courage of Zacchaeus, I can proclaim to the world the love of God that 'saved a wretch like me.'

Thirty-Second Sunday of the Year (A)

The moral attached to today's parable does not suit the story. 'Keep awake therefore, for you know neither the day nor the hour.' The foolish virgins slept, but after all, so did the wise ones. Sleep was not what separated the wise from the fools.

In fact, it would be difficult to see much difference between the two groups until the bridegroom's arrival. They were probably dressed much alike. All of them carried lamps. All of them nodded off.

Just as the wise virgins did not seem at first sight to differ from the foolish, we Christians, generally speaking, do not at first sight seem to differ from our neighbors. We may not even be wiser than they.

The wise virgins were not vigilant, straining their eyes in the dark to see the approach of the bridegroom. Like the foolish virgins, they fell asleep. The difference was that the wise virgins were ready for what would come. They had their oil.

If we look like our neighbors, and do so much that is like what they do, is the difference that we have our oil ready? That the bridegroom might surprise us, but we are ready for action when he does?

Who is the bridegroom? At first glance, we might think that he is Christ, and that we must be ready to welcome his coming in our lives. But, while we must be ready to meet the Lord, this parable is not about Jesus himself, but about the kingdom of God. 'The kingdom of heaven will be like this,' is the way Jesus introduces the parable. He is speaking of the answer to our prayer, 'your kingdom come.'

What is the kingdom? We do not know the details, since it is beyond all that we can imagine or experience in our present life. But we have hints. From the Lord's Prayer, we know that it involves God's will being done, that all we need to sustain life will be given and that forgiveness will be shared. We know it is the reality of life beyond death. From the Eucharist, our deepest experience of the kingdom in this life, we know it means total communion with Christ in offering praise to the Father.

Ultimately, the kingdom is not something to know, but something to experience. So, we pray for that experience, for God to finish the work of salvation.

But, it's taking a long time. Even when we peer vigilantly into the darkness of our world, we don't always see signs that God is coming to us. At times, it seems as if God is not coming at all, that there might not even be a God to come. So we nap, nap without being ready for the kingdom's coming.

Because we do that, when the kingdom does come in its little precursors, we are not ready to recognize it, any more than a virgin with a burnt-out lamp can recognize the groom in the gloom.

Those little precursors are the acts of love and forgiveness that we see around us. They are the people who are not overcome by the darkness, but who carry on with faith and hope, confident that in God's good time they will know that they have been eternally embraced by God.

In order to see and greet these hints of the kingdom, we need to have oil prepared for our lamps. But what is the oil? Lamp oil helps us see in the dark. We need an oil that will enable us to see the coming of the kingdom in our dark world of sin, confusion, suffering and death.

The first way to acquire that oil is through prayer. By spending time becoming friends with God, we learn to recognize the divine footfalls in the darkness of our lives.

The Word of God in Scripture, especially as it is proclaimed in the community of those who wait and pray for the coming of the kingdom, is another source of oil.

Finally, we should keep in mind the words of the British writer George Orwell, 'To see what is in front of one's nose needs a constant struggle.' Signs of God's kingdom are all around us. If we remember that, we will see them and thus build up our supply of oil so that at any time, in any way that God comes to us, we will be ready.

Thirty–Second Sunday of the Year (B)

For most of us, our treasure is probably not measured with coin counting machines, but with clocks. Time is our treasure.

We add one day to the calendar every four years, but some of us feel that we should add an extra hour or two to each day. We are busy. There never seems to be enough time to do all we have to do, let alone all we want to do. We try to do several things at once, 'multi-tasking.'

Not only do I not have enough time, I have less and less of it every moment. I am running out of time. Sooner or later, I will have no more time. Each second brings me one second closer to the end.

Yes, indeed, time is a treasure for me. I have a limited amount of it, and I don't even know how little. I have a lifetime of duties and desires to fit into that rare time, yet it disappears even faster than a poor widow's savings.

Two thousand years ago, Jesus sat opposite the temple treasury to watch people being generous. Today, he might sit across the street from one of those big digital clocks that record the passing tenths of seconds in a blur.

For if I wish to imitate the widow's generosity today, I would not give a few coins or even a big bundle of bills. I would give time.

There is no shortage of uses to which my time could be put. There are lonely people who need someone who will give time to listen to their stories, to join them on strolls, to run errands for them. There are children who need the time of adults in order to learn, to make their dreams come true. These lonely people, these children, may even be in our own homes. Projects and programs to make our world better need the time of talented men and women.

All of that is obvious. Frankly, though, it is easier for me to give money. I do not have the time to spare. However, the widow in the Gospel did not have any money to spare, yet that did not stop her from giving it. How could she do that? After all, she needed those two coins in order to live. How could she do with her money treasure what I find so hard to do with my time treasure?

There are two answers: trust and gratitude. The woman was able to give all that she had because she trusted God. She knew that ultimately all that she had came from God and that no matter what she gave up, nothing would separate her from God's love. She might starve because of her generosity, but God's life-giving love would still embrace her.

This is very different from the scribes against whom Jesus speaks at the start of the Gospel passage, those bigwigs 'who like to parade around in their robes and accept marks of respect in public, front seats in the synagogues, and places of honor at banquets'. They are not willing to trust in God, to trust that in time they would be rewarded. They prefer to seek instant recognition from others now rather than from God later. With that attitude, they cannot risk their treasure, because what they have now is all they expect to have.

The woman knew better. She knew that what she had, her treasure of two coins, was nothing compared to what God offers. So, in gratitude she could give them up.

God offers me eternity. Can I, in gratitude, find ways to offer up my treasure of time?

Thirty–Second Sunday of the Year (C)

A common mistake is to assume that Christianity is about a way of life, a moral system. But before all else, a Christian life is a certain kind of relationship with God through, with and in Jesus Christ. Because we have that relationship, we try to live in a certain way. We know we are loved by God and try to return that love by loving God and all those whom God loves.

One characteristic of that relationship is that it is not ended by death. God's life-giving love is not overwhelmed by my sin and will not be overwhelmed by my death.

The Sadducees were not nonbelievers. In some ways they were more strict in their obedience to the Word of God than others, particularly the Pharisees. The Sadducees pointed out that the Torah, the first five books of the Bible, believed to have been revealed by God to Moses, does not mention anything about life beyond death, let alone resurrection.

For most of the history of the People of God between Moses and Jesus, there was no clear belief in an 'afterlife.' Since the Israelites were surrounded by people like the Egyptians and various Mesopotamian cultures that seemed obsessed with death and its aftermath, this is unusual. Perhaps they had to avoid the issue in order to get their priorities right. The little speculation they did was vague and certainly did not include resurrection until fairly close to the time of Jesus.

That gives us an important message. Faith is primarily about a relationship with God, not about 'getting to heaven' or anything else that smacks of 'what's in it for me'. Abraham, Sarah, Isaac, Jacob, Moses and the prophets were all people whose faith relied upon God's love for them and their love of God in return, not upon a hope of some form of life beyond death.

The Sadducees who face Jesus are a canny bunch. They use a debating device called the *reductio ad absurdum*, taking their opponent's apparently sensible position and drawing it to a conclusion that shows it to be nonsense right from the start.

They bait Jesus by asking about the case of a woman who married seven brothers. While extreme, it is not absolutely outside the realm of possibility. A widow was expected to marry her brother-in-law if she had not yet borne any children to carry on her husband's line. The Sadducees want to know whose wife she will be in the resurrection, or if she would have a husband for each day of the week. They figured that they had shown how ridiculous belief in resurrection could be.

Jesus refutes them by denying their premise, another debating device. He says they are wrong to presuppose that resurrection is experienced in terms of the life we know. Whatever resurrection means, it is not a rerun.

Jesus goes on to use the Torah to show that resurrection is in line with the ancient faith. The voice that spoke to Moses from the burning bush was that of 'the God of Abraham, the God of Isaac and the God of Jacob'. But, since God is 'God not of the dead, but of the living', then Abraham, Isaac and Jacob are alive.

Jesus affirms the resurrection of the dead, but he does not tell us what resurrection is like. He merely says it will not be like the life we know. There will, for example, be no marriage. But, what will there be? He does not say.

We use lots of images when we talk about resurrection: halos, harps, clouds, a banquet (Jesus himself uses this one). We do that because we need images in order to think, pray and preach about the resurrection. But, we know nothing and it appears we are not supposed to know anything. St. Paul has a rather strong answer for anyone who wonders, 'How are the dead raised? With what kind of body do they come?' His abrupt but clear answer: 'Fool!' Apparently, we waste time when we speculate upon the resurrection.

All we need know is that God loves us. In that love we live in spite of sin and evil and will live in spite of death. There are no human words or concepts to explain it. All we can confidently say is that it is far beyond what we can imagine or even hope. We're in for a big surprise.

Thirty-Third Sunday of the Year (A)

Since the talent was a sum beyond anyone's most avaricious dreams, Jesus seems to have liked using it in parables as a metaphor for the infinite love of God.

In today's parable, the master entrusts to his servants a total of eight talents, such an incredible amount that there could be no mistaking the master for anyone but God.

Fourteenth-century translations of Matthew introduced the word 'talent' into English, and within a century the word took on the meaning we usually give it today, an aptitude or ability.

So, a word that once awed people with the immeasurable generosity of God shifted focus. Now, when we hear the word talent, we think not of God, but of ourselves.

The shift was based upon the interpretation of the parable. The master gives each of his servants a sum of money to use. In the same way, God gives each of us life, abilities and opportunities. Some of us use them to increase the measure of God's glory, others do not.

Talents are a treasure, but a responsibility as well. The master is angry with the servant who buries what he received. True, he did not lose it, but he was entrusted with a talent in order to put it to work for the master, not to bury it.

In the Middle Ages, people recognized that the parable was not a once-upon-a-time story, but was about themselves. God has given each of us an inestimable treasure. Calling it by the parable's name for treasure made sense.

However, care is needed using the word. We tend to think of talents as personal possessions and reasons to be praised. We forget that they are not ours, but God's. Whatever talents I have are given to me in trust to be used on God's behalf. I did not make, or even choose, my talents. I merely have use of them.

Does that mean that my talents are insignificant? Of course not. They are gifts from God, a treasure beyond counting. I can use them, abuse them, or bury them as I choose. God will want an accounting, but will not force me to use them in any particular way.

We often speak of trusting God, but today, we are reminded that God trusts us as well. Treasures the world desperately needs have been given to me. No one else has the exact same combination of talents. My talents can be used to fulfill the will of God or even thwart it. Not a single talent is worth less than an uncountable treasure.

We usually consider certain things as talents and overlook others. Artistic or academic ability will get me recognized as talented. But, there are so many other talents that we fail to recognize or take for granted, failing to assign them near-infinite value.

No one is without talents. No matter how weak and fractured the image of God may seem in us, no matter how severe our disabilities, by the very fact that we have life, we know we have talents. Affection is a talent. Service is a talent. Generosity is a talent. The ability to evoke and facilitate the talents of others is a talent. Not talents in the Hollywood sense, but talents in the heaven sense.

In fact, our 'drawbacks' may be our most precious talents, just as Jesus' cross was his glorification. For some people, perhaps suffering is a share in Christ's talent.

We should cultivate an ability to recognize talents, our own and others'. When we do that, two things happen. The first is that in recognizing talents, we can better put them to use for God's kingdom. Overlooked talents may become buried talents. The second is that we begin to understand the generosity of God.

That leads us back to seeing that talent is more about God's generosity than about us. My talents are nothing to brag about any more than breathing is something to brag about. When I use them in a praiseworthy way, the praise may be given to me, but it really belongs to God.

And how do I use the talents God has given me in a praiseworthy way? They are entrusted to me for the sake of the world, as a sign of God's generosity, so I must use them for the sake of the world. It is to us as servants and for the sake of being servants that God gives us talents. Let us not bury them, but put them forth for the whole world.

Thirty-Third Sunday of the Year (B)

I once lived in a house that had a fig tree outside it. It never bore fruit. It certainly never gave me insights into God's Reign. This week's passage from Mark seems like that fig tree. It does not bear fruit. As one scholar wrote about the details of the passage: 'it is not easy to assess either the meaning they had for first-century Christians or the meaning that modern Christians are to draw from them.'

Yet, the first-century Christian who wrote this Gospel felt there was some meaning to be drawn from the passage as a whole, if not from the details. Ever since, the Church has continued to proclaim it, even though the details are either wrong or incomprehensible. Is there some meaning in this passage for our age as well?

In our lives there are events and situations that to us, at least, seem as overwhelmingly terrible as the sun dying or the stars falling. My plans and dreams fail. A relationship is betrayed. One I love suffers. I will die. Natural and man-made disasters destroy livelihoods and lives. War, injustice, violence, corruption, disease and poverty seem too powerful to be driven from our world. When these things strike home with me, the world may carry on, but so far as I am concerned, it may as well have ended.

Situations like that are invitations to despair. Why should I carry on? Why trust in God's love? Why risk loving or forgiving? A sort of spiritual and emotional paralysis can set in. I cease to desire, cease to pray, cease to hope. I may wish I were dead and gone. I may even be tempted to make that happen. The end of a world—whether it be the planet we live on, a society or nation, or my own private world—is a terrible thing.

Is there an alternative to despair? There is hope, of course, but how can I hope when my world is destroyed? Whether another tells me to 'cheer up,' or I say it to myself, I cannot do it. 'Cheer up' is useful advice for small disappointments, but it does not work when a world ends. I want something upon which I can either restore my world or build a new one.

Jesus tells us to learn from the way that seemingly dead trees send forth new shoots. There is something about the world God made that refuses to die forever. The flowing sap and tiny buds remind us that we may have to look hard to see signs of new life, but they are there.

Does that mean that after a bit of time I can expect my world to be reborn as it was, as I want it? Painful experience says 'No!' The fig tree is only a parable, not a paradigm or model.

So, what, then, is the evidence that can draw me from the edge of despair? Parables are nice, but my life is not a parable. It is real.

The most conclusive evidence is in something else that Jesus says. In the midst of destruction, the Son of Man comes. When he comes, 'he will send out the angels, and gather his elect from the four winds, from the ends of the earth to the ends of heaven.'

The risen Lord, the one who has gone through death to life, the conqueror of destruction, is with us when our world is destroyed. He does not reverse the destruction. Instead, his calling us to join him is compensation for all that we must endure. I may not think so, but I must at least have enough trust in the Lord to believe that he, having experienced the end of his world on the cross, knows better than I.

The Good News is not that God will make everything work out as we wish but that he is with us in a special way when it seems our world is ending.

Thirty-Third Sunday of the Year (C)

The people who pointed out the Jerusalem temple to Jesus were overawed. His disciples, after all, were country bumpkins in the big city. They had, perhaps, never seen such magnificence. Since as Jews it was their own temple, they were proud of it and wanted to show it off.

Jesus' prediction in response to their pride, 'the days will come when not one stone will be left upon another', was not quite accurate, or at least not yet. Some stones do remain standing on each other, the famous Western or Wailing Wall of the temple mount, a sort of embankment. But, the temple itself is gone without a trace. It was destroyed by a Roman army in the year 70.

Many of the world's great attractions are, like the Parthenon of Athens or the Roman Colosseum, ruins. Many things that were once great attractions no longer exist. The same will be true of our modern wonders. The Eiffel Tower, the Great Wall of China, St Peter's Basilica and all the rest of our constructions will disappear.

Even nature's wonders will wear out, wash out and be gone. The Himalayas and the Grand Canyon will disappear, as their equivalents and greater have disappeared in the past. Even the earth and our solar system have a fairly accurately predicted life span.

Can you name your great-grandmother's great-grandparents? Probably not. They are gone and forgotten. They were born, they lived, they loved and were loved, they achieved and they died. Will your great-grandchild's great-grandchild know your name, let alone your story?

When Jesus talked of a destruction of the temple so absolute that no sign of its having existed would remain, he could have been talking about anything or anybody. He could have been talking about me. As Isaac Watts's hymn *O God Our Help in Ages Past* puts it: 'Time, like an ever-rolling stream,/ Bears all its sons away;/ They fly forgotten, as a dream/ Dies at the opening day.'

Is that good news or bad? It certainly is hard to think of it as good news. I know that I must die sooner or later (the later the better). But, to enter oblivion, to have my existence, no matter how significant it appears to me or to others, make no difference to the world is more than I want to think about even though there are some things about my life that I am happy to know will disappear forever.

The thought of our disappearance is so distasteful that we seldom think of it. But, as the Church's year draws to an end, we should reflect on the fact that we, too, will draw to an end.

There can be various reactions to our eventual disappearance. The development of cloning techniques has some people thinking that they can somehow be re-created. They forget that cloned people—identical twins—already exist, and they are not the same person. Others live by the ancient dictum, 'Eat, drink and be merry, for tomorrow we die', a saying which goes back to the Bible. Since my time here is short, I may as well enjoy it and not worry about what others may think.

There is some truth in that last attitude, but in a sense that might not seem obvious at first. Thought of my death may indeed free me from worrying about what others think—in order to live a life dedicated to God. If I and the scoffers will all be gone one day, why worry about what they may think? Paradoxically, what terrifies some people can give courage to others.

For the one important fact that solely concentrating upon oblivion omits is God. God is not subject to disappearing, and neither is God's love. Those of us who know we are loved by God will disappear, but we are confident that something else awaits us. In the words of the funeral Mass, 'for your faithful, Lord, life is changed not ended.'

Do I really believe that? Well, sort of. But, there are always doubts. Faith is not certainty, it is a choice. I choose, because of the evidence I have experienced of God's loving help in ages past, to believe that love will not desert me. If I am right, I will know. If I am wrong, I will not know. And in that case, neither being wrong nor having lived at all will matter.

Thirty–Fourth or Last Sunday of the Year, Christ the King (A)

'If you look at a thing nine hundred and ninety–nine times, you are perfectly safe; if you look at it the thousandth time, you are in frightful danger of seeing it for the first time.'

That comment by GK Chesterton suits my experience with today's famous and popular passage about the final judgment.

I have looked at the text of today's Gospel many times. For a long time, I was 'perfectly safe' in doing so. I had it all figured out, and it was a comforting, though challenging message.

We will be judged by Christ on the basis of what we do to serve the poor, the weak, the lost and the lonely. Salvation would be bought by my doing things for others, obeying the law of service. Enough carrots peeled at the soup kitchen, enough visits to the sick, enough hoarseness at a demonstration, and I would be one of Christ's sheep.

But, I began to have some doubts. Perhaps I was nearing the eight hundredth look. The difficulty was the response of the righteous: 'Lord, when was it that we saw you hungry and gave you food, or thirsty and gave you something to drink? And when was it that we saw you a stranger and welcomed you, or naked and gave you clothing? And when was it that we saw you sick or in prison and visited you?'

I could understand why the goats might not recognize Jesus because of their spiritual blindness, but how could his own people not recognize him? How could those who followed him, heard his word, lived his law of love and shared his Eucharist not know him?

Obviously, I had to take another look. Finally, it occurred to me that the reason the righteous sheep did not recognize Christ was the fact that they had not known him in the first place. Matthew was not telling us about the judgment of Christians, but of non–Christians, those who serve Christ without knowing him by serving their neighbors. It was comforting to know that Christ would welcome those who did not believe in him.

What that meant for us Christians was that we had to be even more active, more busy earning our salvation because we have no excuse for not recognizing Christ in the 'least.' So, the judgment of Christians would be a sterner affair. We had to do even more serving or we would find ourselves lined up somewhere behind the goats.

For a hundred looks or so, that was enough.

But, I was getting beyond the nine hundredth look. Things began to look unfair toward us Christians. Unbelievers could get by with good deeds like a bunch of Boy Scouts. We seemed to need extraordinary deeds. What was the advantage of following Christ when salvation was easier for outsiders?

So, more thinking. I eventually realized that my salvation does not depend upon what I do, upon the prerequisites I meet, but upon the love of God. It is in meeting Christ and being embraced by him that we are saved. We do not do good in order to be saved, but because God's love is so overwhelming that we cannot help sharing it.

By now, my looks were getting into the nine hundred eighties or nineties, dangerous territory.

I began to wonder about those 'littlest ones'. Who are they? At first it seemed obvious. They are anyone who suffers hunger, thirst and all the other pains of humanity. Then, the nine hundred ninety-ninth look.

I realized that in Matthew's Gospel, 'little ones' has a very specific meaning. The little ones are not the weak and suffering. They are Christians, the followers of Jesus.

Does that mean that unbelievers are judged by what they do for us Christians? At first thought, that might be nice. That thought did not last long, however. If they serve us, it will be because we are so woebegone that they are moved to pity by us. One thousand!

We must be such followers of the crucified Jesus, giving our strength and even our lives for the sake of others that they will respond to us as the bystander at the crucifixion did who tried to give Jesus something to drink. When we become the little ones, they will serve Christ.

What does that mean for me and for the Church?

Maybe I should have stopped at the nine hundred ninety-ninth look.

Thirty–Fourth or Last Sunday of the Year, Christ the King (B)

Since the American and French revolutions of the eighteenth century, the number of countries with kings and queens has been shrinking. The number of countries where royalty actually rules has shrunk even faster.

Since kings and queens are becoming the stuff of fairy tales and legends, why celebrate a feast declaring Christ to be a king? Certainly Jesus was not a king. He had nothing to do with ruling anyone or anything.

Ironically, this feast was introduced long after kingship's decline began. It is surprisingly new. It is also surprisingly subversive of the way we use power in this world. It is very relevant.

The feast of Christ the King was introduced by Pope Pius XI in 1925, partly in response to the growth of totalitarian and super-nationalistic governments in Europe. Under those governments, dictators claimed and attempted to exercise absolute authority over the thoughts and actions of people. The state, embodied in the ruler or ruling party, was supreme. The duty of citizens was to serve the state. Such ideologies still rule huge portions of the world's people.

In the face of this, the Church declared that the only true ruler of people's minds and hearts is Christ. No earthly power can usurp his authority. No earthly power can treat men and women as tools of power or as 'resources' to be used and abused at the whim of governments or others. Today is the feast of human rights.

It is easy to point out examples in the political realm where individuals are trampled so that others may usurp God's rule over creation. But, it is not just politicians who must recognize that Christ is King.

Where else can we see situations in which the powerful 'lord it over' others? Where else are people used by their 'masters' and made to serve ends that are not appropriate to men and women who are children of God?

Certainly the business world falls into the trap. Some enterprises even talk openly about 'human resource management' as if people were merely assets like machinery or barrels of oil. There are obviously degrading situations of child labor, indentured labor (a fancy name for slavery), the sex trade and labor in health-and life-threatening conditions. But, men and women who sit at desks and make international phone calls can also be treated as if their sole value were in their usefulness to a corporation and its aims.

Even families are challenged by today's feast. We may not even have to leave our own homes to see families that suffer under the dominance of an absolute monarch who may masquerade as a father, a mother, an aunt, an uncle or even a child.

Even the Church is not immune. Some studies have shown that the basic reason men and women leave priesthood or religious life is the abuse of power by 'religious superiors'.

Today the Church says, 'No!' to all such tyrannies. There is only One who has any claim to absolute obedience. That one is Christ. Anyone else who claims such power is a usurper.

Why is that? Isn't it enough to grant that Christ is king in heaven? Isn't his claim to rule on earth 'meddling in internal affairs'? However, in the Incarnation Christ has become a citizen of the world. For this king, there are no foreign relations.

We are images and heirs of God. We are the princes and princesses of Christ the King. Each of us without exception has a dignity that cannot be subordinated to any person, ideology or worldly desire.

Today we say that Christ is King. He is not merely King of Heaven; he is King of the Universe, including you and me. When we say Christ is King, we say we belong to him and to no others. We cannot, then, be used or abused, since that is an attack upon his subjects and his sovereignty.

Thirty–Fourth or Last Sunday of the Year, Christ the King (C)

Through much of history, the wealthy and powerful have sat on chairs while the poor sat on stools, benches, overturned buckets or the ground.

The earliest chairs of which we know were made in ancient Egypt. The ancient Greeks and Romans had a kind of portable chair known as a *cathedra*. Since bishops sat on such chairs, the churches that contained them came to be called cathedrals. When the pope declares something to be infallibly the teaching of the Catholic Church, he is said to be speaking *ex cathedra*, from the cathedra. Catholics even speak figuratively of 'the throne of Peter' to mean the papacy, though the real Peter may never have sat on a chair in his life.

Chairs still show status. The one who runs a meeting or an organization is called the chairperson. Look in any office, and compare the chairs of the executives with those of their secretaries and receptionists. The higher the position, the bigger and better the chair.

We speak of a bishop's see or the Holy See, 'see' coming from a Latin word for a seat. Though priests usually stand to preach, they can, according to the liturgical rules, preach from a chair. Bishops frequently do so. Someone who tells people what to do and how to do it sits.

For a long time, the ruler has been the one who sits. When the ruler stands, no one else may remain seated. This is supposedly the origin of the custom of standing during the Hallelujah Chorus of Handel's oratorio, *Messiah*. When he first heard the music, King George II of Great Britain was supposedly so moved that he stood up. Some claim he was actually bored or had an itch. In any case, everyone else in the audience had to stand as well, and nearly 300 years later audiences around the world continue to do so.

The Feast of Christ the King shows another sort of king. This king is not seated; he is hanging on a cross. This king is not wearing fancy clothing; paintings and carvings to the contrary notwithstanding, he is stark naked. This king is not issuing orders; he is under a death sentence.

One more thing about this king—he is ours.

We are followers of a king who has no throne but the cross. What does that mean for us?

A throne-king, a chair-king, is comfortable. The cross-king has forsaken his own comfort for the sake of his people. His people, too, then, should not be concerned primarily with comfort. We should be willing to face inconvenience, discomfort and even death for the sake of others.

A throne-king, a chair-king, has servants and gives orders. The cross-king is humble. His people, too, then, should be servants of all, willing to help all other men and women.

A throne-king, a chair-king, is in his palace, waiting for his subjects to come to him. The cross-king is out where the world can see and hear him, where the world needs him. His people, too, should be in mission to the world, going wherever the Spirit calls them.

A throne-king, a chair-king, condemns. The cross-king forgives and promises a place in paradise to the thief. His people, too, should be forgiving, should be a sign of heaven's love for all.

A throne-king, a chair-king, sits in isolated majesty, surrounded by his courtiers. The cross king hangs between two thieves in front of a crowd of jeerers, soldiers and curious passers-by. His people, too, should be out among the outcasts and sinners, showing them the love of God.

A throne-king, a chair king, is, in spite of all his grandeur, merely one of us. The cross-king is one of us, but much more. He is God with us. His people should be signs of God to the world.

A throne-king, a chair-king, rules geography and the people in it for a few years. The cross-king is the ruler of heaven and of all men and women of all times and climes forever. His people should live as citizens of heaven, not of the world.

We Christians are courtiers of Christ the King, paying him our homage and allegiance. However, we sometimes forget whose subjects we are. We sometimes sit down.

I often become a chair-Christian. I forget where my King is to be found, so I am willing to limit my life of faith to sitting in church, sitting at home, sitting at work, sitting around as the world rushes by.

But, if I am a servant of the cross-king, of a king who does not sit, then I too must not be a sitter. I must show my loyalty to my king by moving among others as he did, as he does, not to receive homage or reward, but to serve.

Sacred Days:

Major Feasts

January 1: Mary, Mother of God

There are people who assume that there are two Churches, one Christian and the other Catholic, as if Catholics were not Christians.

One day, a man came to the parish I served in Japan. He said he had been puzzling out the difference and wanted to verify his conclusion. He said, 'The difference between Christianity and Catholicism is that Christians worship Jesus Christ and Catholics worship Mary, right?'

I'm not sure he believed my attempt to correct his misunderstanding. After all, there were two statues of Mary outside the church and another inside. Since the Church exists in order to proclaim Christ, we must be more careful about what messages our art, architecture and devotions convey to those with whom we hope to share our faith in the Lord.

Even we Catholics, if we're not careful, sometimes forget that anything we say of Mary is actually something we say about Christ and his people.

Today's feast, which though the doctrine is much older only replaced the Feast of the Circumcision in 1974, is one example.

From the earliest days of the Church, we have struggled to understand and express the reality of the Incarnation. If Jesus be God, can he be fully human? If he be as human as I am, can he be God? In different times and places, and even on different days of my own life, we tend to go back and forth on the issue, sometimes emphasizing the Lord's divinity while forgetting his humanity and at other times emphasizing his humanity while forgetting his divinity. Keeping both truths in mind and heart is difficult.

When the bishops at the Council of Ephesus in 431 declared that Mary is the mother of God, they were correcting the idea that because Christ is God, he could not be a real human being. The council fathers used the one absolutely human trait—we all have mothers—to affirm that Jesus whom we worship as God is a real human being. After all, he has a mom. They were talking about Jesus, not Mary.

(The other side of the conundrum, whether the man Jesus is really God, was the subject of other early ecumenical councils, notably Nicea in 325 and Constantinople in 381.)

But, today's feast is not just about a fifth-century theological dispute. Any feast is about us as well because in our baptism we are united with Christ.

We honor Mary not because she is some near-goddess. We honor her because she wholeheartedly did something we all are called to do. She said 'Yes'.

When God's messenger told her that God had a task, a vocation, for her, Mary responded, 'Let it be done to me as you say.' Her yes-saying made her the mother of God and a model of what the Church is. We are the community of those who in our Baptism have said 'Yes'.

Each of us is presented with the same vocation as Mary. God says to you and to me, 'Make my Son present in the world. Forgive sins. Bring healing. Live with faith that my love is stronger than your death. By word and deed, assure the world of my love.'

And, what answer do we give? Well, in our baptism, we have given the same answer as Mary: 'Yes, Father, I will give your Son a human body, my human body, so that the world might know you.'

The humanity of Christ will be shown today in your humanity, in our humanity. The divinity of Christ will be shown today in his working through you, through me. Today, right here, we are called to be what the Council of Ephesus said of Mary. Today and every day, we are the mothers of God, we are the fathers of God.

February 2: Presentation

The stories of the infancy and childhood of Jesus in the Gospels of Matthew and Luke are not mere once-upon-a-time tales. The evangelists expected those stories to tell something essential about life and faith. The stories said something important twenty centuries ago and they still do.

So, what does the presentation of the infant Jesus in the Jerusalem temple tell us today?

The basic message is a call to a sort of atheism. Luke is showing us that Christians must not believe in any sort of god the rest of the world believes. In fact, real Christianity does not believe in the sort of god some unreflective Christians seem to believe in.

We like our gods to be powerful. Perhaps we feel that if our deity is powerful, then we might share some of that power. While sometimes we actually call those powerful deities 'god', more often than not, we don't use that name. But, from the way we treat them, the amount of time we spend on them, the mental and emotional energy we devote to them and the ways in which we shape our ideas and actions around them show them to be our gods, no matter what we call them.

For some people their god may take the form of money, or a nation, or an economic system, or social achievement, or race, or religion or family. For some people who consider themselves 'good Catholics', it may be a particular form of piety or Church structure. In all these cases, devotees hope to gain special advantages by their devotion.

And the message of the Gospel in Luke's account of the presentation of Jesus in the temple is: become an atheist, renounce your false gods and believe in the one true God revealed in Jesus.

The prophet Malachi says, 'And suddenly there will come to the temple the Lord whom you seek'. The temple is the place where people expect to meet God. Malachi goes on to say that the Lord's coming will be like a refiner's fire, powerful and painful. The Responsorial

Psalm speaks of the entry of the Lord who is 'strong and mighty, the Lord, mighty in battle'.

But, Luke tells us that when the Lord actually does appear in the temple, it is as a powerless baby. And poor. Though it was not, in fact, a requirement for Mary and Joseph to present the child in the temple, for those who chose to do so, the usual offering was a lamb and a dove. Families who could not afford a lamb offered a pair of doves instead, as did the parents of Jesus. So, the Lord comes to his temple poor, powerless and human.

That is not how we expect our gods to be. It takes a special kind of insight to see God present in a poor baby. Or in a grown man hanging on a cross. Simeon had that kind of wisdom. His prayer, which is used every evening as part of the Church's night prayer (and which is worth memorizing for our personal nightly use), praises God because his 'eyes have seen' God's saving presence. In a crowd of people, many of them carrying babies, Simeon could recognize God hidden in a baby blanket.

How could he do that? Luke describes Simeon as a man who was 'righteous and devout, awaiting the consolation of Israel'. In other words, Simeon really believed that God would act to bring consolation to the world's pain and that in order to recognize that action one must be attuned to recognize it by a life of service and prayer.

In his praise, Simeon proclaims the meaning of the new thing God is doing, 'salvation prepared in the sight of all the peoples, a light for revelation to the Gentiles'. The coming of Jesus to the Jewish temple is the beginning of a new age. From now on, all peoples can see more clearly than ever before that God's love is meant for all the world.

We must be imitators of Simeon, recognizing the Lord at work in the world in places and ways that others might miss. In order to do that, we must, like Simeon in the temple, be where the Lord is likely to make his presence known. As in the temple, that presence will be known in the hustle and bustle of everyday life. When we are attentive there, we will see the coming of the Lord, not in power, but in weakness, poverty and love. And then, like Simeon and Anna we must proclaim what we have seen.

June 24: Birth of John the Baptist

The story of the birth of John the Baptist is not much more remarkable than the birth of any of us. True, the story as presented in Luke's Gospel has some details that did not appear in my birth or yours, but the main elements are the same for us as for him.

First, John had a mother and father, as do we all. His parents were religious people, something that is true of many of us. They had friends who celebrated their child's birth with them, something that likely happened at our own births. They came from a culture that had certain customs when it came to naming children.

In the case of Zechariah and Elizabeth, the custom was to name a first-born boy after his grandfather. Coincidently, in my own cultural background the same is common, and so I am named after my grandfathers. But, it is more common among my relatives for parents to choose other names. In John the Baptist's case, people wanted to name him after his own father instead of his grandfather, but his parents chose a totally different name.

The similarities between ourselves and John are not limited to what the Gospel says about his birth. John grew up, as we do. He found a vocation and lived it out. So do we. He was religious, as are many of us. He suffered because of the sin and stupidity of others, as we all have. And he died, as we all will.

The world John lived in was also much like ours. Of course, many things have changed in two thousand years, especially in terms of technology. But, many things are the same. People still love and hate. People still hope and fear. People still bring joy and sorrow into each others' lives. People still harm and help one another. People still wonder about God.

The details are, of course, different—sometimes very different—but similarities between us and John are many.

God was part of John's life. He knew that wherever his life might lead him, whether to the desert of Judea or the palace of Herod, so long as he was faithful to God, all would be well, even if it meant death.

That raises a question for me: Am I similar to John in this as well? Is God really a part of my life?

Of course, God is a part of everyone's life whether we know it or not or admit it or not. But, how aware of that am I from day to day? Is my faith simply a Sunday-morning and nighttime-prayers matter, or do I live as much as possible as someone who knows I am not alone?

If I were to do so, there would be other similarities between me and John.

The first is that like John who recognized Jesus in the crowd that came to be baptized, I would be able to recognize the Lord at work in the world around me.

The second is that I would devote myself to pointing the Lord out to others. Through my deeds and words, I would show them what it means to know 'the Lamb of God who takes away the sins of the world', what it means to know that God is among us.

Yet another is that I would point out when and how our world, how we ourselves, act as if God were not among us. We would remind ourselves that the Lamb of God came to take away the sins of the world because there is, in fact, sin in the world, in our lives.

That might lead to another similarity to John, rejection. Such rejection cost John his life. We may not be brought to that extreme, but we can be sure that if we challenge a world that tries to live without the justice of God, we will pay some price.

And if we live that way it shall lead to a final similarity with John. He is, after all, Saint John, one whose faithfulness to God was matched by God's faithfulness to him. We are born like John. We can live like John. We will die like John. We can be saints like John.

June 29: Peter and Paul

Simon Peter was a Galilean fisherman. Whatever schooling he had was probably limited to learning to read the Bible at his local synagogue.

The evidence we have in the Gospels indicates that he was an impulsive man. He also may not have been as quick of wit as he was of word and action. The Gospels certainly give the impression that he could be pretty dense at times. Perhaps that is one of the reasons Jesus nicknamed him 'Kephas' or 'Peter' (rock).

He was, however, a man whom Jesus could trust to lead the community, a steady rock in the turbulent times ahead for the new Church. Apparently, the other disciples were willing to look upon him as a leader.

After Pentecost, Peter preached in Jerusalem and to the Jewish people. He had some contact with non-Jewish believers in Jesus, but seems to have been ambivalent about how to treat them. Eventually he led the Jerusalem community to accept the outsiders.

Tradition says that he died a martyr on a cross in Rome. Was he living and working among the large Jewish community there, or had he moved beyond them?

Paul was more cosmopolitan from the start, a sophisticate. He came from the Jewish community outside Israel, from the city of Tarsus in present day Turkey, and would have spent his whole life in contact with nonbelievers as well as fellow Jews. He was a Roman citizen, educated in Greek as well as Hebrew.

Unlike Peter, who got a nickname from Jesus, Saul/Paul came by his two names naturally. Like other Jews in the Empire who lived in a non-Jewish milieu, he had a Jewish name and another name for use in Greek or Latin.

Since he spoke Greek, the day-to-day language of the Roman Empire, he could travel around with confidence. He was a trained theologian with connections to the religious establishment in Jerusalem. Yet, he was able to share his faith with Gentiles.

In another difference from Peter, Paul seems to have been hard to get along with. Rather than considering him a leader, most of his companions seem to have left his company after disagreements.

Tradition has him, like Peter, dying in Rome. Since he was a citizen, he would probably have been beheaded rather than crucified.

These two different men, from different backgrounds, living and working in different societies, spent their lives for one thing, the proclamation of the risen Lord Jesus.

It was not an easy vocation. At times, it meant going against the religious and political societies in which they lived. At all times, it meant dedicating themselves wholeheartedly to sharing with their neighbors, whether Jew or Gentile, the good news of Jesus Christ.

We Christians are a varied group. We come from many different nations. We have many different ideas about politics, economics, history and even theology. We have many different hopes and aspirations as well as fears and doubts.

What we have in common with each other as well as with Peter and Paul and all the saints is our faith that Jesus is risen from the dead and offers us a new life that transcends the limits of this world.

We share with Peter and Paul the vocation to proclaim the good news to all the world. Like Peter and Paul, we should not be held back by either the communities in which we live, the cultures in which we were raised or the larger political and social systems of the world.

We do not know, we never know, what the future will bring. What we do know is that God's love is real and that as Christians we are sent into the world to proclaim that good news.

Systems, societies, cultures, nations and such are important, but ultimately our chief vocation is independent of them. Peter and Paul lived and used their different backgrounds and talents to preach their faith in the real world in which they lived.

So can we. So must we. So will we.

August 6: Transfiguration

The Gospel writers intended to show Jesus in his glory as a sign of his ultimate triumph over death, but the Church has traditionally also believed that the story of the Transfiguration is the story of us as well. Our destiny is glory and peace, both on earth and in heaven. For, just as the journey of Jesus to Jerusalem and the Cross would be the road to his glorification, our own destiny is glory. Just as he was glorified in his humanity, so may we be.

Is it coincidental or providential that the Gospel reading for the feast of the Transfiguration mentions bright light, saying that Jesus and his garments became as bright as the sun?

Besides being a feast of the Church, August 6 is a terrible anniversary in human history. On the morning of August 6, 1945, an atomic bomb exploded over Hiroshima, Japan. Eyewitnesses to nuclear explosions describe them, too, as a light as bright as the sun, though followed by darkness as a cloud of smoke, dust and debris covers the sky.

The Hiroshima bombing was the first-ever use of an atomic weapon, and marked the beginning of decades of terror as various nations have joined the so-called 'nuclear club' and others work to develop their own nuclear weapons.

Every one of us has been contaminated as nuclear tests and accidents have polluted our land, air, food, water and bodies with radioactivity. We all suffer as incredible amounts of talent and treasure are wasted on weapons of mass destruction instead of being used to build solutions to poverty, ignorance, disease, environmental degradation, fear and hatred.

Yet, violence seems to be a part of our make-up. Whether we be children hitting one another, or nations warring against each other, or criminals attacking rivals or terrorists attacking strangers, humankind can legitimately be described as a violent species. Much of what passes for 'entertainment' is a glorification of violence. And, even though we use the verb 'play' to describe them, many of our sports and the attitudes of players and spectators are anything but playful.

Glorified children of God or demonic murderers—which are we? Are we both? The title 'Killer Angels' captures our plight.

Might the light of the transfiguration of Jesus before Peter, James and John offer us something to answer the brightness that ends in darkness for our violence-clouded world?

We must not forget that the one who was glorified on the mountain was the man Jesus. If it could happen to him, it could happen to us. Since God has created us for glory, living as glory-bound daughters and sons of God should be easy for us. It is what we were made for. Yet, one of the mystifying things about us is that we devote so much energy to being what we are not.

Turning away from our brothers and sisters, turning away from God, turning away from our true selves must require extra effort. Yet, we (or to be more specific, I) continue to live the difficult way, the way of self-centeredness, the way of selfishness, the way of competition, the way of violence.

The atomic bombing shows what we can be. The transfiguration of Jesus and this feast show us how we should be. If we could accept our destiny and live true to it, what a difference it would make for us and the world!

So, what would living toward glory look like? The life of Jesus, the transfigured one, shows us. Such a life would be at the disposal of others, the life of a servant. It would be a life in which violence toward others, including the quiet violence of using others for our own ends, would be unthinkable. It would be a life of confidence that God's love is stronger than anything we might fear, even death.

Can we live such a life? One man has, and his living it has opened the way to glory for us all.

August 6 shines a bright light on our possibilities both as a human race and as individuals. As individuals, nations and a world, we must choose the path of glory lest we go down the path of destruction.

August 15: Assumption

Every feast of the Church, no matter what its name, is ultimately a celebration of what God has done in Jesus Christ. The Assumption is such a feast, an encouraging reminder of what Christ has done for us and a challenge to live as what we have become through Baptism.

At first glance, the feast appears to be about Mary, and how at her death she was taken into the fullness of life promised in the Resurrection of Christ. If that were all there is to the feast, there would not be much reason for us to celebrate it, especially not to the point of making it one of the few feasts of the Church that is celebrated even when it falls on a Sunday.

We try to be followers of Jesus, living, loving and forgiving as he did. But, we seem to fall short more often than not. When we are discouraged by the weakness of our faith or by our sins, we can be tempted to think that it was easy for Jesus to follow the will of the Father because, after all, he is God the Son. And so, we make excuses for ourselves instead of continuing to provide a model of Christ for the world. That's a dangerous comfort.

The danger is that it can let us assume that the Incarnation was not real, that the Lord was not fully human, with all the temptations and weaknesses that we have. We can begin to think that he was playacting at being a man.

Once we start thinking that way, it is a short step to thinking that our union with him in Baptism is somehow or other incomplete rather than total. The doctrine and feast of the Assumption of Mary are an antidote to that sort of thinking.

When I am tempted to say, 'Well, Jesus was God, so he could love', or 'Jesus is in heaven, but I'm not good enough to join him', the Assumption reminds us that we are wrong. The Assumption deprives us of the illusion that we cannot and need not be signs of Christ to the world. After all, Mary was not God incarnate. She was a woman, as completely human as any other woman or, for that matter, any man.

As completely human as Jesus. And it is as a human that she shares fully in the glory of Christ crucified and risen.

Like Mary, we are completely human. What God has done for her is something God can do, and in fact has done for us. In our baptism, we are united with the glorified Christ, the crucified and risen. This feast, then, is not simply about Mary, it is about us. The Assumption of Mary shows us our own destiny.

And, on this feast the Gospel reading about Mary's visit to her relative Elizabeth shows us the vocation we share with Mary. Luke tells us that after the angel's announcement of her being chosen to bear Christ the first thing Mary did was to travel in haste to her relative Elizabeth. She brought Christ.

We, too, are Christ bearers, and we, too, are sent to bring Christ to our relatives. In other words, to every person who, like us, is a son or daughter of God. They are our sisters and brothers; they are everyone. And, like Mary hastening to Elizabeth, we must recognize that our mission is urgent. Mary hastened to Elizabeth because the older woman also had an important role to play in God's plan for the world. God has dreams, plans and hopes for everyone in the world. And so, like Mary, we go to them to help them know and live their vocations.

When we have done that, we will know like Mary that we will be called blessed because of the great things God does through us. The Magnificat, Mary's prayer at Elizabeth's home, will become our own prayer.

September 14: Triumph of the Cross

Today's feast goes by two names: the Exaltation of the Cross and the Triumph of the Cross.

Triumph? Wasn't Jesus defeated on that Friday afternoon some 2000 years ago? Wasn't it he who suffered torture and execution, abandoned by his followers while his enemies stood by jeering? Wasn't it his adversaries who went home for dinner while he was carried to a tomb?

Yes, Jesus was defeated on the cross. It is nonsense to make believe otherwise. So, why do we call it a triumph? The Jewish leaders triumphed, the Roman administrators triumphed, evil triumphed. Are we making believe the crucifixion of Jesus was not real? Are we going to re-define the word 'triumph' to mean 'whatever happens, good or ill, to me or someone I like'?

That might be a comforting re-definition. After all, we all have our share of what in honesty can only be called defeats. We all enter situations filled with great expectations, but the end is often different. From losing games as a child (or adult) to bad grades, flubbed projects, betrayed hopes, broken marriages, wasting disease and final death, our lives are full of events and situations that it would be nice to be able to call triumphs. Failure is so much a part of our lives that the writer Robert Louis Stevenson said, 'our business in this life is not to succeed, but to continue to fail, in good spirits.'

Is that the best we can manage—a stiff upper lip, 'let's sing on the Titanic' approach to life? I have spent much of my life fooling myself, but I doubt I could carry on that masquerade for long. Defeat is defeat. It hurts. No amount of good spirits will make it otherwise.

Perhaps this feast calls us to take a new look at what we consider to be success and failure. We know that the cross of Jesus was real defeat, but at the same time, we proclaim it as triumph. Could the same be true for other defeats, our own defeats, as well?

How might failure be a triumph in my life? The Japanese have a saying, *nana korobi, ya oki,* 'fall down seven times, get up eight.'

Failure can be a spur to increased efforts that may eventually lead to triumph of some sort. But what if the eighth, ninth and tenth efforts are all failures? Effort is no guarantee of success.

Another Japanese saying is, *kanashii toki no kami danomi*, 'calling on the gods when one is suffering.' Failure can move me to prayer, to reliance upon God. When all my efforts have failed, when it seems there is no hope, when my dreams are nailed to a cross, then I might turn to God. In that sense, defeat becomes victory, because anything that draws me to God is good.

This is true, but not inevitable. We've all seen people who've been driven from God and others by defeat. The anguish parents feel when they see their child suffer may draw them to prayer. It can also drive them to hate God. So, whatever triumph there is in the cross is not to be found in possible minor victories over suffering.

There must be something about the cross itself that is triumph. Its triumph does not come later, after the suffering is over. The Church has always said it was the cross of Jesus, not his empty tomb, that saves.

One of the key messages of the biblical prophets is that God suffers. God is heartbroken over what people do to one another and to themselves when they abandon true faith. When God came among us, the suffering of God and the suffering of humanity were united in Jesus Christ. To suffer is to be like God. The crosses we bear do not merely bring us close to God, they make us like God, the God who suffers.

Does that mean that suffering is good and we should seek it out for ourselves and not strive to ease it for others? No, suffering is not God's will for the world. The suffering of the world breaks God's heart. If for no other reason than out of sympathy for God, we must put an end to suffering.

The triumph of the cross is that, though suffering is always with us and may make us think we are far from God, when we suffer, we share in the life of God. Defeat, then, is victory. The holy Cross triumphs!

November 1: All Saints

Usually, we think of a saint as someone with superhuman endurance in trials, someone who exceeds all we could ever reach in terms of sanctity, someone whom we should strive to emulate with little likelihood of success.

In some cases, we also consider saints to be wonder workers who either when alive or since dead work miracles for us, from finding our car keys to curing cancer. Finally, we say a saint is someone whom the leaders of the Church have declared, canonized, to be a saint.

On this feast when we consider all the saints rather than focusing on one or the other, what do we see? We do, indeed, see examples of heroic faith like Polycarp and Thomas More and the martyr children who sang hymns on their crosses in Japan. We see extraordinary learning and piety as in Thomas Aquinas, Theresa of Avila and Catherine of Siena.

But, is this all we see? We also see Edward the Confessor, canonized by command of the Norman rulers of England to mollify their Anglo–Saxon subjects after Edward failed in his vocation as king and opened the way to the Norman conquest. We see Joan of Arc leading an army in a procession of murder and pillage across the French countryside for the sake of the Kingdom, not of God, but of Charles VII. We see Vincent Ferrer preaching at Jews and then consigning to the torturers those who refused his exhortation to be baptized.

The American satirist Ambrose Bierce was not all wrong when he defined a saint as 'A dead sinner revised and edited.'

To be told to honor this, that or the other saint?—no problem. But to honor *all* saints? That's a bit much to swallow.

Is a saint someone who does extraordinary things for the sake of God? Sometimes, but not always. Might then, a saint be someone in whom God does extraordinary things? That makes a big difference.

Sanctity is not something people do, it is something God does. God works through the holy and the hateful, the wise and the witless, the attractive and the abhorrent. They do not even have to agree to God's using them—the fact that the infants murdered by Herod have a feast of their own reminds us of that.

And what does God do with that motley crew? One thing is to show us that in every age, in every circumstance, God continues to work in the world. God's love and the work of the Holy Spirit were not limited to some Golden Age when men and women were superhuman. Nor were they limited to the lifetime of Jesus.

In that case, remembering all saints becomes a reminder that God can be, and in fact is at work in the time, place and life which I live.

That is the reason that in the early days of the Church, 'saints' were not people separated out from among the rest of Christians. All Christians were called saints.

So, am I one among all the saints? Well, I suppose if some of the other people who have been declared saints can be, I guess I can fit in somehow or other.

But, it's an uncomfortable thought, thinking of myself as a saint. I don't match up to the good ones, and I want nothing to do with the bad ones, in part because I don't want to admit that I fit into their company better than I wish. Perhaps that is a reason we abandoned the practice of calling ourselves saints.

As a Christian, I have been chosen by God to be a herald of God's love. I may do that by word or deed, or I may only show it by being a sign of how tolerant God is in putting up with me, with having the divine message depend upon such as me.

One of the admonitions I heard uncomfortably often in my adolescence was, 'Act your age.' Perhaps I have a similar admonition given to me in the reminder today that all saints includes me. 'Act your sainthood.'

In my baptismal union with Christ, I am one of the saints. Knowing that, perhaps I can make better choices about the sort of saint I will be.

November 2: All Souls

In many places, the feast of All Souls is known as some variation of 'The Day of the Dead'. People recall and pray for their deceased family members and friends, sometimes visiting their tombs and graves.

Less often do we recall that we ourselves are certainly on the way to being among the departed. It is estimated that more than 100 billion people, 93 percent of us, have already died, and the billions alive today and yet to be born will join them. The death rate for humanity is, was and always will be one hundred percent, and that includes me and you

So, the feast of All Souls tells us something about ourselves.

On November 1, we celebrated All Saints Day, reminding ourselves that saints are not simply people who have churches named after them and feast days on the Church's calendar. St. Paul uses the word saint as a title for all those who would later be known as Christians. In our baptism, we are united with Christ and with the People of God, and are therefore part of the communion of saints.

All Souls Day is, in some ways, a further reflection upon our sainthood. But, it is so as a reminder of something else. The feast might be called All Sinners Day, for it is a day to recall that though we are called to sanctity and eternal life, we are not the saints we might be, the saints we hope to become.

We need help. Freedom from sin and death is not something we can achieve, earn or deserve any more than we can achieve, earn or deserve life. It is a gift from God.

So, we pray for the dead, that their sins not deprive them of the fullness of life and sanctity for which God gave them life. And, we pray for the dying, which is all of us, that we, too, might receive the fullness of life and sanctity for which God gave us life.

Of course, we don't need a special day to do that. We can and should pray for and with the dead as well as for ourselves at all times. But, there is a good reason to have a feast like today, a day on which our sisters and brothers throughout the world are consciously united with us, and we with them, in such prayer.

I could not exist without other people. I depend at every moment upon others whom I do not know. I flick a switch, and the work of engineers, miners, clerks and others gives me light. I take a bite of food, and receive a gift from farmers, truck drivers, and vendors. Not only are these men and women my family, they, like I, will one day join the rest of humanity in death.

I exist thanks to hundreds of thousands of ancestors of whom I know nothing. The uniqueness of each of those people (and even pre-humans) is a part of me. Genetically, culturally, socially, linguistically and even spiritually I would be a different person if even one of them had been different. Rather, I would not be a different person, I simply would not be.

Not only do I depend upon others, they depend upon me. Men and women alive today rely in some way upon my work, service, prayers or friendship. And on this day I recall that even the dead rely upon me.

Just as we ask friends to pray for us, the dead have a claim on our prayers. After all, we are their family. The dead also have a right to expect us to not waste the heritage they have given us, their part in us. When I live as the person God made me through all those men and women, I become part of the fulfillment of their lives.

So, today we pray for the dead, our brothers and sisters who have gone before us. We ask God to bless them. We offer thanks for the lives they lived and ask forgiveness for their sins.

We ask, too, that in their communion with us, they might pray for us, that we, like they, may be forgiven our sins and might one day join them in the fullness of life in Christ.

I think of heaven as a huge reunion, when I will at last meet all those men and women upon whom I have depended and who have depended upon me and we will rejoice in the life–giving love of God that worked through us all. It will be the ultimate Feast of All Souls.

November 9: Dedication of the Lateran Basilica

Every Sunday is a celebration of the Resurrection, and so the Church rarely celebrates any other feast on a Sunday. Whenever a feast falls on a Sunday, it is usually dropped for that year. There are a few exceptions: some feasts that commemorate key events in the life of Christ, a few saints like Mary, John the Baptist, Peter and Paul. And, there is a building.

Today's feast of the Dedication of the Lateran Basilica in Rome is not only a major feast, it even 'bumps' Sunday. At first glance, this appears one of the craziest things in the Church's calendar of worship.

The land on which the church stands and a building that was on it may have been given to Pope Miltaides by the Roman Emperor Constantine, perhaps in time for a synod of bishops that was held in Rome in 313, the year the persecution of Christianity by the empire officially ended. The basilica was dedicated by Pope Sylvester in 324. The original building is long gone, and occupied only a small part of the present basilica, which is the cathedral of the diocese of Rome, and therefore the pope's cathedral church.

Because it is the pope's cathedral, officially called the Archbasilica of the Most Holy Savior and Saints John the Baptist and the Evangelist at the Lateran, a plaque on the front of it declares it to be the 'mother church' of all the other churches in the world.

And, perhaps it is in that 'family' that we can find some sense in celebrating the dedication of a building on the weekly feast of the Resurrection.

When the Church was born, Christians gathered in their homes to celebrate the Eucharist. This was similar to Jewish practice, where even today major celebrations like Passover are celebrated at home with friends and family rather than in a synagogue.

As the Church grew, communities became too large to gather in homes or even in converted houses like one that was discovered by archaeologists in Dura-Europos in Syria. Increasingly, Christians began to use buildings designed in the basilica style. Basilicas were generally rectangular halls with three aisles and were places where legal matters were discussed and decided and business was conducted. This style is the one we still think of as 'normal' for a church.

So, the conversion and construction of basilicas for Christian use was a sign of the Church's growth. That is the first thing we can celebrate on this feast, the growth of the Church that continues even today.

Though for the most part we have found the basilica style satisfactory, it is not without problems, problems we have especially recognized and have tried to alleviate today.

The major problem is that with large numbers and a rectangular layout, our worship can, and often does, become a spectators' activity. As Winston Churchill once said, 'We shape our buildings, and afterwards our buildings shape us.' Architects struggle to find ways to accommodate large numbers of people doing what is originally intended to be a family meal.

This may be the second thing that today's feast can celebrate, the Church's willingness to adopt and adapt from the world around us. Styles of buildings, vestments, music, activity and even theology have over the years shifted, and those shifts are usually influenced by the culture and society in which they take place.

This may, in fact, be one of the major attributes of Catholic Christianity, a willingness (too often forgotten or betrayed) to take into our life and worship anything that shows that the Holy Spirit is at work in the world around us.

And finally, this feast of one church building in Rome reminds us that we can and should appreciate and celebrate all the buildings in which we gather as a community. Those buildings, whether they be lowly huts or grand basilicas, are our homes. It is in them that we hear the Word of God proclaimed. It is in them that we share the Eucharist. It is in them that we are baptized, that we marry, that we are mourned. They enable us to become a community at worship, and we turn them into the house of God.

www.ingramcontent.com/pod-product-compliance
Ingram Content Group UK Ltd.
Pitfield, Milton Keynes, MK11 3LW, UK
UKHW041304180426
11947UKWH00009B/680